RENAISSANCE DRAMA

New Series XXI ☙ 1990

Renaissance Drama

New Series XXI

Disorder and the Drama

Edited by Mary Beth Rose

Northwestern University Press and

The Newberry Library Center for Renaissance Studies

EVANSTON 1990

209053

Editorial Note

R*ENAISSANCE DRAMA,* an annual publication, is devoted to understanding the drama as a central feature of Renaissance culture. Coverage, so far as subject matter is concerned, is not restricted to any single geographical area. The chronological limits of the Renaissance are interpreted broadly. Essays are encouraged that explore the relationship of Renaissance dramatic traditions to their precursors and successors; have an interdisciplinary orientation; explore the relationship of the drama to society and history; and examine the impact of new forms of interpretation on the study of Renaissance plays.

Volume XXI (1990), "Disorder and the Drama," includes essays that discuss Renaissance dramatic representations of violence, crime, public strife, and political mayhem, and essays that explore the ways in which chaos is ritualized to contain and/or encourage social, political, and religious disorder. As editor I am very grateful to members of the Editorial Committee. Special thanks are due to Manuscript Editor Alma A. MacDougall for her diligence and imagination.

Volume XXII (1991) will include essays concerned with any topic related to Renaissance drama.

Volume XXIII (1992) will focus on essays concerned with "Renaissance Drama in an Age of Colonization." The deadline for submission is January 15, 1992. Manuscripts should be submitted with stamped, self-addressed envelopes.

Renaissance Drama conforms to the stylistic conventions outlined in the most recent *MLA Style Manual.* Scholars preparing manuscripts for submission should refer to this book. Submissions and inquiries regarding future volumes should be addressed to Mary Beth Rose, *Renaissance Drama,* The Newberry Library, 60 West Walton Street, Chicago, Illinois 60610.

Mary Beth Rose
Editor

Contents

RENAISSANCE DRAMA

New Series XXI 1990

Charivari and the Comedy of Abjection in Othello

MICHAEL D. BRISTOL

Iᶠ ᴄᴇʀᴛᴀɪɴ ʜɪꜱᴛᴏʀʏ ᴘʟᴀʏꜱ can be read as rites of "uncrowning" then *Othello* might be read as a rite of "unmarrying." The specific organizing principle operative here is the social custom, common throughout early modern Europe, of charivari.[1] The abusive language, the noisy clamor under Brabantio's window, and the menace of violence in the opening scene of the play link the improvisations of Iago with the codes of a carnivalesque disturbance or charivari organized in protest over the marriage of the play's central characters. Charivari does not figure as an isolated episode here, however, nor has it been completed when the initial onstage commotion ends.[2] Despite the sympathy that Othello and Desdemona seem intended to arouse in the audience, the play as a whole is organized around the abjection and violent punishment of its central figures.

Charivari was a practice of noisy festive abuse in which a community enacted its specific objection to inappropriate marriages and more generally exercised a widespread surveillance of sexuality. As Natalie Davis has pointed out ("Reasons of Misrule"), this "community" actually consists of young men, typically the unmarried ones, who represent a social principle of male solidarity that is in some respects deeply hostile to precisely that form of institutionally sanctioned sexuality whose standards they are empowered to oversee.[3]

3

As a violent burlesque of marriage, charivari represents the heterosexual couple in grotesquely parodic form. The bride, frequently
depicted by a man dressed as a woman, will typically be represented
as hyperfeminine. The groom, against whom the larger share of social
animosity is often directed, is invariably represented as a type of
clown or bumpkin. In addition, the staging of a charivari requires a
master of ceremonies, a popular festive ringleader whose task is the
unmaking of a transgressive marriage (Neill). Even in its standard
form, a full-blown charivari would be a disturbing spectacle to witness. The charivari that forms the comical substructure of *Othello* is
even more powerfully troubling, because here the role of the clownish
bridegroom is conflated with a derisory and abusive image of "The
Moor."

The following analysis sketches out an interpretation of *Othello* as
a carnivalesque text.[4] Carnival is operative as something considerably
more than a novel decor for the *mise-en-scène* or an alternative the-
matics for interpretation. The play's structure is interpreted sche-
matically as a carnivalesque derangement of marriage as a social
institution and as an illustration of the contradictory role of heterosexual desire within that institution. The grotesque character of this
popular festive scenario is heightened by its deployment of the stereo-
typical figure of an African, parodically represented by an actor in
blackface. Heterosexual desire is staged here as an absurdly mutual
attraction between a beautiful woman and a funny monster.

At the time of the play's earliest performances, the supplementary
character of Othello's blackness would be apparent in the white actor's
use of blackface to represent the conventionalized form of "The
Moor." In the initial context of its reception, it seems unlikely that
the play's appeal to invidious stereotypes would have troubled the
conscience of anyone in the audience. Since what we now call racial
prejudice did not fall outside prevailing social norms in Shakespeare's
society, no one in the early audience would have felt sympathy for
Othello simply on grounds that he was the victim of a racist society.[5]
It is far more probable that "The Moor" would have been seen as
comically monstrous. Under these conditions the aspects of charivari
and of the comical abjection of the protagonists would have been
clear to an audience for whom a racist sensibility was entirely normal
(Newman).

At the end of the sixteenth century racism was not yet organized as a large-scale system of oppressive social and economic arrangements, but it certainly existed in the form of a distinctive and widely shared *affekt-complex*. Racism in this early, prototypical, form entails a specific physical repugnance for the skin color and other typical features of black Africans. This sensibility was not yet generalized into an abstract or pseudoscientific doctrine of racial inferiority, and for this reason it would have been relatively difficult to conceive of a principled objection to this "commonsensical" attitude. The physical aversion of the English toward the racial other was rationalized through an elaborate mythology, supported in part by scriptural authority and reinforced by a body of popular narrative (Jordan, Tokson). Within this context, the image of the racial other is immediately available as a way of encoding deformity or the monstrous.

For Shakespeare and for his audience the sensibilities of racial difference are for all practical purposes abstract and virtually disembodied, since the mythology of African racial inferiority is not yet a fully implemented social practice within the social landscape of early modern Europe. Even at this early stage, however, it has already occurred to some people that the racial other is providentially foreordained for the role of the slave, an idea that is fully achieved in the eighteenth- and nineteenth-century institution of plantation slavery and in such successor institutions as segregation and apartheid. The large-scale forms of institutional racism that continue to be a chronic and intractable problem in modern societies are, of course, already latent within the abstract racial mythologies of the sixteenth century, since these mythologies enter into the construction of the social and sexual imagery both of the dominant and of the popular culture. In more recent contexts of reception the farcical and carnivalesque potentiality of the play is usually not allowed to manifest itself openly. To foreground the elements of charivari and comic abjection would disclose in threatening and unacceptable ways the text's ominous relationship to the historical formation of racism as a massive social fact in contemporary Europe, and in the successor cultures of North and South America as well as in parts of the African homeland itself. Against this background the text of *Othello* has to be construed as a highly significant document in the historical constitution both of racist sensibility and of racist political ideology.

As a seriocomic or carnivalesque masquerade, the play makes visible the normative horizons against which sexual partners must be selected and the latent social violence that marriage attempts to prevent, often unsuccessfully, from becoming manifest. To stage this action as the carnivalesque thrashing of the play's central characters is, of course, a risky choice for a director to make, since it can easily transform the complex equilibrium of the play from tragedy to *opera buffa.* Although the play is grouped with the tragedies in the First Folio and has always been viewed as properly belonging to this genre, commentators have recognized for a long time the precarious balance of this play at the very boundaries of farce.[6] *Othello* is a text that evidently lends itself very well to parody, burlesque, and caricature, and this is due in part to the racial otherness of its protagonist (Levine 14–20, Neill 391–93).

The relationship of marriage is established through forms of collective representation, ceremonial and public enactments that articulate the private ethos of conjugal existence and mark out the communal responsibilities of the couple to implement and sustain socially approved "relations of reproduction." In the early modern period the ceremonial forms of marriage are accompanied (and opposed) by parodic doubling of the wedding feast in the forms of charivari.[7] This parodic doubling is organized by a carnivalesque wardrobe corresponding to a triad of dramatic agents—the clown (who represents the bridegroom), the transvestite (who represents the bride), and the "scourge of marriage," often assigned a suit of black (who represents the community of unattached males or "young men").[8] Iago of course is neither unattached nor young, but part of his success with his various dupes is his ability to present himself as "one of the boys." Iago's misogyny is expressed as the married man's *ressentiment* against marriage, against wives in general, and against his own wife in particular. But this *ressentiment* is only one form of the more diffuse and pervasive misogyny typically expressed in the charivari. And of course Iago's more sinister function is his ability to encourage a kind of complicity within the audience. In a performance he makes his perspective the perspective of the text and thus solicits from the audience a participatory endorsement of the action.

The three primary "characters" in charivari each has a normative function in the allocation of marriage partners and in the regulation of sexual behavior. These three figures parody the three persons of the wedding ceremony—bride, groom, and priest. The ensemble performs a travesty of the wedding ceremony itself. The ringleader or master of ceremonies may in some instances assist the partners in outwitting parental opposition, but this figure may also function as a nemesis of erotic desire itself and attempt to destroy the intended bond. In the actual practice of charivari, the married couple themselves are forced to submit to public ridicule and sometimes to violent punishment (Ingram, Muchembled). In its milder forms, a charivari allows the husband and wife to be represented by parodic doubles who are then symbolically thrashed by the ringleader and his followers.

This triad of social agents is common to many of Shakespeare's tragedies of erotic life, and it even appears in the comedies. Hamlet stages "The Murder of Gonzago" partly as a public rebuke to the unseemly marriage of Claudius and Gertrude (Davis, "Reasons of Misrule" 75). This is later escalated to a fantasy of the general abolition of the institution of monogamy, "I say we will have no moe marriage" (3.1.148). Hamlet's situation here expresses the powerful ambivalence of the unattached male toward marriage as the institutional format in which heterosexual desire and its satisfaction are legitimated. His objection to the aberrant and offensive union of mother and uncle is predicated on the idealization of marriage and in this case on the specific marriage of mother and father. This idealization is, however, accompanied by the fantasy of a general dissolution of the institution of monogamy back into a dispensation of erotic promiscuity and the free circulation of sexual partners. A similar agenda, motivated by a similar ambivalence, is pursued by Don John in *Much Ado about Nothing,* and by Iachimo in *Cymbeline.*

The argument I hope to sketch out here requires that readers or viewers of *Othello* efface their response to the existence of Othello, Desdemona, and Iago as individual subjects endowed with personalities and with some mode of autonomous interiorized life. The reason for such selective or willful ignorance of some of the most compelling features of this text is to make the determinate theatrical surfaces visible. To the extent that the surface coding of this play is openly manifested, the analysis presented here will do violence to the existence of the characters in depth. I believe that the withdrawal of empathy and of identification from the play's main characters is difficult, not least because the experience of individual subjectivity as we have come to know it *is* objectively operative in the text. It has been suggested, in fact, that the pathos of individual subjectivity was actually invented by Shakespeare, or that this experience appears for the first time in the history of Western representation in that great sociocultural laboratory known as Elizabethan drama (Belsey, Brecht).

Whether this view is accurate or not, however, there is the more immediate difficulty that we desire, as readers and viewers, to reflect on and to identify with the complex pathos of individual subjectivity as it is represented in Shakespeare's oeuvre. This is especially so, perhaps, for professional readers and viewers, who are likely to have strong interests in the experience of the speaking/writing subject and in the problematic of autonomy and expressive unity. The constellation of interests and goal-values most characteristic of the institutional processing of literary texts has given rise to an extremely rich critical discourse on the question of the subject; it is precisely the power and the vitality of this discourse that makes the withdrawal of empathy from the characters so difficult. But when we acknowledge the characters not only as Othello, Desdemona, and Iago, but also as components in a carnivalesque "wardrobe" that is inscribed within this text, then this wardrobe assigns them the roles of clown, transvestite, and "scourge of marriage" in a charivari.

The clown is a type of public figure who embodies the "right to be other," as M. M. Bakhtin would have it (*Dialogic Imagination* 158–67), since the clown always and everywhere rejects the categories made available in routine institutional life. The clown is therefore both criminal and monster, although such alien and malevolent aspects are more often than not disguised. Etymologically "clown" is related to "colonus"—a farmer or settler, someone not from Rome but from the agricultural hinterland. As a rustic or hayseed the clown's relationship to social reality is best expressed through such contemporary idioms as "He's out of it!," "He doesn't know where it's at!," or simply "Mars!" In the drama of the early modern period a clown is often by convention a kind of country bumpkin, but he is also a kind of "professional outsider" of extremely flexible social provenance. Bakhtin has stressed the emancipatory capacity of the clown function, arguing that the clown mask embodies the "right to be other" or *refus d'identité*. However, there is a pathos of clowning as well, and the clown mask may represent everything that is socially and sexually maladroit, credulous, easily victimized. And just as there is a certain satisfaction in observing an assertive clown get the better of his superiors, so is there also satisfaction in seeing an inept clown abused and stripped of his dignity. This abuse or "thrashing" of the doltish outsider provides the audience with a comedy of abjection, a social genre in which the experience of exclusion and impotence can be displaced onto an even more helpless caste within society.

To think of Othello as a kind of blackface clown is perhaps distasteful, even though the role must have been written not for a black actor, but with the idea of black makeup or a false-face of some kind. Othello is a Moor, but only in quotation marks, and his blackness is not even skin deep but rather a transitory and superficial theatrical integument. Othello's Moorish origins are the mark of his exclusion; as a cultural stranger he is, of course, "out of it" in the most compelling and literal sense. As a foreigner he is unable to grasp and to make effective use of other Venetian codes of social and sexual conduct. He is thus a grotesque embodiment of the bridegroom—an exotic, monstrous, and funny substitute who transgresses the norms associated with the idea of a husband.

To link Othello to the theatrical function of a clown is not necessarily to be committed to an interpretation of his character as a fool. Othello's folly, like Othello's nobility and personal grandeur, is a specific interpretation of the character's motivation and of his competence to actualize those motives. The argument here, however, is that the role of Othello is already formatted in terms of the abject-clown function and that any interpretation of the character's "nature" therefore has to be achieved within that format. The eloquence of Othello's language and the magnanimity of his character may in fact intensify the grotesque element. His poetic self-articulation is not so much the *expression* of a self-possessed subject but is instead a form of discursive indecorum that strains against the social meanings objectified in Othello's counter-festive *persona*. Stephen Greenblatt identifies the joke here as one of the "master plots of comedy," in which a beautiful young woman outwits an "old and outlandish" husband (234). Greenblatt reminds us here that Othello is functionally equivalent to the gull or butt of an abusive comic action, but he passes over the most salient feature of Othello's outlandishness, which is actualized in the blackface makeup essential to the depiction of this character. Greenblatt's discretion is no doubt a political judgment rather than an expression of a delicacy of taste. To present Othello in blackface, as opposed to presenting him just as a black man, would confront the audience with a comic spectacle of abjection rather than with the grand opera of misdirected passion. Such a comedy of abjection has not found much welcome in the history of the play's reception.

The original audience of this play in Jacobean England may have had relatively little inhibition in its expression of invidious racial sentiments, and so might have seen the derisory implications of the situation more easily. During the nineteenth century, when institutional racism was naturalized by recourse to a "scientific" discourse on racial difference, the problem of Othello's outlandishness and the unsympathetic laughter it might evoke was "solved" by making him a Caucasoid Moor, instead of a "veritable Negro" (Newman 144). Without such a fine discrimination, a performance of *Othello* would have been not so much tragic as simply unbearable, part farce and part lynch-mob. In the present social climate, when racism, though still very widespread, has been officially anathematized, the possibility of a blackface Othello would still be an embarrassment and a scandal, though presumably for a different set of reasons. Either way, the element of burlesque inscribed in this text is clearly too destabilizing to escape repression.

If Othello can be recognized as an abject clown in a charivari, then the scenario of such a charivari would require a transvestite to play the part of the wife. In the context of popular culture in the early modern period, female disguise and female impersonation were common to charivari and to a variety of other festive observances (Davis, "Women on Top"). This practice was, among other things, the expression of a widespread "fear" of women as both the embodiment of and the provocation to social transgression. Within the pervasive misogyny of the early modern period, women and their desires seemed to project the threat of a radical social undifferentiation (Woodbridge). The young men and boys who appeared in female dress at the time of Carnival seem to have been engaged in "putting women in their place" through an exaggerated pantomime of everything feminine. And yet this very practice required the emphatic foregrounding of the artifice required for any stable coding of gender difference. Was this festive transvestism legitimated by means of a general misrecognition of the social constitution of gender? Or did the participants understand at some level that the association of social badness with women was nothing more than a patriarchal social fiction that could only be sustained in and through continuous ritual affirmation?

Female impersonation is, of course, one of the distinctive and extremely salient features of Elizabethan and Jacobean dramaturgy, and yet surprisingly little is known of how this mode of representation actually worked (Rackin). The practice of using boy actors to play the parts of women derives from the more diffuse social practice of female impersonation in the popular festive milieu. Were the boy actors in Shakespeare's company engaging in a conventional form of ridicule of the feminine? Or were they engaged in a general parody of the artifice of gender coding itself? A transvestite presents the category of woman in quotation marks, and reveals that both "man" and "woman" are socially produced categories. In the drama of Shakespeare and his contemporaries, gender is at times an extremely mobile and shifting phenomenon without any solid anchor in sexual identity. To a considerable degree gender is a "flag of convenience" prompted by contingent social circumstances, and at times gender identity is negotiated with considerable grace and dexterity. The convention of the actor "boying" the woman's part is thus doubly parodic, a campy put-down of femininity and, at another level, a way to theorize the social misrecognition on which all gender allocations depend.

Desdemona's "femininity" is bracketed by the theatrical "boying" of his/her part. This renders her/his sexuality as a kind of sustained gestural equivocation, and this corresponds to the exaggerated and equivocal rhetorical aspect of Desdemona's self-presentation. As she puts it, "I saw Othello's visage in his mind" (1.3.252); in other words, her initial attraction to him was not provoked by his physical appearance. The play thus stipulates that Desdemona herself accepts the social prohibition against miscegenation as the normative horizon within which she must act. On the face of it she cannot be physically attracted to Othello, and critics have usually celebrated this as the

sign of her ability to transcend the limited horizons of her accultur-
ation. These interpretations accept the premise of Othello as physically undesirable and therefore insinuate that Desdemona's faith is
predicated on her blindness to the highly visible "monstrosity" of
her "husband." In other words, her love is a misrecognition of her
husband's manifestly undesirable qualities. Or is it a misrecognition
of her own socially prohibited desire? Stanley Cavell interprets her
lines as meaning that she saw his appearance in the way that he saw
it, that she is able to enter into and to share Othello's self-acceptance
and self-possession (129ff.). In this view Desdemona is a kind of
idealization of the social category of "wife," who can adopt the husband's own narrative fiction of self as her own imaginary object.
Desdemona is thus both a fantasy of a sexually desirable woman and
a fantasy of absolute sexual compliance. This figure of unconditional
erotic submission is the obverse of the rebellious woman, or shrew,
but, as the play shows us, this is also a socially prohibited *métier*
for a woman. In fact, as Greenblatt has shown in his very influential
essay, the idea that Desdemona might feel an ardent sexual desire for
him makes Othello perceive Iago's insinuations of infidelity as plausible and even probable (237–52). The masculine imagination whose
fantasy is projected in the figure of Desdemona cannot recognize
itself as the object of another's desire.

   Like all of Shakespeare's woman characters, Desdemona is an impossible sexual object, a female artifact created by a male imagination
and objectified in a boy actor's body. This is, in its own way, just as
artificial and as grotesque a theatrical manifestation as the blackface
Othello who stands in for the category of the husband. What is
distinctive about Desdemona is the way she embodies the category
of an "ideal wife" in its full contradictoriness. She has been described
as chaste or even as still a virgin and also as sexually aggressive, even
though very little unambiguous textual support for either of these
readings actually exists.[9] Her elopement, with a Moor no less, signals
more unequivocally than a properly arranged marriage ever could
that the biblical injunction to leave mother and father has been ful-
filled. It is probably even harder to accept the idea of Desdemona as
part of a comedy of abjection than it is to accept Othello in such a
context. It is, however, only in such a theatrical context that the

hyperbolic and exacerbated misrecognition on which marriage is founded can be theorized.

At the level of surface representation then, the play enacts a marriage between two complementary symbols of the erotic grotesque. This is a marriage between what is conventionally viewed as *ipso facto* hideous and repellent with what is most beautiful and desirable. The incongruity of this match is objectified in the theatrical hyper-embodiment of the primary categories of man and woman or husband and wife. It is not known to what extent Elizabethan and Jacobean theater practice deliberately foregrounded its own artifice. However, the symbolic practice of grotesque hyper-embodiment was well known in popular festive forms such as charivari. The theatrical coding of gender in the early modern period is still contaminated by the residue of these forms of social representation.

The marriage of grotesque opposites is no more a private affair or erotic dyad than a real marriage. Marriage in the early modern period, among many important social classes, was primarily a dynastic or economic alliance negotiated by a third party who represents the complex of social sanctions in which the heterosexual couple is inscribed.[10] The elopement of Desdemona and Othello, as well as their reliance on Cassio as a broker or clandestine go-between, already signals their intention deliberately to evade and thwart the will of family interests. To the extent that readers or viewers are conditioned by the normative horizons that interpret heterosexual love as mutual sexual initiative and the transcendence of all social obstacles, this elopement will be read as a romantic confirmation of the spiritual and disinterested character of their love (Luhmann). However, it can also be construed as a flagrant sexual and social blunder. Private heterosexual felicity of the kind sought by Othello and Desdemona attracts the evil eye of erotic nemesis.[11]

The figure of erotic nemesis and the necessary third party to this union is Othello's faithful lieutenant, Iago. It is Iago's task to show both his captain and his audience just how defenseless the heterosexual couple is against the resources of sexual surveillance. The romantic lovers, represented here through a series of grotesque distortions, do not enjoy an erotic autonomy, though such erotic autonomy is a misrecognition of the socially inscribed character of "private" sexuality. His abusive and derisory characterizations of the couple, together with his debasement of their sexuality, are a type of social commentary on the nature of erotic romance. The notion of mutual and autonomous self-selection of partners is impugned as a kind of mutual delusion that can only appear under the sign of monstrosity. In other words, the romantic couple can only "know" that their union is based on mutual love *and on nothing else* when they have "transcended" or violated the social codes and prohibitions that determine the allocation of sexual partners.

Iago is a Bakhtinian "agelast," that is, one who does not laugh. He is, of course, very witty, but his aim is always to provoke a degrading laughter at the follies of others rather than to enjoy the social experience of laughter *with* others. He is a de-mythologizer whose function is to reduce all expressivity to the minimalism of the *quid pro quo*. The process represented here is the reduction of quality to quantity, a radical undifferentiation of persons predicated on a strictly mechanistic, universalized calculus of desire. Characters identified with this persona appear throughout Shakespeare's oeuvre, usually in the guise of a nemesis of hypocrisy and dissimulation. Hamlet's "I know not 'seems'" (1.2.76) and Don John's "it must not be denied but I am a plain-dealing villain" (*Much Ado about Nothing* 1.1.31) are important variants of a social/cognitive process that proclaims itself to be a critique of equivocation and the will to deception. It is ironic, of course, that these claims of honesty and plain dealing are so often made in the interests of malicious dissimulation. What appears to be consistent, however, in all the variants of this character-type, is the disavowal of erotic attachment and the contemptuous manipulation of the erotic imagination.

The supposedly "unmotivated" malice enacted by this figure is puzzling, I believe, only when read individualistically. Is Iago envious of the pleasure Othello enjoys with Desdemona, or is he jealous of Othello's supposed sexual enjoyment of Emilia? Of course, both of these ideas are purely conjectural hypotheses that have no apparent bearing on Iago's actions. In any case, Iago shows no sustained commitment to either of these ideas, as numerous commentators have pointed out. Nevertheless, there is an important clue to understanding Iago as a social agent in these transitory ruminations. Iago seems to understand that the complex of envy and jealousy is not an aberration within the socially distributed erotic economy, but is rather the fundamental precondition of desire itself. Erotic desire is not founded in a qualitative economy or in a rational market, but rather in a mimetic and histrionic dispensation that Iago projects as the envy-jealousy system (Agnew 6–7 et passim). In this system men are the social agents, and women the objects of exchange. Iago's actions are thus socially motivated by a diffuse and pervasive misogyny that slides between fantasies of the complete abjection of all women and fantasies of an exclusively masculine world.

Iago's success in achieving these fantasies is made manifest in the unbearably hideous tableau of the play's final scene. If the play as a whole is to be read as a ritual of unmarrying, then this ending is the monstrous equivalent of a sexual consummation. What makes the play unendurable would be the suspicion that this climax expresses all too accurately an element present in the structure of every marriage. This is an exemplary action in which the ideal of companionate marriage as a socially sanctioned erotic union is dissolved back into the chronic violence of the envy-jealousy system. Iago theorizes erotic desire—and thus marriage—primarily by a technique of emptying out Othello's character, so that nothing is left at the end except the pathetic theatrical integument, the madly deluded and murderous blackface clown. Desdemona, the perfect wife, remains perfectly submissive to the end. And Iago, with his theoretical or pedagogical tasks completed, accepts in silence his allocation to the function of sacrificial victim and is sent off to face unnamed "brave punishments."

Finita la commedia. What does it mean to accept the *mise-en-scène* of this play? And what does it mean to *know* that we wish it could be otherwise? To the extent that we want to see a man and a woman defying social conventions in order to fulfill mutual erotic initiatives, the play will appear as a thwarted comedy, and our response will be dominated by its pathos. But the play also shows us what such mutual erotic initiatives look like from the outside, as a comedy of abjection or charivari. The best commentators on this play have recognized the degree to which it prompts a desire to prevent the impending debacle and the sense in which it is itself a kind of theatrical punishment of the observers.[12] This helpless and agonized refusal of the *mise-en-scène* should suggest something about the corrosive effect on socially inscribed rituals of a radical or "cruel" theatricality.

The idea of theatrical cruelty is linked to the radical aesthetics of Antonin Artaud. However, the English term "cruelty" fails to capture an important inflection that runs through all of Artaud's discussion of theater. The concept is derived from words that mean "raw" or "unprocessed." In French *"cruaute"* expresses with even greater candor this relationship with *"le cru"* and its opposition to *"le cuit."* Cruelty here has the sense of something uncooked, or something prior to the process of a conventional social transformation or adoption into the category of the meaningful (Artaud 42 et passim). *Othello,* perhaps more than any other Shakespeare play, raises fundamental questions about the institutional position and the aesthetic character of Shakespearean dramaturgy. Is Shakespeare raw—or is he cooked? Is it possible that our present institutional protocol for interpreting his work is a way of "cooking" the "raw" material to make it more palatable, more fit for consumption?

The history of the reception of *Othello* is the history of attempts to articulate ideologically correct, that is, palatable, interpretations. By screening off the comedy of abjection it is possible to engage more affirmatively with the play's romantic *liebestod.* Within these strategies, critics may find an abundance of meanings for the tragic dimension of the play. In this orientation the semantic fullness of the text is suggested as a kind of aesthetic compensation for the cruelty of its final scenes. Rosalie Colie, for example, summarizes her interpretation with an account of the play's edifying power.

> In criticizing the artificiality he at the same time exploits in his play, Shakespeare manages in *Othello* to reassess and to reanimate the moral system and the psychological truths at the core of the literary love-tradition, to reveal its problematics and to reaffirm in a fresh and momentous context the beauty of its impossible ideals. (167)[13]

The fullness of the play, of course, is what makes it possible for viewers and readers to participate, however unwillingly, in the charivari, or ritual victimization of the imaginary heterosexual couple represented here. Such consensual participation is morally disquieting in the way it appears to solicit at least passive consent to violence against women and against outsiders, but at least we are not howling with unsympathetic laughter at their suffering and humiliation.

Colie's description of the play's semantic fullness is based in part on her concept of "un-metaphoring"—that is, the literalization of a metaphorical relationship or conventional figuration. This is a moderate version of the notion of theatrical cruelty or the unmaking of convention that does not radically threaten existing social norms. In other words, the fate of Desdemona and Othello is a cautionary fable about what happens if a system of conventional figurations of desire is taken literally. But the more powerful "un-metaphoring" of this play is related not to its fullness as a tragedy, but to its emptiness as a comedy of abjection. The violent interposing of the charivari here would make visible the *political* choice between aestheticized ritual affirmation and a genuine refusal of the sexual *mise-en-scène* in which this text is inscribed.

Othello occupies a problematic situation at the boundary between ritually sanctioned reality and theatrically consensual fiction. Does the play simply depict an inverted ritual of courtship and marriage, or does its performance before an audience that accepts its status as a fiction also invite complicity in a social ritual of comic abjection, humiliation, and victimization? What does it mean, to borrow a usage from the French, to "assist" at a performance of this text? At a time when large-scale social consequences of racist sensibilities had not yet become visible, it may well have been easy to accept the formal codes of charivari as the expression of legitimate social norms. In later contexts of reception it is not so easy to accept *Othello* in the form of a derisory ritual of racial and sexual persecution, because the social experience of racial difference has become such a massive scandal.

The history of both the interpretation and the performance of *Othello* has been characterized by a search for consoling and anaesthetic explanations that would make its depictions of humiliation and suffering more tolerable. On the other hand, some observers, like Horace Howard Furness, have been absolutely inconsolable and have even refused to countenance the play.[14] The need for consolation is of course prompted by the sympathy and even the admiration readers and spectators feel for the heterosexual couple who occupy the center of the drama. The argument I have tried to develop here is not intended to suggest that the characters do not deserve our sympathy. Nevertheless, *Othello* is a text of racial *and* sexual persecution. If the suffering represented in this drama is to be made intelligible for us, then it may no longer be possible to beautify the text. It may be more valuable to allow its structures of abjection and violence to become visible.

Notes

1. See Neely, *Broken Nuptials*. On charivari, see Le Goff and Schmitt, Thompson, and Underdown 99–103.

2. Laroque; see also Nelson and Haines 5–7.

3. On the topic of "male solidarity" see Sedgwick.

4. Bakhtin, *Rabelais and His World* 145–96 and passim; see also his *Dialogic Imagination* 167–224 and Gaignebet.

5. Hunter, "Elizabethans and Foreigners" and "Othello and Colour Prejudice." See also Jones and Orkin.

6. Rymer 2: 27. See also Snyder 70–74.

7. See Alford; Belmont; Davis, "Charivari"; Grinberg; and Bristol.

8. For the importance of "youth groups" and of unmarried men see Davis, "The Reasons of Misrule."

9. Arguments for a chaste or virginal Desdemona are found in Nelson and Haines as well as in Janton. The idea of a sexually aggressive Desdemona is to be found in Greenblatt 237ff. and in Booth.

10. On the "triangular" character of erotic desire see Girard 1–52.

11. Dumouchel and Dupuy; see also Siebers.

12. In addition to Cavell and Greenblatt see, for example, Burke; Neely, "Women and Men in *Othello*"; Parker; Snow; and Stallybrass.

13. For other recuperative readings within quite different normative horizons see, for example, Newman; Barber and Wheeler 272–81; Heilman; Holland 197–216; and Kirsch 10–39.

14. Furness found the play horrible, and wished Shakespeare had never written it (2: 149, 156). See also Cavell 98ff.

Works Cited

Agnew, Jean-Christophe. *Worlds Apart: The Market and the Theater in Anglo-American Thought, 1550-1750*. Cambridge: Cambridge UP, 1986.

Alford, Violet. "Rough Music or Charivari." *Folklore* 70 (1959): 505–18.

Artaud, Antonin. *The Theater and Its Double*. Trans. Mary Caroline Richards. New York: Grove, 1958.

Bakhtin, M. M. *The Dialogic Imagination*. Trans. Caryl Emerson and Michael Holquist. Austin: U of Texas P, 1981.

———. *Rabelais and His World*. Trans. Hélène Iswolsky. Cambridge: MIT P, 1968.

Barber, C. L., and Richard P. Wheeler. *The Whole Journey: Shakespeare's Power of Development*. Berkeley: U of California P, 1986.

Belmont, Nicole. "Fonction de la dérision et symbolisme du bruit dans le charivari." Le Goff and Schmitt 15–21.

Belsey, Catherine. *The Subject of Tragedy: Identity and Difference in Renaissance Drama*. London: Methuen, 1985.

Booth, Stephen. "The Best *Othello* I Ever Saw." *Shakespeare Quarterly* 40 (1989): 332–36.

Brecht, Bertolt. *The Messingkauf Dialogues*. Trans. John Willett. London: Methuen, 1965.

Bristol, Michael D. "Wedding Feast and Charivari." In his *Carnival and Theater: Plebian Culture and the Structure of Authority in Renaissance England*. New York: Methuen, 1985. 162–78.

Burke, Kenneth. "*Othello*: An Essay to Illustrate a Method." *Hudson Review* 4 (1951): 165–203.

Cavell, Stanley. *Disowning Knowledge in Six Plays of Shakespeare*. Cambridge: Cambridge UP, 1987.

Colie, Rosalie. *Shakespeare's Living Art*. Princeton: Princeton UP, 1974.

Davis, Natalie Zemon. "Charivari, honneur et communauté à Lyon et à Genève au XVIIᵉ siècle." Le Goff and Schmitt 207–20.

———. "The Reasons of Misrule: Youth Groups and Charivaris in Sixteenth-Century France." *Past and Present* 50 (1971): 49–75.

———. "Women on Top: Symbolic Sexual Inversion and Political Disorder in Early Modern Europe." *The Reversible World: Symbolic Inversion in Art and Society*. Ed. Barbara A. Babcock. Ithaca: Cornell UP, 1978. 147–90.

Dumouchel, Paul, and Jean-Pierre Dupuy. *L'Enfer des choses: René Girard et la logique de l'économie*. Paris: Seuil, 1979.

Furness, Horace Howard. *Letters*. Ed. Horace Howard Furness Jayne. 2 vols. Boston: Houghton, 1922.

Girard, René. *Deceit, Desire, and the Novel: Self and Other in Literary Structure*. Trans. Yvonne Freccero. Baltimore: Johns Hopkins UP, 1965.

Greenblatt, Stephen. *Renaissance Self-Fashioning: From More to Shakespeare*. Chicago: U of Chicago P, 1980.

Grinberg, Martine. "Charivaris au Moyen Age et à la Renaissance. Condamnation des remariages ou rites d'inversion du temps?" Le Goff and Schmitt 141–47.

Heilman, Robert. *Magic in the Web: Action and Language in* Othello. Lexington: U of Kentucky P, 1956.

Holland, Norman. *The Shakespearean Imagination: A Critical Introduction*. Bloomington: U of Indiana P, 1964.

Hunter, G. K. "Elizabethans and Foreigners." *Shakespeare Survey* 17 (1964): 37–52.

———. "Othello and Colour Prejudice." *Proceedings of the British Academy* 53 (1967): 139–63.

Ingram, Martin. "Le charivari dans l'Angleterre du XVIᵉ et du XVIIᵉ siècle. Aperçu historique." Le Goff and Schmitt 251–64.

Janton, Pierre. "Othello's Weak Function." *Cahiers Elisabéthains* 34 (1988): 79–82.

Jones, Eldred D. *Othello's Countrymen: The African in English Renaissance Drama.* Oxford: Oxford UP, 1965.

Jordan, Winthrop D. *White over Black: American Attitudes toward the Negro, 1550–1812.* Chapel Hill: U of North Carolina P, 1968.

Kirsch, Arthur C. *Shakespeare and the Experience of Love.* Cambridge: Cambridge UP, 1981.

Laroque, François. "An Archaeology of the Dramatic Text: *Othello* and Popular Traditions." *Cahiers Elisabéthains* 32 (1987): 13–35.

Le Goff, Jacques, and Jean-Claude Schmitt, eds. *Le charivari: Actes de la table ronde organisée à Paris (25–27 avril 1977) par l'Ecole des Hautes Etudes en Sciences Sociales et le Centre National de la Recherche Scientifique.* Paris: Mouton, 1977.

Levine, Lawrence W. *Highbrow/Lowbrow: The Emergence of Cultural Hierarchy in America.* Cambridge: Harvard UP, 1988.

Luhmann, Niklas. *Love as Passion: The Codification of Intimacy.* Trans. Jeremy Gaines and Doris L. Jones. Cambridge: Harvard UP, 1986.

Muchembled, Robert. "Des conduites de bruit au spectacle des processions. Mutations mentales et déclin des fêtes populaires dans le Nord de las France (XV^c–XVI^c siècle)." Le Goff and Schmitt 229–36.

Neely, Carol Thomas. *Broken Nuptials in Shakespeare's Plays.* New Haven: Yale UP, 1985.

———. "Women and Men in *Othello*: 'What should such a fool / Do with so good a Woman?'" *The Woman's Part: Feminist Criticism of Shakespeare.* Ed. Carolyn Ruth Swift Lenz, Gayle Greene, and Carol Thomas Neely. Urbana: U of Illinois P, 1980. 211–39.

Neill, Michael. "Unproper Beds: Race, Adultery, and the Hideous in *Othello.*" *Shakespeare Quarterly* 40 (1989): 383–412.

Nelson, T. G. A., and Charles Haines. "Othello's Unconsummated Marriage." *Essays in Criticism* 33 (1983): 1–18.

Newman, Karen. "'And wash the Ethiop white': Femininity and the Monstrous in *Othello.*" *Shakespeare Reproduced: The Text in History and Ideology.* Ed. Jean E. Howard and Marion F. O'Connor. New York: Methuen, 1987. 143–62.

Orkin, Martin. "Othello and the 'Plain Face' of Racism." *Shakespeare Quarterly* 38 (1987): 166–88.

Parker, Patricia. "Shakespeare and Rhetoric: 'Dilation' and 'Delation' in *Othello.*" *Shakespeare and the Question of Theory.* Ed. Patricia Parker and Geoffrey Hartman. London: Methuen, 1985. 54–74.

Rackin, Phyllis. "Androgyny, Mimesis, and the Marriage of the Boy Heroine on the English Renaissance Stage." *PMLA* 102 (1987): 29–41.

Rey-Flaud, Henri. *Le charivari: Les rituels fondamentaux de la sexualité.* Paris: Payot, 1985.

Rymer, Thomas. *A Short View of Tragedy. Shakespeare: The Critical Heritage.* Ed. Brian Vickers. 6 vols. London: Routledge, 1974–81. 2: 25–59.

Sedgwick, Eve Kosofsky. *Between Men: English Literature and Male Homosocial Desire.* New York: Columbia UP, 1985.

Shakespeare, William. *The Riverside Shakespeare.* Gnl. ed. G. Blakemore Evans. Boston: Houghton, 1974.

Siebers, Tobin. *The Mirror of Medusa.* Berkeley: U of California P, 1983.

Snow, Edward A. "Sexual Anxiety and the Male Order of Things in *Othello.*" *English Literary Renaissance* 10 (1980): 384–412.

Snyder, Susan. *The Comic Matrix of Shakespeare's Tragedies.* Princeton: Princeton UP, 1979.

Stallybrass, Peter. "Patriarchal Territories: The Body Enclosed." *Rewriting the Renaissance: The Discourses of Sexual Difference in Early Modern Europe.* Ed. Margaret W. Ferguson, Maureen Quilligan, and Nancy J. Vickers. Chicago: U of Chicago P, 1986. 123–42.

Thompson, E. P. "Rough Music: Le Charivari Anglais." *Annales: Economies, sociétes, civilizations* 27 (1972): 285–312.

Tokson, Elliot H. *The Popular Image of the Black Man in English Drama, 1550–1688.* Boston: Hall, 1982.

Underdown, David. *Revel, Riot, and Rebellion: Popular Politics and Culture in England, 1603–1660.* Oxford: Clarendon, 1985.

Woodbridge, Linda. *Women and the English Renaissance: Literature and the Nature of Womankind, 1540–1620.* Urbana: U of Illinois P, 1984.

Slander for Slander in
Measure for Measure

M. LINDSAY KAPLAN

IN JUNE 1596 two men were brought before the Star Chamber for "coseninge diuers yonge gentlemen" in a fraudulent loan and commodity scheme. The defendants were found guilty and sentenced to be imprisoned, fined twenty pounds, and whipped four times around the city. They were also to be placed in the pillory with papers attached which literally wrote the crime on the perpetrators so their disgrace could be read by all. To this humiliating and harsh punishment William Burghley suggested an explicitly theatrical addition: "The Lord Treasurer 'would haue those y^t make the playes to make a Comedie hereof, & to acte it wth these names . . .'" (Hawarde 48). There is no evidence that Burghley's proposal was acted upon, but the suggestion shows that he clearly appreciated the capacity of a play to expose the defendants and warn others by its example. Paradoxically, while the state understood that dramatic humiliation served its interests in deterring criminal activity, it nevertheless condemned theatrical impersonation, when not sponsored by the state, as slander.[1]

In *Measure for Measure,* the duke of Vienna stages a dramatic exposure of his subjects, acted not merely "wth [their] names," but with the persons themselves. While he ostensibly leaves his realm to

23

effect a change in the enforcement of the fornication statutes, and to avoid any slanderous backlash such an action might occasion, by the play's end he is clearly more concerned with humiliating his subjects and subordinating them stringently to his authority. The one character who resists being chastened, Lucio, has to be forcibly removed from the stage before he is silenced; although the duke charges Lucio with fornication, he is ultimately punished for "Slandering a prince" (5.1.521). However, the duke condemns Lucio not because the latter's slanders malign the ruler's good government, but because Lucio exposes the state's own slanderous practices. In this essay I will first discuss how slander figured as theater in political and poetical practice in late sixteenth- and early seventeenth-century England, and then turn to an analysis that brings these attitudes to bear on *Measure for Measure*.

* * *

In Renaissance England, conventional methods of punishment were scarcely less dramatic than the "Comedie" proposed by Burghley; in the absence of a centralized instrumental power, the state relied on representational power to maintain order (Greenblatt 44). In *Discipline and Punish,* Michel Foucault argues that public ritualized executions served a larger purpose than the mere chastisement of a criminal. The manner in which death sentences and corporal punishments were meted out carried a symbolic meaning, often representing an aspect of the crime in the correction: "the tongues of blasphemers were pierced, the impure were burnt, the right hand of murderers was cut off" (45).[2] Spectators viewing the administration of such penalties could read the crime from the corresponding punishment.

Theatrical exposure in the form of humiliating and violent public punishments ostensibly served to chastise the criminal, but its real value lay in the effect such displays were thought to have on the audience of potential offenders.

In the ceremonies of the public execution, the main character was the people, whose real and immediate presence was required for the performance. An execution that was known to be taking place, but which did so in secret, would scarcely have had any meaning. The aim was to make an example, not only by making people aware that the slightest offence was likely to be punished, but by arousing feelings of terror by the spectacle of power letting its anger fall upon the guilty person. (Foucault 57–58)

While Foucault focuses here on the terrifying aspect of punitive spectacles, he acknowledges elsewhere the dishonor inherent in such ceremonies.[3] Lawrence Stone notes that punishment by dishonor was particularly effectual in sixteenth- and seventeenth-century England:

One of the most characteristic features of the age was its hyper-sensitive insistence upon the overriding importance of reputation. Many of the punishments of the day, the stocks, the pillory, the apology read out in the market-place, were based upon the theory that public humiliation was a more effective penalty than a swingeing fine. (25)

All public punishment—from the scaffold to the pillory—operated on the premise that the humiliation of the criminal acted as a future deterrent for witnesses of the event. This calculated theatrical exposure served to disgrace both the offender and his offense in the eyes of the public.

To the extent that punishment worked to make the criminal infamous, it essentially functioned as defamation. In fact, the English legal system as a whole functioned as a type of institutionalized slander, in both the punishment and the indictment of criminals. In the Middle Ages, justices of the peace depended on reports from local inhabitants to inform them of crimes committed. In turn, the justices of the peace were expected to give these petitions to the grand jury, who would hand down an indictment if they determined the accusation was true. By the sixteenth century,

[t]here was still no way in which the government could itself initiate criminal proceedings. . . . It ordered arrest and trial on the *information* of private persons, without getting a grand jury to confirm the charges. . . . In early Stuart times an average county might have as many as twelve professional informers working in cooperation with the clerk of the peace, each bringing twenty or so prosecutions to quarter-session, and some directing rudimentary detective agencies. (Harding 76–77)

Thus the system at its most fundamental level was based on the criminal accusations of one private citizen by another, with cases brought to trial without the more objective deliberations of a disinterested grand jury.[4]

One's reputation or standing in the community was of the utmost importance when authorities were searching out suspects. Bad fame was considered evidence enough to suspect someone of a crime. If someone possessing a bad reputation was in fact deserving of it, then it was logical that he or she be questioned when a crime was committed. However, while the informations and imputations brought against a suspect could be true, they could also be motivated by personal hatred, a desire to harass or vex, or a malicious impulse to slander.

A rather more dubious proceeding than information, though it had ancient roots, was trial upon 'record.' It was in part an extension of the old principle that notoriety was adequate to accuse a man—and even condemn him. (Harding 77)

The distinction between a valid accusation of a crime and a spiteful defamation was difficult to maintain in the absence of an impartial judicial procedure to initiate criminal proceedings.

Similarly, the state's reliance on various forms of defamation could just as easily work against, instead of for, its interests. In cases of guilt by notoriety, infamous accusations could be turned against the state.

J.P.s sometimes had authority to arrest on suspicion. . . . [T]he analogous king's witness of rebellion was no less than incontrovertible, so that it was found politically convenient to condemn rebels on the king's record. . . . The families of the noble victims of this doctrine that notoriety to the king equalled condemnation, naturally claimed that it was contrary to law; and it was certainly dangerous. The practice was . . . turned against the Crown, which found its ministers, from the end of the fourteenth century right on to the eighteenth, being impeached by parliament on the same basis of 'notorious crimes'. (Harding 77–78)

The cruelty and humiliation of public executions could likewise redound to the infamy of the state and not the criminal. Foucault's observations on the reversibility of an execution's intended effect, though made with regard to conditions in eighteenth-century France, are corroborated by events in early Renaissance England.

In these executions, which ought to show only the terrorizing power of the prince, there was a whole aspect of the carnival, in which rules were inverted, authority mocked and criminals transformed into heroes. The shame was turned round; the courage, like the tears and the cries of the condemned, caused offence only to the law. (61; see also 58–69 passim)

The popularity of John Foxe's *Acts and Monuments* demonstrates the extent to which public opinion could side with the "criminal" (as martyr) against the popish state.[5] Likewise, Elizabeth's "anger" over the execution of Mary Queen of Scots, following her tacit approval of the sentence, indicates her desire to dissociate herself from the event and avoid popular disapproval. The execution of the inordinately popular earl of Essex was privately performed within the Tower grounds to avoid eliciting sympathy among his supporters. In spite of this precaution, Essex's executioner was almost mobbed leaving the Tower and ballads singing Essex's praises appeared immediately after his death (Bowen 160–62). Thus, the state's use of slander, specifically dramatic public exposures, relied for its success on the very people such spectacles were meant to control, and upon whose acquiescence it could not depend.[6]

Because defamatory displays constituted an important, if unstable, mechanism of royal power, the monarchy was determined to regulate unauthorized dramatic criticism that could be turned against the state. One of the first proclamations Elizabeth made after her accession prohibited unlicensed interludes and plays, especially on religion and policy. The 16 May 1559 order forbids the playing of "all manner interludes," either publicly or privately, unless they be licensed. In giving her charge to the licensing officers, the queen instructs them to deny permission of performance to those plays

wherein either matters of religion or of the governance of the estate of the commonweal shall be handled or treated being no meet matters to be written or treated upon but by men of authority, learning and wisdom, nor to be handled before any audience, but of grave and discreet persons. . . . (Hughes and Larkin 2: 115–16)

Elizabeth does not categorically condemn "interludes," even when they touch on matters of church and state; the proclamation seems to suggest that certain "men of authority" are in fact capable of writing on these issues for the appropriate audience. She is here less concerned about the medium itself, than about those beyond her authority writing unlicensed plays which might threaten the monarchy by challenging its own representational power.

The monarchy identified theatrical impersonation of actual people, especially figures of state, as slander to distinguish it from the state's own practice of humiliating exposure. In his *Treatise of the Court of Star Chamber,* the seventeenth-century barrister William Hudson includes impersonation in the chapter devoted to defining "Libelling and Scandalous Words":

> Libels are of several kinds; either by scoffing at the person of another in rhyme or prose, or by the personating him, thereby to make him ridiculous. (100)

In May 1601, with the Essex crisis barely behind them, the Privy Council ordered an investigation of a report that

> certaine players [in Middlesex] . . . do represent upon the stage in their interludes the persons of some gentlemen of good desert and quallity that are yet alive under obscure manner, but yet in such sorte as all the hearers may take notice both of the matter and the persons that are meant thereby. (Chambers 4: 332)

The council ordered the county justices of the peace to forbid the performance of the play because it clearly had not been "perused and allowed" by the appropriate authorities and thus could "minister . . . occasion of offence or scandal."[7] Because such "occasion[s]" could lead to duels or even riots, the Star Chamber defined them as criminal offenses that fell within its jurisdiction,

> for although the libel be made against one, yet it incites all those of the same family, kindred, or society to revenge, and so tends *per consequens* to quarrels and breach of the peace, and may be the cause of shedding blood.[8]

In these cases, the truth did not constitute a defense because a factual accusation could prove more inflammatory than a lie.[9]

In the chapter on libel Hudson offers an example of dramatic defamation—"The personating of the earl of Lincoln in a play" (101)—

that was successfully redressed through appropriate legal channels. Most of the documents related to *Lincoln v. Dymock* are missing from the Public Record Office, but one of the depositions which remains provides an apparently thorough account of the play.[10] The Star Chamber records reveal a prodigious number of cases in which both Lincoln and Edward Dymock are named. In this instance Dymock, a neighbor of the earl's, was charged with producing a play in August 1601 in which Lincoln is portrayed as being carried off by the devil. Lincoln is ridiculed further when he is named heir in the fool's will and inherits the latter's wooden dagger. Dymock insured his play an audience by inviting neighbors to a venison feast, after which the skit was performed. His intent was clearly to discredit and humiliate the earl by means of theatrical slander. The Star Chamber recognized the threat of this instance of unauthorized theatrical criticism and, according to Hudson, severely punished the play's perpetrators.

An infamous example from the public theater of the threat of even a veiled theatrical impersonation is the staging of *Richard II* (presumably Shakespeare's) during the Essex rebellion (February 1601). William Lambarde's now familiar account of Elizabeth's remarks (August 1601) on the performance indicates that she understood the implied menace of this attempt to cast her in the role of the monarch deposed by a popular nobleman.[11] The April 1601 proclamation offering a reward for information about authors of "libels . . . tending to the slander of our royal person and state" would have included unauthorized dramatic representations as well as written and verbal attacks (Hughes and Larkin 3: 233). Even before the 1601 uprising, Jonson was required to excise the climax of *Every Man Out of His Humour* because it staged a confrontation, and a flattering one at that, of the queen and a satirist (Barish 137).

Poets and their defenders understood that plays and slander were linked by the common operation of public exposure. However, dramatic disclosure was defended on the grounds that it assisted the established order by condemning vice and promoting virtue. In book 1 of *The Arte of English Poesie* George Puttenham gives a "historical" account of the function of poetry. Its first role was to praise the gods; its second was not, as one might suppose, to praise good men, but to correct vice. The purpose of "Poesie *Dramatick* reprehensive"

(34) was to foster virtue and order, and thus promote the aims of the state. Dramatic satire was "the first and most bitter inuectiue against vice and vicious men" (31). The poets of the time disguised themselves as satyrs or silvans, "as if the gods of the woods . . . should appear and recite those verses of rebuke" (31). Comedy and tragedy were developed as more persuasive means of correcting abuses; instead of a dramatic narration, the characters of the plot themselves represented the action, creating a more verisimilar, and thus convincing, effect.

However, while comedies "debated the matters of the world, some-times of [the poets'] priuate affaires, sometimes of their neighbours," tragedies exposed corrupt tyrants, "their miserable ends painted out in playes and pageants, to shew the mutabilitie of fortune, and the iust punishment of God in reuenge of a vicious and euill life" (33). Puttenham does not directly sanction criticism of princes; he insists that tragedy concern itself with their behavior only after their deaths. Nevertheless, in the section on the praise of princes, he suggests a slightly different perspective. Rulers, because they are "of greater moment," must conform to a higher standard of virtue than "any inferior sort of men."

> Wherefore the Poets being in deede the trumpetters of all praise and also of slaunder (not slaunder, but well deserued reproch) were in conscience & credit bound next after the diuine praises of the immortall gods, to yeeld a like ratable honour to all such amongst men, as most resembled the gods by excellencie of function. . . . (35)

Puttenham deliberately permits his first thought, "slaunder," to remain alongside his afterthought, "well deserued reproch," which serves to redefine the former. Aware that contemporary opinion equated reproaching the prince with slander, Puttenham tries to make the case that poetic correction is justified by precedent. Thus, according to its "history," while dramatic poetry can assist the state in reproving vice, it also maintains the ability to criticize the state.[12]

The English monarchy was anxious to control for its own aims the theater's power to criticize and expose; independent attempts to deploy this medium were distinguished as slanders. However, this was not a battle between the state's truth and the theater's slander, but a struggle to determine which institution would have control over dramatic defamation. The ability to humiliate, expose, and reprehend offenders—and thus to prevent others from offending—was claimed by both poets and the state. While drama that criticized the state or challenged the status quo was labeled slander and condemned, dramatic slander that supported the ends of the state was condoned. Although the rhetoric of the authorities who attempted to control slander represents it as a threat to the peace of the realm, in fact the operation of slander constitutes (as we have seen) the state's own methods of punishment and maintaining dominion. This is the argument of Shakespeare's *Measure for Measure*.

At the close of *Measure for Measure* Duke Vincentio pardons all of his offending subjects with the exception of Lucio: "And yet here's one in place I cannot pardon" (5.1.497). He is punished, like Angelo and Claudio, ostensibly for fornication, and is forced to marry the prostitute who bore his child. However, when Lucio complains that "Marrying a punk, my lord, is pressing to death, / Whipping, and hanging" (5.1.520–21), the duke reveals in his reply that Lucio is being punished for an altogether different crime: "Slandering a prince deserves it." The duke is clearly much more concerned about enforcing laws against criticism of the ruler than laws against fornication that he let slip, by his own admission, for fourteen years (1.3.21).

Lucio is a slanderer, charging the ruler with licentiousness, drunkenness, and stupidity (3.2.115ff.); similar imputations of a ruler's moral improbity brought several of Elizabeth's subjects to grief.[13] However, Lucio's accusations become relatively innocuous when compared to the slanders spoken elsewhere in the play, which pose a direct threat to the authority of the ruler:

> My business in this state
> Made me a looker-on here in Vienna,
> Where I have seen corruption boil and bubble
> Till it o'errun the stew: laws for all faults,
> But faults so countenanc'd that the strong statutes
> Stand like the forfeits in a barber's shop,
> As much in mock as mark.
>   (5.1.314–20)

Paradoxically enough, this is spoken by the duke himself in a public space in front of many of his subjects. Why is Vincentio so angered by the fabrications Lucio alleges in private when he himself publishes a direct critique of the state in full hearing of his subjects? The duke condemns Lucio not so much for impugning his authority, but for competing with it. Lucio poses a threat to the state precisely because he usurps the duke's ability to deploy slanders.

In order to understand the relationship between Lucio and Vincentio we need to know who the former is and what he represents. In the dramatis personae of the First Folio Lucio is listed as "a fantastique."[14] An examination of both the etymology of the term and its context in sixteenth-century literary theory suggests that fantasy is considered the source of poetic inspiration, and that a fantastic represents the figure of the poet. Furthermore, contemporary thought connects the fantastic with both a revealing function and with state policy.[15]

In his *Defense of the "Comedy" of Dante* (1587), Jacopo Mazzoni distinguishes between the intellective power that produces conceptions in conformity with the nature of objects, and the fantastic or imaginative power that is fitted to generate and create.[16]

Phantasy is the true power over poetic fables, since she alone is capable of those fictions which we of ourselves are able to feign and put together. From this of necessity it follows that poetry is made up of things feigned and imagined, because it is founded on phantasy. (387)

Mazzoni believes that poetry is based on credibility rather than truth, and is therefore a subdivision of the sophistic. Recognizing that this characterization carries a negative connotation, he makes a defense of sophistry,

which, though it propounds to the intellect things that are feigned, yet does not disorder the will, but rather in every way . . . makes it comfortable with the just. . . . And if it should appear to any one that it does merit blame because of disordering the intellect with falsity, I say that such an one should know that the ancient gentile philosophers . . . praise this disorder of the intellect in certain things, when it was directed to a proper end. For this reason Plato holds that the magistrate should be able to lie to his citizens for the sake of some public good. . . . Now I say phantastic poetry regulated by the proper laws is part of this ancient sophistic, since it also propounds feigned things to our intellect in order to regulate the appetite and many times contains beneath the husk of the fiction, the truth of many noble conceptions. (369–70)

Mazzoni defends the fictional and fantastic elements of poetry by claiming that the state uses the same means to effect good ends. He even demonstrates how poetry was used by the ancients to regulate the different classes in society: the comic to make artificers laugh and forget their wretched state, the heroic to embolden soldiers and make them better warriors, and the tragic for the magistrates to keep them from being too ambitious and proud (382–83). This argument suggests that the poet and the statesman work by the same means to achieve the better ordering of society.

In *The Arte of English Poesie* Puttenham also makes a strong argument for the symbiosis of poetry and government by referring to historical precedent. In former ages, good poets

were highly esteemed and much fauoured of the greatest Princes. . . . [N]or this reputation was giuen them in auncient times altogether in respect that Poesie was a delicate arte, and the poets them selues cunning Prince-pleasers, but for that also they were thought for their vniuersall knowledge to be very sufficient men for the greatest charges in their common wealthes, were it for counsell or for conduct, whereby no man neede to doubt but that both skilles may very well concurre and be most excellent in one person. (16–17)

In the course of this discussion Puttenham lists several rulers who were poets, including Julius Caesar, and other poets who were considered capable of governing, such as Horace. However, the poets of Puttenham's England no longer enjoy this esteem. Like Mazzoni, his contemporaries connect the fantastical with poetry, but with a less flattering comparison:

For as well Poets and Poesie are despised, . . . [and] who so is studious in th'Arte or shewes him selfe excellent in it, they call him in disdayne a *phantasticall:* and a light headed or phantasticall man (by conuersion) they call a Poet. (Puttenham 18)

In the passage that follows, Puttenham explains that the fantastic is commonly misunderstood. He likens it to a mirror: "There be . . . glasses that shew thinges exceeding faire and comely, others that shew figures very monstrous & illfauored." If the fantasy is disordered it can hinder the sound judgment and discourse of the brain; but that part being well affected . . . the inuentiue parte of the mynde is so much holpen, as without it no man could deuise any new or rare thing: and where it is not excellent in his kind, there could be no politique Captaine, nor any witty enginer or cunning artificer, nor yet any law maker or counsellor of deepe discourse. (18–19)

Those persons whose imaginations are in disarray are known as "*phantastici,*" but

such persons as be illuminated with the brightest irradiations of knowledge . . . are called . . . *euphantasiote,* and of this sorte of phantasie are all good Poets, . . . all Legislators Polititiens & Counsellours of estate, in whose exercises the inuentive part is most employed and is to the sound & true iudgement of man most needful. (19–20)

Thus Puttenham links what is good in the fantastic poet with the minister of state in an effort to demonstrate that the former provides the same valuable function for society.

Another aspect of the fantastic that would have been available to Shakespeare and his contemporaries derives from the etymology of the word. According to the *Oxford English Dictionary,* "fantasy" finds its root in the Greek *phantasia,* "a making visible," *phantazein,* "to make visible," and *phanein,* "to show." The fantastic could therefore be understood both as the faculty of imagination and as sensuous perception.[17] In other words, it could reveal the truth as well as create an illusion—like Mazzoni's suggestion that the fantastic "many times contains beneath the husk of the fiction, the truth of many noble conceptions" (370).

The fantastic's revealing function is very similar to the way in which dramatic defamation uncovers embarrassing claims about a person. In the second scene of *Measure for Measure,* Lucio displays how his creative wit discloses the flaws of his companions. In a conversation with two gentlemen, he notes and illustrates the hypocrisy of one in the tale of the sanctimonious pirate. When the first gentleman attempts to defend himself, Lucio turns the latter's retorts into a self-incrimination:

1 GENT.
. . . I had as lief be a list of an English kersey, as be piled, as thou art pilled, for a French velvet. Do I speak feelingly now?

LUCIO

I think thou dost: and indeed, with most painful feeling of thy speech. I will, out of thine own confession, learn to begin thy health; but whilst I live, forget to drink after thee.

1 GENT.

I think I have done myself wrong, have I not?

2 GENT.

Yes, that thou hast, whether thou art tainted or free.

(1.2.31–40)

Like the mirror in Puttenham's discussion of the fantastic, Lucio accurately reflects his low-life surroundings in this episode. However, in 1.4 he demonstrates his adaptability to other environments.[18]

Lucio's speeches to Isabella in the convent retain the wittiness of his earlier language ("Hail virgin, if you be" [1.4.16]), but are presented in a diametrically different format. Attending to the decorum of his surroundings, he addresses her in blank verse, which expresses both moral restraint and ornamental formality.

> I would not, though 'tis my familiar sin,
> With maids to seem the lapwing, and to jest
> Tongue far from heart, play with all virgins so.
> I hold you as a thing enskied and sainted
> By your renouncement, an immortal spirit,
> And to be talk'd with in sincerity,
> As with a saint.
>   (1.4.31–37)

His language reveals something about Isabella's character that, judging from her response, she is uncomfortable about acknowledging: "You do blaspheme the good, in mocking me" (38). However, Lucio's solicitousness for her piousness and chastity foreshadows Isabella's own behavior later on in the play.

Lucio's ability to reflect and reveal something about the other characters has a dramaturgical aspect as well.[19] When Isabella's first plea to Angelo is met with refusal, she accepts his answer and turns to leave. Lucio convinces her to stay, and proceeds to block her movements and supply her lines in an effort to improve her performance:

> Give't not o'er so.—To him again, entreat him,
> Kneel down before him, hang upon his gown;

> You are too cold. If you should need a pin,
> You could not with more tame tongue desire it.
> To him, I say.
>
> (2.2.43–47)

He continues to coach Isabella throughout the rest of her audience with Angelo, providing encouragement and advice: "Ay, touch him: there's the vein" (70); "Art avis'd o' that? More on 't" (133). Finally, at the appropriate moment, he gives her the cue to exit: "Go to: 'tis well; away" (157).

Lucio's staging of Isabella's request is disastrously successful, placing her in an impossible dilemma. However, her passionate plea does strike a chord in Angelo that forces him, at least ostensibly, to capitulate to her request. If his promise is not finally kept, it is not because Isabella's importuning is a failure. Rather, it is a tribute to Lucio's talents that she is able to move the deputy as much as she does; Angelo had every intention of refusing all requests to pardon Claudio, even Escalus's (2.1.1–31), and Isabella was convinced she would fail even before she met the deputy (1.4.75–76, 78). Most important here is that Lucio's fantastical direction discloses an aspect of Angelo's character with which the deputy himself had never come to terms.

However, Lucio's most effective performance as a fantastic occurs in his remarks concerning or scenes with the duke, about whom he appears to know quite a bit. At the opening of 1.2 Lucio demonstrates that he is apprised of the latest gossip on the duke's mission, but in his discussion with Isabella later in the act, he indicates that he is not taken in by the rumors:

> The Duke is very strangely gone from hence;
> Bore many gentlemen—myself being one—
> In hand, and hope of action: but we do learn,
> By those that know the very nerves of state,
> His giving out were of an infinite distance
> From his true-meant design.
>
> (1.4.50–55)

It is impossible to know if Lucio does have contacts in the government or whether he simply fabricates this explanation. What is significant about this statement is that it provides a remarkably accurate account of the duke's plans. Lucio continues to express his fantastical insights in his conversation with the disguised duke in 3.2. Several critics have noted that Lucio's speculations are uncanny in their accuracy.[20] Vincentio, disguised as a friar or mendicant, is figuratively "in Rome" (86), and does in fact "usurp the beggary he was never born to" (90). Lucio's fantastical descriptions of Angelo's "creation" do contain a grain of truth in them; in fact, his remarks parallel comments the duke has made to Friar Thomas about the deputy's preciseness (1.3.50–54).

Although the account of Angelo strikes the disguised duke as funny, it marks the point at which Lucio's fictions become slanders.[21] While Vincentio ignores this criticism of his deputy, he lashes out when Lucio shifts his attention to the absent duke. Lucio's first fantastical slander of the duke portrays him as lascivious: "He had some feeling of the sport; he knew the service; and that instructed him to mercy" (3.2.115–16). The suggestion that the duke is promiscuous seems blatantly untrue; after all, he tells Friar Thomas in 1.3 that the "dribbling dart of love" never pierced his "complete bosom" (2–3), and later in 3.2, disguised as a friar, he condemns with vehement disgust the act Pompey's occupation promotes:

> Do thou but think
> What 'tis to cram a maw or clothe a back
> From such a filthy vice. Say to thyself,
> From their abominable and beastly touches
> I drink, I eat, array myself, and live.
> (20–24)

Yet the duke freely admits that he is responsible for the present licentiousness of Vienna (". . . 'twas my fault to give the people scope" [1.3.35]), and is unwilling to rectify the problem himself— thus the necessity for appointing Angelo. By the play's end the lapse still has not been redressed; Vincentio pardons rather than punishes the fornicators. Lucio's witticisms here pinpoint what seems to be a significant inadequacy in the duke's actions as a ruler.

The two pronouncements on the duke's character that follow in 3.2, that he is "A very superficial, ignorant, unweighing fellow" (136), and that he "would have dark deeds darkly answered" (171), also contain elements of truth. If Angelo was appointed in order to enforce the fornication law, the duke could scarcely have selected a more disastrous candidate; his decision appears distinctly ill considered, especially with as qualified a candidate as Escalus at hand. That Vincentio would answer "dark deeds darkly" also seems borne out by the fact that he prefers an indirect method of alleviating Vienna's troubles, both in authorizing a deputy to solve its problems and in his own behind-the-scenes manipulation of the situation. Again, these apparently fictitious remarks contain truths that call into question the duke's ability to rule, and therefore they constitute seditious slander.

Lucio's most astute insight about the duke is that the latter is a fantastic too (see 3.2.89 and 4.3.156). An examination of the duke's actions shows them to be almost identical to Lucio's, with one difference. If Lucio's fictions have had the limited effect of revealing the flaws in other characters' personalities, the duke's elaborate plans constitute a full-scale exposure of Viennese society.

The duke's first action in the play is to announce his imminent departure and appoint Angelo as his deputy: "In our remove, be thou at full ourself" (1.1.43). The choice seems oddly inappropriate; why should Escalus, who is "first in question," be Angelo's "secondary" (1.1.46)? As we discover in 1.3, this appointment and the duke's hasty departure are part of a strategy of fictions he plans to deploy. Vincentio claims that his self-imposed absence from the ducal seat is a way of bringing his subjects back into a closer observance of the statutes prohibiting fornication. Because it would appear too tyrannous to enforce laws that he let "slip," he has appointed Angelo as his substitute:

> Who may in th'ambush of my name strike home,
> And yet my nature never in the fight
> To do in slander.
>
> (1.3.41–43)

Although the duke expresses disapproval of and disgust for illicit sex in his scenes with Juliet and Pompey (2.2 and 3.2), his scheme to couple Mariana and Angelo indicates that he is not above making use of it to further his own ends. His main motive for selecting a deputy is not so much to rectify the law but to protect his reputation; his anxiety about public opinion is made clear by its reiteration throughout his later speeches.

But the duke offers another motive for choosing Angelo. Vincentio professes to know Angelo's real worth and ability:

> There is a kind of character in thy life
> That to th'observer doth thy history
> Fully unfold. . . .
>
> (1.1.27–29)

However, he suggests to Friar Thomas that the deputy's character might not jibe with his history:

> Lord Angelo is precise;
> Stands at a guard with Envy; scarce confesses
> That his blood flows; or that his appetite
> Is more to bread than stone. Hence shall we see
> If power change purpose, what our seemers be.
>
> (1.3.50–54)

In fact, the duke already does know from Angelo's history that he has been less than just in his dealings with Mariana. While the duke is careful to keep his own reputation from exposure ("I love the people, / But do not like to stage me to their eyes" [1.1.67–68]; "I have ever lov'd the life remov'd" [1.3.8]), he is very eager to discover if Angelo's reputation is all it seems to be. The duke's decision to spy on Angelo in the guise of a friar suggests a strategic fiction which will put to the test—and possibly debunk—the substitute's apparent virtuousness.

Vincentio's suspicions about his deputy are confirmed when he overhears Isabella's disclosure of Angelo's terms for her brother's pardon. The disguised duke, who moments earlier while shriving Claudio did not indicate he felt the sentence was unjust, begins constructing an elaborate plan to save the prisoner and expose Angelo. When he asks Isabella what she plans to do, she replies: "If ever [the duke] return, and I can speak to him, I will open my lips in vain, or discover his government" (3.1.191–93). The novice's accusation of Angelo would seem to spill over into a complaint of the duke's own government. The friar/duke suggests a strategy which will effectively focus the blame entirely on the deputy. Because Angelo has only propositioned Isabella, he can avoid the accusation; the duke devises

a plan which will allow his substitute to incriminate himself fully
and provide Vincentio with the opportunity to expose the crime.

In conversations with Isabella (3.1.257ff.) and Mariana (4.1.71ff.)
the duke justifies the use of deception by demonstrating the benefits
the scheme will effect. However, while he plans to save Isabella's
brother and provide restitution for Mariana, Vincentio's primary aim
is to humiliate Angelo. Once he proposes the plan to Isabella, the
disguised duke starts setting the stage, as it were, for Angelo's exposure by making several apparently offhand remarks to a variety of
characters. When Elbow mentions that he must take Pompey before
Angelo, the friar/duke replies: "That we were all, as some would
seem to be, / From our faults, as faults from seeming, free!" (3.2.37–
38). At the end of this scene, in a discussion in which Escalus mentions
Angelo's severity, the duke responds:

If his own life answer the straitness of his proceeding, it shall become him
well: wherein if he chance to fail, he hath sentenced himself.

(3.2.249–51)

In 4.2, when the provost displays momentary anger at Angelo's "bitterness," the friar/duke chides him:

Not so, not so; his life is parallel'd
Even with the stroke and line of his great justice.
He doth with holy abstinence subdue
That in himself which he spurs on his power
To qualify in others; were he meal'd with that
Which he corrects, then were he tyrannous;
But this being so, he's just.

(77–83)

The effect of these comments is to heighten the tension and resentment that already exist around Angelo so that his final exposure will
be all the more mortifying.

Further evidence of the duke's attempts to expose and slander
Angelo, instead of simply rectifying the situation, is his manipulation
of Isabella. Although Vincentio finds a way to preserve Claudio's life
when Angelo refuses to grant the promised pardon, the disguised
duke informs Isabella only that the deputy has ordered her brother's

execution. Predictably enough, Isabella is infuriated by Angelo's treachery, and again the duke shapes her anger to suit his purposes. He dissuades her from confronting the deputy immediately, counseling her instead to slander Angelo in front of an audience:

> . . . you shall have your bosom on this wretch,
> Grace of the Duke, revenges to your heart,
> And general honour.
>
> . . . .
>   . . . [T]o the head of Angelo
> Accuse him home and home.
>
>   (4.3.134–35, 142–43)

Vincentio then insures that a number of witnesses will observe this accusation by sending letters to Angelo and his friends, instructing the former to proclaim that anyone recently wronged seek redress at the gates of the city and requesting the attendance of the latter upon his return.

It is puzzling that, given his own fear of slander, the duke would want to denounce Angelo. He was initially motivated to select a deputy because of his anxiety about his own reputation (1.3.39–43); the public exposure of his substitute's incompetence would appear to reflect badly on him. Vincentio is deeply disturbed by Lucio's slanders in 3.2, yet the duke is also responsible for spreading rumors about his own absence. If he is so anxious to avoid slander, why does the duke seem to promote it?

The duke makes his most vehement denunciation of slander in act 4, while lamenting the ruler's inability to avoid detraction. The great are represented as inextricably connected to defamation, which maintains a limpet-like hold on authority:

> O place and greatness! Millions of false eyes
> Are stuck upon thee: volumes of report
> Run with these false, and most contrarious quest
> Upon thy doings: thousand escapes of wit
> Make thee the father of their idle dream
> And rack thee in their fancies.
>
>   (4.1.60–65)

However, this association of slander with the ruler reverses from a juxtaposition of rumor and ruler to an identification of the duke with

defamation personified. Although the duke's explicit meaning indicates that his subjects' surveillance and misrepresentation threaten
the ruler, his language suggests his ability to spy on and defame them.
The Arden edition (99) notes the similarity of the metaphor in lines
60–62 to the description of Fame in Jonson's *Poetaster* (1601):

> . . . Looke, how many plumes are plac't
> On her huge corps, so many waking eyes
> Sticke vnderneath: and (which may stranger rise
> In the report) as many tongues shee beares,
> As many mouthes, as many listning ears.
>
> (5.2.85–89)

The eyes of a slanderous audience fixed on the duke can also be read
as eyes attached to, and looking out from, his own body. "[P]lace
and greatness" are transformed into an allegorical figure of bad fame—
defamation—in a description which presents authority as being covered with eyes just as Fame is depicted by Jonson.[22] The ruler is not
so much the victim of slander as its source.

The duke's role as slanderer is most clearly presented in the last
act of the play.[23] When he returns undisguised to Vienna, Vincentio
receives Isabella's accusations of Angelo with an apparently suspicious
ear. He concludes that she has been "suborn'd against [Angelo's] honour / In hateful practice" (5.1.109–10) and dismisses her valid claims
as false imputations. She is consequently arrested for her defamation:

> To prison with her! Shall we thus permit
> A blasting and a scandalous breath to fall
> On him so near us? This must needs be a practice.
>
> (5.1.124–26)

The duke proceeds to accuse Friar Lodowick (his disguised persona),
Friar Peter, and Mariana, along with Isabella, of plotting to defame
his deputy. He leaves the latter two in Angelo's hands to be punished:
"stir not you till you have well determin'd / Upon these slanderers"
(5.1.257–58). The irony here is that the duke is behind this "practice,"
which results in the slandering of his deputy.

When Vincentio returns disguised as Friar Lodowick, he speaks the
most destructive sedition in the play:

> My business in this state
> Made me a looker-on here in Vienna,
> Where I have seen corruption boil and bubble
> Till it o'errun the stew: laws for all faults,
> But faults so countenanc'd that the strong statutes
> Stand like the forfeits in a barber's shop,
> As much in mock as mark.
>
> (5.1.314–20)

Escalus, realizing the danger this speech poses to the established order, immediately calls for the friar's arrest: "Slander to th'state! / Away with him to prison!" (320–21)

What does the duke—who throughout the play attests to his desire to avoid slander—gain by such a manifest self-slander? The result of his dramatic and defamatory epiphanies is to batter the majority of his subjects into submission and silence. By posing as a slanderer and promoting slander, the duke maneuvers practically all of the characters present into positions of subservience: Angelo, Escalus, Isabella, the provost all ask for his pardon; and Mariana, Barnardine, and Claudio are completely indebted to him. If Vincentio's original intention in leaving Vienna was to reassert his authority, he would appear to be largely successful.

The duke's appointment of Angelo posed a threat of self-slander, but it was a carefully calculated risk. Vincentio clearly had no intentions of selecting a candidate who was conspicuously well equipped for the job. All of Escalus's actions demonstrate that he could be both a just and merciful ruler; in the duke's absence, his expertise and compassion would have made him more popular than his superior.[24] Angelo, on the other hand, was bound to be unpopular whether he succeeded, because he enforced the law too harshly, or failed, as he did. The deputy's service falls so short of even Vincentio's abilities that the latter's authority is enhanced profoundly by comparison.

Vincentio's control over his subjects appears so absolute as to approach omniscience. Angelo articulates this sense of the duke's power when his guilt is discovered near the play's end.

> O my dread lord,
> I should be guiltier than my guiltiness
> To think that I can be undiscernible,

When I perceive your Grace, like power divine,
Hath looked upon my passes.

(5.1.364–68)

The ruler, as God's temporal representative, is endowed with a transcendent authority; the duke's disguise as a friar, which allows him
omniscience over his subjects, serves to emphasize this point. The
duke possesses something of the eclipsing authority of divine power
that Puttenham ascribes to satiric poets; he describes them as

disguised persons vnder the shape of *Satyres* as who would say, these terrene
and base gods being conuersant with mans affaires, and spiers out of all their
secret faults: had some great care ouer man, & desired by good admonitions
to reforme the euill of their life, and to bring the bad to amendment by those
kinde of preachings, whereupon the Poets inuentours of the deuise were
called *Satyristes*. (31)

Vincentio is a kind of "terrene god" who spies out and exposes the
vices of his subjects and his substitute. While the apparent function
of his role as "satyriste" is the reformation of vice in Vienna, the
duke's ultimate motive in using the power of satiric exposure is to
reaffirm his own authority.

James I was an eloquent and frequent articulator of the relationship
of monarch to deity. In a February 1604–05 charge to the judges and
justices of the peace, he describes the ruler's divine right: "the kinge's
Matie, as it were inheritabel & descended from god, hathe absolutelye
monarchicall power annexed inseperablye to his Crowne & diademe"
(Hawarde 188). This privilege gave the king, according to James,
absolute power in the reign and reformation of his kingdom:

. . . his Ma$^{tie's}$ pleasure & express Charge ys that the vulgar shall not leape
into his throne & reforme any contempte herein, but shall Complaine to the
maiestrate & he shall prouyd for yt, and his Matie will exacte a verye exacte
accounte at his handes [from officers who neglect] . . . his Ma$^{tie's}$ pleasure
herein. (Hawarde 162)

James clearly felt it the king's sole right to criticize the state. In his
Basilikon Doron he identifies a fault common to all of his subjects,
"which is, to iudge and speake rashly of their Prince" (27). This
comment comes at the end of a list of reproofs of his subjects' short-
comings, in which, as he explains to Prince Henry,

... I haue not spared to be something Satyricke, in touching well quickly the faults in all the estates of my kingdome: But I protest before God, I doe it with the fatherly loue that I owe to them all; onely hating their vices, whereof there is a good number of honest men free in euery estate. (27)

In James's view, the king's position enables him to criticize his people and discourage their criticism of him.

However, the duke's determination to expose every character on the stage extends the ruler's right to criticize beyond his ability to justify it. In so doing, Vincentio completes his humiliation of his onstage audience, transforming them from welcoming spectators into chastened criminals. By silencing his subjects, the duke eradicates not only the slander, but also the affirmation of his actions. When the audience itself is deliberately put in the position of the disgraced criminal, it has no choice but to identify with the criminal against the ruler. Foucault's comments on public execution are applicable to this moment of public humiliation in which the spectators not only sympathize with the criminal, but become him: "out of the ceremony of the public execution, out of that uncertain festival in which violence was instantaneously reversible, it was [the solidarity between audience and criminal] much more than the sovereign power that was likely to emerge with redoubled strength" (63).

The monarch's right to "satirize" his realm must also stop short of intentionally appointing corrupt officials. In fact, according to James, the ruler's ability to restrain popular criticism of the state is dependent upon the appointment of just magistrates who will address such grievances. Officers who fail to fulfill their duties by allowing subjects' complaints to go unredressed—and who thus run the risk of encouraging disparagement of the state—will be called into account by the king. Contemporary legal theory also suggests that the ruler's right to criticize and expose did not include the ability to slander his realm by the selection of incompetent substitutes. In the early seventeenth century, libels of a magistrate or a public person were perceived by the Star Chamber to jeopardize the security of the state: "'Let all men ... take heed how they complayne in words against any magistrate for they are gods'" (Holdsworth 5: 208–09). In the case *De Libellis Famosis* Edward Coke states that libel against a magistrate is a greater offense than against a private person, for it concerns not only the breach of the peace, but also the scandal of Government; for what greater scandal of Government can there be than to have corrupt or wicked magistrates to be appointed and constituted by the King to govern his subjects under him? And greater imputation to the State cannot be, than to suffer such corrupt men to sit in the sacred seat of justice, or to have any meddling in or concerning the administration of justice. (251)

Ferdinando Pulton makes a similar observation in his *De Pace Regnis et Regni* (1609):

... libelling, secret slandring or defaming ... against a publicke magis-trate ... is a great sca[n]dal & offence to the king, his chief magistrates, & the whole gouernment of the realm, to assigne such an officer to rule & gouern others, who himself is void of gouernme[n]t, & shal deserue to be impeached with such crimes as he shalbe taxed with, or shall be imputed vnto him by such an infamous libell. (1Bv)

Although the gist of these statements is that this serious offense is the fault of the slanderer, both Coke and Pulton seem to suggest that the real threat to the peace of the realm lies with the king who appoints an incompetent magistrate.

In naming and then condemning an incompetent deputy, the duke opens his government up to the slanders he himself articulates in act 5. His subsequent condemnation of Lucio for "Slandering a prince" (5.1.521) calls into question his own defamatory practice. Angelo is punished for hypocrisy, for failing to chastise in himself the vices he so vehemently prosecuted in others.[25] By the doctrine of *lex talionis* that Vincentio sets out in the course of the play, the duke must also correct his own vice in castigating Lucio's slanders. His ultimate goal—to reassert his authority and reputation in Vienna, "And yet [his] nature never in the fight / To do in slander" (1.3.42–43)—fails in his alienation of the very spectators he wished to impress.

Thus, just as the "fantastical duke of dark corners" effects the several exposures of his subjects, Lucio's presence also serves to expose the duke. Vincentio's ability to spy out men's secret faults seems to be aptly described by Puttenham, but we must remember that the passage quoted above referred to poets, not rulers. Lucio is equally capable of discovering the duke's "secret faults." He does so figuratively when he claims that the disguised duke was no true friar (5.1.261–63), and then literally when he unmasks "Friar Lodowick"

(5.1.349–53).[26] Finally, Lucio's punishment for slander exposes the duke's own defamatory practices.

Lucio's slanders of the duke are dangerous precisely because they ultimately expose the danger of the duke's slanders. *Measure for Measure* shows that the state's dramatic slander is more hazardous than the poet's. In fact, attempts to discredit the slanderous aspects of the theater could redound against the state by calling into question the ruler's own use of theatrical power to expose and punish. The duke's attempt to ballast his authority by means of theatrical slander is undermined by his punishing Lucio's slanders. In its dramatization of the duke's actions, *Measure for Measure* employs the state's own methods of exposure to criticize the arbitrariness of its response to theater, and to warn that the greater peril of theatrical slander lies in the ruler's, not the theater's, abuse of it.

Notes

1. Although distinctions among libel, slander, sedition, and scandal were taking shape in sixteenth- and seventeenth-century English law, the terms were still frequently interchanged; take for example this 1581 statute making it a felony to "devise and write, print or set forth, any manner of book, rhyme, ballad, letter, or writing containing any false, seditious or slanderous matters to the defamation of the Queen's majesty" (Bowen 89). Speaking such words constituted a felony on the second conviction, suggesting that verbal imputations were considered a lesser offense (Holdsworth 4: 511–12). The Star Chamber also appears to have been more concerned with written defamation, but both written and spoken defamation were considered criminal if the imputation resulted in a breach of the peace (Coke 250–52). The common law courts did not make a consistent distinction between libel and slander as written and spoken defamation until 1660 (Baker 373). The term "libel" was usually understood in the Renaissance as a criminal form of defamation; "slander" was generally used to indicate a tort or private injury. In this essay, I nevertheless tend to privilege the term "slander" because it was used frequently in contemporary parlance, and almost exclusively by Shakespeare in *Measure for Measure,* to describe both criminal and civil defamation.

2. Similar punishments were carried out in sixteenth- and seventeenth-century England, as is evidenced by the amputation of Philip Stubbes's right hand as punishment for libeling Elizabeth in *The Discoverie of a Gaping Gulf;* William Prynne lost his ears (connected with rumor and libel) and the initials "SL"—seditious libeler—were carved on his cheek to punish his oblique criticism of Charles I and Henrietta Maria in *Histriomastix.* I am indebted to Richard Burt for kindly allowing me to read an unpublished manuscript in which he discusses such mutilations in an analysis of censorship and the body in the works of Ben Jonson.

3. "... [T]orture forms part of a ritual. It is an element in the liturgy of punishment and meets two demands. It must mark the victim: it is intended, either by the scar it leaves on the body, or by the spectacle that accompanies it, to brand the victim with infamy; even if its function is to 'purge' the crime, torture does not reconcile, it traces around or, rather, on the very body of the condemned man signs that must not be effaced; in any case, men will remember public exhibition, the pillory, torture and pain duly observed. And, from the point of view of the law that imposes it, public torture and execution must be spectacular, it must be seen by all almost as its triumph" (34). Foucault notes the greater importance of torture in France (and most of Europe), where the legal procedure up until the punishment was kept secret, as opposed to England, where trials by jury were open to the public; in the Continental system, torture publicly enacted the private trial (35–47).

4. The earliest definition of defamation in England—the false imputation of a crime—was formed by the ecclesiastical courts. While the scope of defamation was narrowed and altered once the common law courts began hearing slander cases in the early 1500s, this original definition remained actionable (Helmholz xiv, lxxvii). The fact that words endangering life or liberty were considered defamatory derived from the idea that the accusation of a crime could damage one's reputation by resulting in "arrest and trial, or seizure by the lord; and in some cases ... imprisonment ... [or] loss of credit with persons who had stopped dealing with the plaintiff as a result of the scandal" (Baker 366). The latter half of the sixteenth century witnessed an enormous increase in slander suits as the common law courts (specifically, Queen's Bench and Common Pleas) extended their jurisdiction to include defamation, previously handled in ecclesiastical and local courts. Words that resulted in a temporal loss for the plaintiff constituted slander; damages were the gist of the action. Specific categories of defamatory words were delineated; false accusations that endangered life or liberty, allegations of professional incompetence, or imputations of certain diseases were all considered actionable. Truth was an absolute defense; if the imputation could be verified then no action would lie. In an attempt to stem the flood of actions on the case for slander, the common law judges introduced several interpretive strategies which enabled them to dismiss cases by construing the imputations as not actionable (Baker 364–73; Holdsworth 5: 205–07).

By the beginning of the seventeenth century the introduction of a category of criminal defamation created tensions and contradictions with the development of the common law definitions of the term. Words that led to a breach of the peace constituted criminal defamation according to the Star Chamber definition. Thus the plaintiff did not have to prove damages, and the truth of the claim was immaterial. Here, the justices were not as much concerned about limiting the number of libel suits as halting violent social unrest. The Star Chamber formulated a redress for provocative words in part to provide a legal alternative to duelling that would compensate for damaged reputations (Holdsworth 5: 208–11).

In this essay, I concern myself more with the criminal rather than the tort definition of defamation, and with the Star Chamber's development of this category. The claim I make that the state operated by means of institutionalized slander cannot be completely supported by the fact that true accusations could constitute libel, for in the normal course of legal procedure, state-sanctioned accusations of crime would not be seen to pose a threat to the peace, even if such charges did result in violence. However, my point here is to show that accusations made and punishments inflicted by the state functioned structurally as slander; that is, the aim of such methods was to humiliate individuals publicly by means of assertions of criminality. Official attempts to define as slander private imputations against citizens or the state show that the Star Chamber was concerned to criminalize defamation in order to distinguish it from state practice. The Privy Council was anxious to control defamation by deploring the power of language to criticize and expose, both because slander constituted in part state power, and because it was also a weapon that could be turned against the state.

5. A copy of the 1570 edition of Foxe's book was commanded to be placed in every English church, along with the Bible (Foxe 1: 64).

6. For a related and more rigorous discussion of the instability of audience reception, with regard to issues of authorial intention, subversion, and the market for plays in the seventeenth century, see Burt.

7. According to the *OED,* slander finds its root in the word *scandal.* The definition of scandal indicates that infamy is the result of one's own disgraceful behavior; however, in the sixteenth century, scandal is also defined as slander, in which false imputations bring about infamy. This apparent contradiction in the etymology of slander/scandal is present in conflicting legal definitions of defamation. In a civil case when damages were the gist of the suit, the imputation had to be false to constitute slander. However, in a criminal case where maintaining the peace was the court's concern, a true accusation was considered just as, if not more, likely to lead to violence, so the truth of the imputation was irrelevant. Thus, the plaintiff in a slander suit could be the victim of a false accusation, according to the common law definition of the tort, or could be complaining about the exposure of infamous behavior, according to the Star Chamber's criminal definition.

8. From Edward Coke's *De Libellis Famosis* (251). See also Holdsworth (5: 208–12) and Pulton: "I have thought it good to begin with the very roote and principall cause of [offenses to the realm], which are Menaces, Threatnings, and other bitter words, beeing as streames gushing out of contentious spirits, and venomous tongues, their naturall fountaines and springheads, from whence do ensue sometimes Assaults, Batteries, Riots, Routs . . ." (1Br).

9. "[F]or as the woman said, she would never grieve to have been told of her red nose if she had not one indeed" (Hudson 2: 103). Edward Coke spells out this concept more fully: "It is not material whether the libel is true, or whether the party against whom it is made, be of good or ill fame; for in a settled state of Government the party grieved ought to complain for every injury done him in an ordinary course of law, and not by any means to revenge himself, either by the odious course of libelling, or otherwise . . ." (251).

10. I was lucky enough to find this document while searching through the earl of Lincoln's Star Chamber litigation; to my knowledge, this case referred to by Hudson has remained undiscovered until now.

11. In perusing a list of documents from the Tower with the antiquary, Elizabeth is reported by Lambarde to have hesitated over Richard II's reign and said "'I am Richard II. know ye not that?' W.L. [replied] 'Such a wicked imagination was determined and attempted by a most unkind Gent. the most adorned creature that ever your Majestie made.' Her Majestie [responded] 'He that will forget God, will also forget his benefactors; this tragedy was played 40^{tie} times in open streets and houses.'" See Peter Ure's introduction to the Arden *Richard II* (lix). Leeds Barroll argues against using this anecdote as evidence that the state found the theater subversive. While I agree that other historical narratives must be examined before drawing conclusions about Lambarde's account, I believe that the documents set out in this essay suggest that the Privy Council was concerned about theatrical impersonation, especially of persons of rank. Elizabeth's claim that "this tragedy was played 40^{tie} times" is surely an exaggeration, but one which registers a clear anxiety during a time of social unrest about being impersonated in the figure of a deposed king. Barroll doesn't disprove that dramatic impersonation threatens the state; he shows that the written word was held to pose a greater threat. He demonstrates that some of the conspirators responsible for commissioning the performance of *Richard II* were punished while the players were not; it makes perfect sense that the state would condemn those who used the drama for seditious purposes, while ignoring the players who were merely hired and performed the play without a certifiably treasonous intent.

12. See also the section on eclogues: poets "deuised the Eglogue . . . [so as] vnder the vaile of homely persons, and in rude speeches to insinuate and glaunce at greater matters, and such as perchance had not bene safe to haue beene disclosed in any other sort . . . " (38).

13. There is evidence in the records of sixteenth-century Essex that "unfavorable or irreverent remarks about the sovereign," such as accusing the queen of being a whore or of bearing and murdering illegitimate children, received very harsh penalties, even though such comments did not directly incite to rebellion (Samaha 70).

14. Reginald Lawson sees Lucio as behaving "according to the 'trick' or fashion of his group. A fantastic is defined variously by Elizabethans as 'an improvident young gallant'; 'an effeminate fool'; . . . 'and one that is so neere a kin to the foole, that they cannot marry without a license from the Pope' . . . " (262). Mary Lascelles claims that this epithet for Lucio should not be attributed to Shakespeare: "The Folio attaches lists of Actors' (i.e. characters') names to seven plays. Mr. Crompton Rhodes supposes them to derive from papers which served some useful purpose in the theatre, as 'a remembrancer for casting, or as a catalogue to a bundle of written parts.' (*Shakespeare's First Folio*, Oxford, 1923, p. 118.) This supposition as to their provenance does not necessarily connect them with the dramatist, and the list for *Measure for Measure* contains one word to which there is no Shakespearian parallel. Lucio is called 'a fantastique'—meaning, presumably, a fop. Shakespeare uses the adjective fantastic in a corresponding sense: 'To be fantastic may become a youth' (*Two Gentlemen,* II.vii.47); but his form for the noun is fantastico: 'such antic, lisping, affecting fantasticoes' (*Romeo and Juliet,* II.iv.30). I believe that we should not associate this list with him, nor build on it any

surmise as to the form in which he found his plot, or left his play" (165). Lascelles is probably justified in her assumption that Shakespeare would have used the term "fantastico" to indicate a simpering gallant. However, I do not see either Lucio or the duke, who is described as "fantastical" in the course of the play, as a fop. I wish to suggest another definition of fantastic that would have been available to Shakespeare, one which applies to both the duke and Lucio and that, regardless of the authenticity of the dramatis personae, is supported by the text of the play. J. M. Nosworthy's comment on Lucio's designation as a "fantastic" in his edition of *Measure for Measure* suggests the direction my argument will take: "The word may imply a fop, but in Lucio's case it seems more likely to signify someone with an unbridled fantasy or imagination" (154).

15. One intriguing appearance of the fantastic should at least be mentioned here, although its relevance to *Measure for Measure* is tenuous. Related to legislation punishing witchcraft and the invocation of evil spirits (which laws by the way enjoyed a renaissance during the early years of James I's reign) were the mid-sixteenth-century statutes directed against false and fantastical prophecies. "The making of such prophecies was declared to be felony in 1541–42; and after the repeal of this statute in 1547 such prophecies were made misdemeanours by statutes of 1549 and 1562–63. The reason for the enactment of these two latter statutes and probably of the first-named also, was the fact that these prophecies were made for the purpose of stirring up rebellion" (Holdsworth 4: 511). A later statute on the containment of masterless men (39 Eliz. 4) classed as vagabonds anyone "using any subtile Crafte or unlawful Games and Playes, or fayning themselves to have knowledge in Phisiognomye, Palmestry or other like crafty Scyence, or pretending that they can tell Destenyes Fortunes or such other like fantastical Imagynacons; . . . all Fencers Bearewards comon Players of Enterludes and Minstrells wandring abroade (other then Players of Enterludes belonging to any Baron of this realme . . .)" (Ribton-Turner 128).

16. Little is known about Mazzoni's reception in England before Milton. I include Mazzoni in this discussion to indicate that contemporary literary theory was developing a specific definition of the fantastic. Puttenham's similar account suggests either that he had read Mazzoni, or that this understanding of the word was already circulating among literary theorists in sixteenth-century England.

17. "The senses of *phantasia* from which the senses of the word in the mod. langs. are developed are: 1. appearance, . . . spectral apparition, phantom . . . ; 2. the mental process or faculty of sensuous perception; 3. the faculty of imagination. These senses passed through OF into Eng., together with others (as delusive fancy, false . . . notion, caprice . . .). . . . The shortened form FANCY, . . . had in the time of Shakespere become more or less differentiated in sense. After the revival of Gr. learning, the longer form was often spelt *phantasy* and its meaning was influenced by the Gr. etymon" (*OED*, s.v. "fantasy").

18. Lucio's status as gentleman-soldier allows him a certain amount of mobility up and down the social scale. His name also suggests his ability to reflect what surrounds him. The Italian *luce* means "light," as well as "looking-glass" (*Lysle-Gualtieri Disionario*).

19. See Lawry for the suggestion that Lucio functions as director in 2.2 (225).

20. Summarized in Spencer (17–18). He argues that the text does not provide a motivation for Lucio's actions toward the duke if he did know the latter was in disguise. I would agree with him in part, but this does not nullify the fact that Lucio does speak the truth here. Shakespeare may be playing with the notion of "fantastic" as it related to such supernatural knowledge as predicting the future (see note 15 above). At any rate, my analysis of his character focuses on his function in the play with regard to the duke, so I tend to concentrate on the allegorical, rather than psychological, significance of his behavior.

21. Insulting language about a magistrate was considered defamatory because it posed a threat to the peace of the realm by calling into question the ruler's judgment. As Edward Coke states in *De Libellis Famosis*, ". . . what greater scandal of Government can there be than to have corrupt or wicked magistrates to be appointed and constituted by the King to govern his subjects under him?" (251). I will discuss at a later point and in greater detail the significance of this theory for the duke's actions.

22. Jonson's depiction of Fame is a translation of Virgil's description of Fama in *Aeneid* 4.181–83: "monstrum horrendum, ingens, cui quot sunt corpore plumae, / tot vigilies oculi subter (mirabile dictu), / tot linguae, totidem ora sonant, tot subrigit auris." Depictions of Fame often showed her covered with sense organs; the "Rainbow portrait" of Elizabeth (c. 1600) represents her in a dress embroidered with ears and eyes, symbolizing Fame (Strong 84–85, plate xvii). In the stage direction to the Induction of *2 Henry IV,* Rumour enters "painted full of tongues."

23. The duke's slanders against his subjects take on the same mixed sense that the competing legal definitions of defamation had. Although some of the accusations he makes are true and others are false—like the criminal and tort definitions of slander— nevertheless they both serve the same intended end: to humiliate publicly his victims.

24. Escalus's name might be derived from "scale," with roots in the German word for "balance." It is probably more closely linked to the Latin *scala,* indicating "staircase, ladder, standard of measurement." The Latin root is also related to *scandere,* "to climb," and thus to such words as "ascend" and "scandal." The duke wouldn't have "measured up" to Escalus's superior leadership, which would have resulted in a scandal for the ruler.

25. See Bawcutt for a discussion of the duke's condemnation of Angelo on the basis of the latter's hypocrisy. Although I disagree with the article's sympathetic attitude toward the duke, I find its account of where he finds fault with Angelo particularly convincing.

26. Lucio's apparent ability to "see through" the duke is emphasized in the language as well as the action of this moment: "You must be hooded, must you? Show your knave's visage, with a pox to you! Show your sheep-biting face, and be hanged an hour! Will't not off?" (5.1.350–53). The Arden note on "sheep-biting face" suggests there is a grain of truth in the midst of this fantastical formulation: "'sheep-biter', i.e. a dog or wolf that attacked sheep, was a common epithet for a dangerous rogue, especially a sanctimonious one." In his ostensible attempts to defend his state from the dangers of slander, Vincentio actually poses a greater threat to order in the realm.

Works Cited

Baker, J. H. *An Introduction to English Legal History.* 2nd ed. London: Butterworths, 1979.

Barish, Jonas A. *The Antitheatrical Prejudice.* Berkeley: U of California P, 1981.

Barroll, Leeds. "A New History for Shakespeare and His Time." *Shakespeare Quarterly* 39 (1988): 441–64.

Bawcutt, N. W. "'He who the sword of heaven will bear': The Duke versus Angelo in *Measure for Measure.*" *Shakespeare Survey* 37 (1984): 89–97.

Bowen, Catherine Drinker. *The Lion and the Throne: The Life and Times of Sir Edward Coke.* Boston: Atlantic–Little, Brown, 1956.

Burt, Richard A. "''Tis Writ by Me': Massinger's *The Roman Actor* and the Politics of Reception in the English Renaissance Theatre." *Theatre Journal* 40 (1988): 332–46.

Chambers, E. K. *The Elizabethan Stage.* 4 vols. Oxford: Clarendon, 1923.

Coke, Edward. "De Libellis Famosis." *Reports,* bk. 5. *The English Reports,* King's Bench Division, bk. 6. Ed. Max A. Robertson and Geoffrey Ellis. Edinburgh: William Green, 1907. 77: 250–52.

Foucault, Michel. *Discipline and Punish: The Birth of the Prison.* Trans. Alan Sheridan. New York: Vintage, 1979.

Foxe, John. *Acts and Monuments.* Ed. George Townsend. 3rd ed. 8 vols. London, 1870.

Greenblatt, Stephen. "Invisible Bullets: Renaissance Authority and Its Subversion, *Henry IV* and *Henry V.*" *Political Shakespeare: New Essays in Cultural Materialism.* Ed. Jonathan Dollimore and Alan Sinfield. Ithaca: Cornell UP, 1985. 18–47.

Harding, Alan. *A Social History of English Law.* Gloucester, MA: Smith, 1973.

Hawarde, John. *Les reportes del cases in Camera Stellata, 1593 to 1609.* Ed. William Paley Baildon. London: Privately printed, 1894.

Helmholz, R. H., ed. *Select Cases on Defamation to 1600.* Publications of the Selden Society, vol. 101. London: Selden Soc., 1985.

Holdsworth, W. S. *A History of English Law.* 16 vols. Boston: Little, Brown–Methuen, 1927–66.

Hudson, William. *A Treatise of the Court of Star Chamber.* London, 1791–92. Vol. 2 of *Collectanea Juridica.* Ed. Francis Hargrave. 2 vols. 1791–92.

Hughes, Paul L., and James F. Larkin, eds. *Tudor Royal Proclamations.* 3 vols. New Haven: Yale UP, 1964–69.

James I. "Basilikon Doron." *The Political Works of James I.* Ed. Charles H. McIlwain. Cambridge: Harvard UP, 1918. 3–52.

Jonson, Ben. *Poetaster.* Vol. 4 of *Works.* Ed. C. H. Herford and Percy and Evelyn Simpson. Oxford: Clarendon, 1925–52.

Lascelles, Mary. *Shakespeare's* Measure for Measure. Folcroft, PA: Folcroft, 1953.

Lawry, J. S. "Imitations and Creation in *Measure for Measure.*" *Shakespeare and the Arts.* Ed. Cecile Williamson Cary and Henry S. Limouze. Washington, DC: UP of America, 1982. 217–29.

Lawson, Reginald. "Lucio, in *Measure for Measure.*" *English Studies* 19 (1937): 259–64.

Lincoln v. Dymock. Public Record Office. STAC5 L/34/37.

Lysle-Gualtieri Disionario. Turin, 1851.

Mazzoni, Jacopo. "On the Defense of the *Comedy* of Dante." *Literary Criticism: Plato to Dryden.* Ed. Allan H. Gilbert. 1940. Detroit: Wayne State UP, 1962. 359–403.

Nosworthy, J. M., ed. *Measure for Measure.* By William Shakespeare. Harmondsworth: Penguin, 1969.

Pulton, Ferdinando. *De Pace Regnis et Regni.* London, 1609.

Puttenham, George. *The Arte of English Poesie.* Ed. Gladys Doidge Willcock and Alice Walker. Cambridge: Cambridge UP, 1936.

Ribton-Turner, C. J. *A History of Vagrants and Vagrancy.* 1887. Montclair, NJ: Patterson Smith, 1972.

Samaha, Joel. "Gleanings from Local Criminal-Court Records: Sedition amongst the 'Inarticulate' in Elizabethan Essex." *Journal of Social History* 8 (Summer 1975): 61–79.

Shakespeare, William. *Measure for Measure.* Ed. J. W. Lever. The Arden Shakespeare. London: Methuen, 1965.

———. *King Richard II.* Ed. Peter Ure. 5th ed. London: Methuen, 1961.

Spencer, Christopher. "Lucio and the Friar's Hood." *English Language Notes* 3 (1965): 17–21.

Stone, Lawrence. *The Crisis of the Aristocracy.* Abridged ed. London: Oxford UP, 1967.

Strong, Roy C. *Portraits of Queen Elizabeth I.* Oxford: Clarendon, 1963.

Staging Pardon Scenes:
Variations of Tragicomedy

JANET M. SPENCER

> Our scene is alt'red from a serious thing,
> And now chang'd to "The Beggar and the King."
> —*Richard II* 5.3.79–80

FOLLOWING UPRISINGS, Tudor and Stuart monarchs authorized public spectacles which represented (and, when successful, effected) the reestablishment of their authority, thus turning the occasion of unrest into a display of power. The most obvious of these dramas, of course, was the public execution. The leaders of the revolt would be returned to the site of the rebellion or to their hometowns, where they were ceremoniously hung, drawn, and quartered; for months afterwards, throughout the territory participating in the unrest, the victims' remains would be displayed as memorials to the sovereign's justice (and power) on the eaves of public buildings or on poles lining the major thoroughfares into town. Through public execution and the subsequent display of the dismembered bodies of its victims, the government used ritualized violence to turn the bodies of the rebellious into material symbols of its own superior (because successful) power.[1]

The execution, however, was not the only drama used by the Tudors and Stuarts to restore order. An equally viable display of power was the spectacle of mercy, dramatized in the public pardon. The two are closely related in the ways that they stage the state's power to exercise capital punishment and also *not* to exercise it. Michel

Foucault explains the relationship among executions, pardons, and the mediation of sovereign power:

The sovereign was present at the execution not only as the power exacting the vengeance of the law, but as the power that could suspend both law and vengeance. He alone must remain master, he alone could wash away the offences committed on his person; although it is true that he delegated to the courts the task of exercising his power to dispense justice, he had not transferred it; he retained it in its entirety and he could suspend the sentence or increase it at will. (*Discipline* 53)

As Foucault describes the relationship, the royal pardon exemplifies the same totality of power of monarch over subject as did the execution.

Unlike executions, however, pardons are displays of state power which end happily, often achieving by comic means what executions accomplish in the mode of tragedy. As Natalie Davis explains in her discussion of pardon tales in sixteenth-century France, "the pardon could change the tragic situation of unpremeditated killing and expected execution into the tragi-comedy of reprieve and peaceful reconciliation" (57). Indeed, as Foucault indicates, the "comedy" of the scene need not, for all that, be less a display of power; when publicly staged by the state, pardon scenes were dignified, solemn affairs which ended in a celebration of royal clemency. Like John Fletcher's definition of tragicomedy, the public pardon "wants deaths, which is inough to make it no tragedie, yet brings some neere it, which is inough to make it no comedie" ("To the Reader" lines 20–23). Also like their dramatic counterparts, royal pardons must stage conflict in order to produce the requisite happy ending. The will of the prince must be brought into conflict with that of the court system before the mercy of pardon can override the death penalty exacted by law. Foucault's totalizing account of sovereign power understates the tensions that the staging of this conflict between the judiciary and monarch, justice and equity presents. Several intermediary conflicts may occur before the need for pardon is even made known to the monarch, but Foucault's emphasis on the final public spectacle takes no notice of the layers of patronage and factional conflict that may direct or limit the monarch's knowledge and decisions—and, therefore, his power.[2] Davis argues that the French kings actively used this type of conflict to strengthen their sovereignty, a sovereignty limited—as in England—by a long tradition of the delegation of royal power to the courts. By the fifteenth century, the French king had established his monopoly over the right to pardon, a right once shared with dukes and seigneurial justices. The pardon provided an opportunity for the king to demonstrate the extent of his sovereignty by pushing his will beyond the strict bounds of law, extending the scope of his prerogative powers (Davis 52, 58n179).

When staged in the public playhouses outside London, however, the tragicomic proceedings of the royal pardon scene often received disruptively and self-consciously *comic* treatments capable of questioning royal power, or at least of revealing the layers of conflict which limit it. This almost parasitic relationship between actual royal pardons and their mimetic treatments is intriguing; Stephen Greenblatt argues that "the actor simulates what is already understood to be a theatrical representation. . . . [T]he spectacular royal pardons that were understood by observers to be theatrical occasions were staged as theatrical occasions in plays such as *Measure for Measure*" (*Negotiations* 10). Both epistolary and dramatic representations of royal pardon scenes revel in this theatricality; extant accounts of pardons are explicitly theatrical and frequently use terms like "comedy" and "tragicomedy" in their descriptions to emphasize the generic difference between the scenes of legally deserved execution and unmerited pardon.

Though mutually dependent, the two dramas did not always coexist without friction. Clearly the state used public spectacles to salvage what it could of its dignity and authority, challenged by recent revolt; in staging a public pardon, the prince metaphorically descends upon the scene of judgment—the *deus ex machina*—and rearranges what had seemed an inevitable concluding act. The drama enhances the monarch's position by identifying his or her authority with God's: it is both more powerful and more merciful than the legal system which had sentenced the rebels to death. Comic treatments of royal pardons, however, resist participating unreservedly in the state's fiction of power, refusing to represent rebellion merely in order to contain it. The tragicomic element of the royal pardon could also function more like the mongrel genres Sidney decried than the sovereignty-enhancing pastoral tragicomedy à la Guarini. State pardon scenes

mingle kings and commoners, bringing the monarch and the subject
into vital, but at times unpredictable, contact. If all goes according
to plan, the latter walks away from the encounter with life restored,
the former with power and mercy applauded.[3] But royal spectacles,
because of their very nature, were vulnerable to the unexpected. As
demonstrated in *Measure for Measure,* spectators like Lucio might
suddenly decide to become players and speak, unbidden; other players, like Barnardine, might mar the spectacle by playing their pre-
scribed parts, but sullenly. As a mixed genre, tragicomedy can test
the boundaries that define the class structure and legitimate sovereign
power; it is a mode that is as capable of revealing the limits of
sovereignty as of extending them.

Comparing the pardon scenes of *Richard II* and *Measure for Measure* to representations of their ceremonial counterparts suggests that
the comic elements of those scenes expose limitations on the monarch's prerogatives that are suppressed in epistolary accounts of actual
royal pardons.[4] These comic moments appear, I suspect, not because
the dramatists were attempting to recapture the spirit of rebellion
itself but to expose aspects of weakness and self-interest barely suppressed in historical accounts which presented royal pardons instead
as displays of godlike power and disinterested mercy. In particular,
Shakespeare's metatheatrical pardon scenes reassert the players'
authority over the domain of spectacle, *of playing,* by exposing the
theatrical basis of the royal practice they represent.[5] By inserting
comedy—the genre of the people—into representations of spectacles
of royal power, playwrights carnivalize their subject matter, producing
scenes replete with the ambivalence of popular festivity. The comic
staging of pardon scenes exposes the political realism of pardon,
reveals the gears and chains of the machine, thus enabling these scenes
to resist the easy mystification of royal power that was the ulterior
motive behind public pardons and executions in the immediate after-
math of rebellion.

Shakespeare's representation of Aumerle's pardon in *Richard II* is
oddly self-conscious in announcing its generic associations in Henry's
rhymed couplet, "Our scene is alt'red from a serious thing, / And
now chang'd to 'The Beggar and the King.'" Henry's couplet, however, does more than just emphasize the theatrical nature of the event
it simulates. It captures the logical essence of every pardon scene:

each pardon scene, historical or dramatic, must contain its obligatory beggar and its king. In studying the interaction between actual royal pardons and their comic representation on stage, I will focus first on the beggar's role, represented by Cardinal Wolsey in Henry VIII's 1517 pardon of the Evil May Day rioters and by the duchess of York in *Richard II,* and will conclude by looking at the role of a would-be absolutist king—who, like Bottom, would play all the parts himself—represented by James I in the 1603 pardon of the Bye conspirators and by Duke Vincentio in *Measure for Measure.*

I

In 1517 Cardinal Wolsey played the beggar's part in a regal scene in which he implored Henry VIII to pardon four hundred Londoners arrested following the Evil May Day riot. A letter from Nicholas Sagudino to Alvise Foscari provides an impressive account of the "alteration" of scene effected by the king's pardon; he tells Foscari that Henry VIII

came one day to a place distant half a mile hence, with his court in excellent array, the right reverend Cardinal being there likewise, with a number of lords, both spiritual and temporal, with their followers, in a very gallant trim. And his majesty, being seated on a lofty platform, surrounded by all those lords, who stood, he caused some four hundred of these delinquents, all in their shirts and barefoot, and each with a halter round his neck, to be brought before him; and on their presenting themselves before his majesty, the Cardinal implored him aloud to pardon them, which the King said he would not by any means do: whereupon said right reverend Cardinal, turning towards the delinquents, announced the royal reply. The criminals, on hearing that the King chose them to be hanged, fell on their knees, shouting "Mercy!" when the Cardinal again besought his majesty to grant them grace, some of the chief lords doing the like. So at length the King consented to pardon them, which was announced to these delinquents by said right reverend Cardinal with tears in his eyes; and he made them a long discourse, urging them to lead good lives, and comply with the royal will. . . . And when the Cardinal told them this, that the King pardoned them, it was a fine sight to see each man take the halter which hung from his neck, and throw it in the air; and they jumped for extreme joy, making such signs of rejoicing as became their escape from such peril. (*Letters and Papers* II, [ii], 3259)

Sagudino adds, "It was a very fine spectacle, and well arranged, and the crowd of people was innumerable." As Bolingbroke once observed in a similar situation, "Such is the breath of kings" (*Richard II* 1.3.215). A well-arranged scene: just how thoroughly arranged, just how scripted was it? Did the audience perceive Henry's relenting as spontaneous—or calculated? Did the prisoners know their parts—or guess them? Were the halters felt to be the actual signs of potential punishment—or mere props? The answers to these questions are beyond our grasp, but the theatrical terms of Sagudino's presentation compel the asking.

Clearly, when staged with this level of attention to ceremony, especially if punctuated with the ritual and rhythm of suspense, a pardon scene could serve the same purpose as the spectacle of execution. The suspense generated by preceding the pardon with its denial would create a painful impression of the monarch's absolute power of destruction over the bodies of the offenders. Sagudino's account exposes the dissymmetry between the bare backs and bare feet of the four hundred supplicants and the "excellent array" of Henry's court; the empowered class is allowed to gaze upon the bare bodies of those subject to its ultimate penalties while concealing its own embodiedness beneath the rich fabrics which symbolized wealth, social position, public office. Forty leaders of the uprising had already been executed, and the gibbets were still displaying their mutilated, criminalized body parts; as a result, it is quite likely that the prisoners played out their roles with real intensity.

Sagudino's letter is not, of course, a source for *Richard II* or any other Elizabethan play. However, *The Book of Sir Thomas More* does depict an occasion immediately prior to the pardon Sagudino's letter describes.[6] In the play version, More quells the same riot and personally undertakes to obtain a pardon for the rioters; the letter presents the public ceremony in which Wolsey and Henry VIII take center stage (and credit) for the pardon. That the comic dramatic version—whether or not it was ever staged—places the focus of the scene on a man who was himself executed later for defying the king marks the extent of the difference between epistolary representations of the public face of pardon and dramatic re-presentations.[7]

The contrast between Sagudino's account and that in *Sir Thomas More* is so clear as to seem almost intentional. While Sagudino's spectacle gives due attention to its low characters and has a celebratory conclusion, it is not entirely comic: it is neither inclusive in ethos nor humorous in tone. The players' account of the same incident, in contrast, is rich in fellow-feeling and low comedy. The rebels' lines maintain a suspicion of constituted authority; Doll threatens that unless More keeps his promise to secure the king's pardon, "by the Lord Ile call thee a plaine Conie catcher" (sc. 6, lines 499–500). The play's depiction of the rebellion itself is interrupted by another pardon scene, in which More procures a cutpurse's pardon by enacting a "merrie iest" at the justice's expense. More requires the convicted thief to lift Justice Suresbie's purse to reprove the justice for displacing blame from the thief to his victim, who had—according to the justice—lured the thief to his crime by boasting of the money he kept about him. The thief, weighing the task More has set him (in lines marked for omission), determines to cooperate with the jest: "I see the purpose of this Gentleman / is but to check the fol<lie> of the Iustice, / for blaming oth<er>s in a desperate case, / wherin hims<elfe> may fall as soone as any" (2.198–201). While we may speculate concerning the reason these lines were marked for omission, they do seem thematically appropriate in reproving the "follie" of a system of justice that uses scapegoating spectacles of punishment and pardon to evade recognition of its own inadequacies. In this manner, the Lifter-Suresbie incident interrupts and, perhaps, interprets the account of the Evil May Day rebellion and pardon; the celebratory conclusion we might expect after reading Sagudino's letter is marred because the royal pardon arrives too late to save one of the rebels and, of course, will not come at all for More in the final act.[8]

The most noticeable difference between the two accounts of the Evil May Day pardon arises from the fact that in the play version Henry VIII remains an offstage presence whose absence from the representation of the pardon permits a fuller expression of the inclusive drive of comedy. In the end, the social hierarchy is reinforced, but not in the extreme measure of the royal spectacle recorded in Sagudino's letter. By making Justice Suresbie the victim of More's jest and reproving the officials' excessive haste in executing the leader of the rebellion, the play greatly minimizes the hierarchical distinctions even while reinforcing them. The medieval cycles with their combination of procession and pageant equally affirmed both the hierarchy and unity of the social body (James 22); in these two accounts of the May Day pardon, we see these two functions of spectacle beginning to diverge as the auspices of the royal or civic spectacles and of theatrical performances become increasingly (though not entirely) separated. Royal spectacles of punishment aim to reinforce the hierarchy of the body by purging the social body of contamination through the expiation of punishment or the generosity of pardon; the comic treatment of these spectacles in plays undercuts hierarchy, emphasizing instead the unity of the social body, by exacting a gentler penance before it forgives or by identifying king with commoner, justice with thief.

This shift in emphasis upon hierarchy or unity becomes clear in a comparison of the beggar's role in Sagudino's account and in *Richard II*. Although Wolsey is rarely recorded celebrating mass, on the state occasion described by Sagudino he demonstrates his mastery of the liturgy of power, performing a priestly role as mediator that emphasizes the gulf between subject and king in the act of bridging it. Initially, Shakespeare's scene of pardon in *Richard II* similarly highlights the gulf between Henry and his subjects as Aumerle prostrates himself, vowing, "For ever may my knees grow to the earth, / My tongue cleave to my roof within my mouth, / Unless a pardon ere I rise or speak" (5.3.30–32). Even though the more gruesome elements of treason executions were routinely commuted to mere beheadings for nobility, Aumerle cannot avoid using anatomical imagery; confronted with the written evidence of his treason, he linguistically severs the offending hand, pleading, "I do repent me, read not my name there, / My heart is not confederate with my hand" (5.3.52–53). Later in the scene, Aumerle's father condemns his treason in images recalling a traitor's death:

> It was, villain, ere thy hand did set it down.
> I tore it from the traitor's bosom, King;
> Fear, and not love, begets his penitence.
>   (5.3.54–56)

In his breathless urgency to denounce his own son, York uses the pronoun *it* three times in the first two lines above, switching antecedents each time, referring to Aumerle's heart, his name, and the document respectively. Having seen York discover the bond in the previous scene, the audience would follow York's meaning easily enough, yet the cumulative effect of the syntax also evokes the image of the executioner tearing the traitor's heart from his bosom. As John Bellamy informs us, after the victim of a state execution had been cut down,

> there followed next the abscission of the victim's "members" (genitals), in order, Coke tells us, to show his issue was disinherited with corruption of blood; then there came the slitting of the stomach, the putting out of his entrails and the cutting out of the heart. . . . Until this point many of the victims were still conscious. (204–05)

Even though Henry confirms Aumerle's pardon, York presses the case against his own son by using another figure of dismemberment which recalls the tortuous scene of execution:

> If thou do pardon, whosoever pray,
> More sins for this forgiveness prosper may.
> This fest'red joint cut off, the rest rest sound;
> This let alone will all the rest confound.
> (5.3.83–86)

While Aumerle may not wear the hangman's noose around his neck as did the May Day rebels, Elizabethan audiences, accustomed to viewing the tragedies of that "other" scaffold, would certainly have recognized equivalent portents of execution in these lines.

Henry seizes on the conflicting appeals of father and son as an opportunity to enhance his power by emphasizing the contrast between York's loyalty and Aumerle's treachery, redeploying the image of treason as a corrupter of blood:

> O heinous, strong, and bold conspiracy!
> O loyal father of a treacherous son!
> Thou sheer, immaculate, and silver fountain,
> From whence this stream through muddy passages
> Hath held his current and defil'd himself!
> Thy overflow of good converts to bad,
> And thy abundant goodness shall excuse
> This deadly blot in thy digressing son.
> (5.3.59–66)

In magnifying York's loyalty, Bolingbroke legitimates his own authority by rewriting Aumerle's loyalty to Richard as treachery; in pardoning Aumerle, he establishes his power by demonstrating his control over the fates of his subjects.

If Henry's pardon alters Aumerle's scene of judgment to a tragicomedy, the scene also alters for Henry with the entrance of the duchess. As the duchess labors for her son's pardon, she also, inadvertently, revives the power of genealogy perverted by Henry's (and her husband's) disloyalty to Richard. The duchess assumes Wolsey's role as intercessor, but, unlike Wolsey, she undermines rather than enhances Henry's power as the solemn rites of pardon disintegrate into a farce that diminishes rather than enhances the dissymmetry between subject and sovereign. A stronger contrast to Sagudino's account of Henry VIII's scene of pardon is hardly imaginable; Henry surrenders control over the scene to his aunt when he realizes that the only way to control her is to accede to the very letter—not to mention pronunciation—of her suit:

> K. HEN.
> Good aunt, stand up.
>   DUCH.
>   Nay, do not say "stand up";
> Say "pardon" first, and afterwards "stand up."
> . . . .
> The word is short, but not so short as sweet,
> No word like "pardon" for kings' mouths so meet.
>   YORK.
> Speak it in French, King, say *"pardonne moy."*
>   DUCH.
> Dost thou teach pardon pardon to destroy?
> Ah, my sour husband, my hard-hearted lord,
> That sets the word itself against the word!
> Speak "pardon" as 'tis current in our land,
> The chopping French we do not understand.
> . . . .
>   K. HEN.
> Good aunt, stand up.
>   DUCH.
>   I do not sue to stand;
> Pardon is all the suit I have in hand.
>   K. HEN.
> I pardon him as God shall pardon me.

> DUCH.
> O happy vantage of a kneeling knee!
> Yet am I sick for fear, speak it again,
> Twice saying "pardon" doth not pardon twain,
> But makes one pardon strong.
> > K. HEN.
> > > With all my heart
> I pardon him.
> > DUCH.
> > A god on earth thou art.
> > > (5.3.111–36)

The duchess is simultaneously a figure from comedy and a representative of the old order; with her couplet-cued entrance, the scene takes on a tone of mock-seriousness in which generic questions become political ones.[9]

On another level, Shakespeare incorporates into the scene the familiar structure of his romantic comedies, as Henry sides with the feminine forces of the duchess in overturning the harsh authority of father over son by pardoning where York would have him condemn (Tennenhouse 81). Shakespeare found in the chronicles York's discovery of the conspiracy, Aumerle's out-riding his father to court to seek mercy, and their audience with Henry; what he added to their account was the duchess's role in the two scenes: *the comedy.* As cardinal, Wolsey's intercession elevates Henry VIII by undergirding the regal decorum of the scene with a religious legitimation of royal judicial powers; in contrast, as the unruly woman, the duchess's intercession undermines Henry's regality by introducing the leveling force of carnivalesque comedy to the scene of pardon. With her entrance the scene takes on a duality of tone similar to that achieved in the best of the comic scenes of the mystery cycles. All of the standard typologies operate: the king as God, the suppliant as Christ, the offender as fallen man.[10] But simultaneously, carnivalesque inversions recast the king as beggar and the beggar as his queen; Henry is both God and fallen man. The resulting scene generates conflicting responses; the legitimating religious imagery of the pardon scene cannot transcend the blatant, comic counterstatements in a way that successfully endorses Henry's role as God's substitute, a veritable god on earth. The creaking of the gears and chains as Henry's throne descends from the "heavens" counterpoints the legitimating effect of the duchess's final line. The pardon, ultimately, is seen to be good theater.

The duchess's insistence on Henry's divine status would have provided a more fitting summation for Henry VIII's pardon of the four hundred May Day rioters in 1517. There Henry VIII, with Wolsey pleading before him in a cardinal's full regalia, would have been so elevated by the theatrics of the spectacle of pardon that he could well have seemed like "a god on earth." In its context in *Richard II*, however, the duchess's analogy only recalls Henry's own: "I pardon him as God shall pardon me," forcing the audience to identify him simultaneously as judge and offender (a conflict of identity explored at length in *Measure for Measure*). Instead of emphasizing the dissymmetry between subject and king, Shakespeare has structured the scene to erase it, by momentarily emphasizing Henry's and Aumerle's shared need of pardon. After all, both sought to unseat a monarch. In light of Henry's attempt to exonerate his betrayal of Richard by criminalizing Aumerle's loyalty, one can hardly resist quoting Sir John Harington's famous epigram: "Treason never prospers. What's the reason? / If it prospers none dares call it treason." To Henry's credit, however, he does at least (unlike Angelo) pardon as he would be pardoned.

Marshaling the figures of inversion against him, the duchess's comedy of "The Beggar and the King" undermines Henry's efforts to legitimate his new identity. Before her entrance, Henry had attempted to appropriate the symbols of genealogy to legitimate his own authority by using the rhetoric of generosity to invert the normal process of corruption of blood. Rather than allowing Aumerle's treason to result in the corruption of the family line (symbolized in executions by castration), Henry argues that York's "abundant goodness shall excuse / This deadly blot in thy digressing son" (5.3.65–66). The duchess's comic conflict with York exposes the illegitimacy of Henry's authority by contrasting the mutability of political loyalties with the constancy of maternal love. York's "abundant goodness," after all, was comprised by his betrayal of Richard. The duchess stresses the sincerity of her appeal for pardon in opposition to her husband's hypocrisy:

> Pleads he in earnest? Look upon his face:
> His eyes do drop no tears, his prayers are in jest,

His words come from his mouth, ours from our breast;

. . . .

His prayers are full of false hypocrisy,
Ours of true zeal and deep integrity.

(5.3.100–108)

Her accusations are those commonly leveled against actors, masters of hypocrisy, who do everything not "in earnest" but "in jest"; the marvelous irony that she and Aumerle are also being played by actors whose eyes "do drop no tears" only adds to the comic dimension of the scene, schooling the audience to suspect all staged events—including royal spectacles—of hypocrisy.

By casting the duchess as an unruly comic beggar rather than a humble suppliant like Wolsey, Shakespeare uses her to prevent Henry from consolidating his control of the legitimating symbols of royal authority. Neither he nor her husband is able to control her. In the topsy-turvy world of "The Beggar and the King," husbands cannot control wives, men cannot dominate women, and kings cannot rule their subjects. After all, a wife who can ride as fast as her husband need not stay at home. In playing out the role of the unruly woman, the duchess succeeds, at least for a time, in inhibiting the power of the king to pronounce a pardon, robbing him of his voice by her own loquacity. Her comically stubborn verbosity demonstrates that when kings would not (or cannot) maintain their will by physical force, they are dependent upon the willingness of their subjects to *be* subjects. So too, at the comic extreme, Duke Vincentio—having traded the symbols of his authority for the anonymity of a friar's habit—is dependent upon his powers of persuasion to gain the cooperation of his subjects and is ultimately discomfited by Barnardine's unwillingness "to die to-day for any man's persuasion" (*Measure for Measure* 4.3.59–60).

It is not only comic intransigence that wins royal pardons, however; Sagudino's letter also tells us that, since no strangers were killed in the uprising, "the people cannot bear that forty of their countrymen should be so cruelly hanged and quartered" (*Letters and Papers* II, [ii], 3259). The execution of a further four hundred might have led to renewed riot, this time directed against the king, not foreigners. Henry VIII issued a similar general pardon after the 1537 Pilgrimage of Grace, being advised by his council that it would help restore "perfect tranquility" (Bellamy 219). It seems that sometimes kings pardoned because they could not do otherwise. As Stephen Greenblatt has observed of James I's pardon of the Bye conspirators:

The cheering had stopped after the first three executions, for if some anxiety is salutary, it may also go too far and evoke not obedience but a sullen withdrawal into discontented silence or even an outburst of rash rebellion. These scenarios are at most only partially and superficially in the control of the authorities; if at such times the prince seems to manipulate the anxieties of others, he inevitably discloses his own half-buried fears. (*Negotiations* 136–37)

Greenblatt is not the first to read fear behind apparent benevolence in a royal pardon; when offered redress of grievances in exchange for dismissing their rebel forces in *2 Henry IV,* Mowbray cautions, "But he hath forc'd us to compel this offer, / And it proceeds from policy, not love" (4.1.145–46). Westmoreland insists, "This offer comes from mercy, not from fear," and persuades the rebels to consider the offer (4.1.148). Hastings concludes the rebel debate:

> Besides, the King hath wasted all his rods
> On late offenders, that he now doth lack
> The very instruments of chastisement,
> So that his power, like to a fangless lion,
> May offer, but not hold.
>
> (4.1.213–17)

That the rebels find themselves betrayed by Prince John's false offer of peace results directly from their acceptance of the official reading of the offer, not an inability to conceive of mercy as a cloak for weakness.

When the king's power is constrained, whether by fear of revolt after Evil May Day or by superior military force as at Flint Castle, the audience may be led to share the puzzlement of the peasant in More's epigram and ask, "Is that the King? . . . He seems to me to be a man in an embroidered garment" (qtd. in Greenblatt, *Self-Fashioning* 27). In the ballad of King Cophetua and the Beggar-maid, the king becomes so enamored of the beggar that she is able to control him; thus, in the ballad the topos of the beggar and king adds true role-inversion to the leveling force seen in More's epigram.[11] Richard himself refers to the beggar and king topos at his deposition, demystifying the royal office in the act of surrendering it:

> I find myself a traitor with the rest;
> For I have given here my soul's consent
> T' undeck the pompous body of a king;
> Made glory base, [and] sovereignty a slave;
> Proud majesty a subject, state a peasant.
>
> (4.1.248–52)

The contrast Richard draws between "proud majesty" and a peasant was visibly present in Sagudino's account of Henry VIII's pardon scene; the contrast between Henry's well-arrayed court and the stripped bodies of the condemned was part of the spectacle's legitimation of his power over their lives. The mystical, "pompous" body of the king ideologically captured the difference between the sovereign and his subject that justified his power. Once "undecked," the king's body seemed no different from the peasant's, problematizing the legitimacy of their roles.[12] In spite of Henry's early attempts to use the pardoning of Aumerle to demonstrate and legitimate his power, the interlude of "The Beggar and the King" unravels his efforts. Henry "begs" his aunt to stand, she him to pardon; although we know his intent to pardon, the fact that she does not stand until he has re-pronounced it—twice—leaves us wondering whom the scene ultimately casts as beggar, whom as king. And, of course, "Who is king?" is the central question of the last half of the play.

Henry IV figured significantly in fifteenth- and sixteenth-century legal debates concerning the doctrine of the king's two bodies and royal succession. Understanding this neglected scene is crucial to interpreting the role of legal doctrine in *Richard II*. The syntax of Henry's couplet, "Our scene is alt'red from a serious thing, / And now chang'd to 'The Beggar and the King,'" recalls the popular Elizabethan proverb, "'The case is altered,' quoth Plowden." As Marie Axton has demonstrated in her application of the theory of the king's two bodies to dramatic discussions of the Elizabethan succession problem, appearances of the proverb "sometimes comment on a simple change of circumstances but more often indicate a change of identity which the law would recognize" (29). By having Henry echo the

proverb here, Shakespeare may be alerting his audience to consider
the scene in light of the legal theory concerning changes in royal
identity propounded by Plowden but popularized in numerous succession treatises (Axton passim).

Early in her reign Elizabeth sought to invalidate a grant of land
from the duchy of Lancaster made by Edward VI in his minority.
Ernst Kantorowicz explains that upon "unkinging" Richard in 1399,
Henry IV refused to merge the duchy of Lancaster with the property
of the crown, an action

> which became a *cause célèbre* and prompted the judges in the days of Plow-
> den to make their most subtle distinctions concerning the king's two bodies,
> led the royal judges as early as 1405 to formulate clearly the difference
> between things *que appertaine al Corone* and those belonging to the king
> *come auter person,* the latter a good anticipation of what was to be called
> in Tudor times the king's "body natural." Under Henry V, Parliament decided
> that the king could leave his property by will but could not bequeath his
> kingdom. . . . (370)

The queen lost her case; as Axton interprets the decision, the justices
succeeded in affirming "their allegiance by exalting the Queen's body
politic while at the same time they frustrated the wishes of her body
natural" (16).

Henry IV, therefore, was associated not merely with succession
debates and the distinctions drawn between the king's two bodies
but also and more particularly with the king's natural body. In the
opening scene of *Richard II,* Bolingbroke steps forward to accuse
Mowbray of treason, insisting that "what I speak / My body shall
make good upon this earth" (1.1.36–37). To press his charges further,
he disclaims "the kinred of the King" and lays aside his "high blood's
royalty" (1.1.70–71). Thus his earliest words in the play associate
him with the concept of the natural body, distancing him from the
royal lineage. Richard is also careful to emphasize the distance
between Bolingbroke and himself, declaring his own impartiality by
insisting that "Were he my brother, nay, my kingdom's heir, / As he
is but my father's brother's son, / . . . / He is our subject, Mowbray;
so art thou" (1.1.116–17, 122). One act later, Bolingbroke returns
from banishment to seek his natural inheritance—the titles and properties the historical figure sought by special legislation to hold sep-

arately after his accession. His ensuing encounter with York provides
an almost comic instance of the utter contrast between Henry's natural power (and his growing army) and York's impotence as the
representative of the body politic:

> Com'st thou because the anointed King is hence?
> Why, foolish boy, the King is left behind,
> And in my loyal bosom lies his power.
> Were I but now lord of such hot youth
> As when brave Gaunt, thy father, and myself
> Rescued the Black Prince . . .
>
>   .   .   .   .
> O then how quickly should this arm of mine,
> Now prisoner to the palsy, chastise thee,
> And minister correction to thy fault!
>   (2.3.96–105)

The play unquestionably demonstrates the superiority of Henry's
power; the pardon scene, however, questions its legitimacy and
exposes his attempts to use a rewriting of the principle of genealogy
and a self-serving display of mercy to legitimate a succession not
authorized by natural descent.

Since Henry has already pardoned Aumerle before the duchess's
entrance, the real conflict of the pardon scene concerns whether or
not he can meet the challenge of her genre-shifting, demystifying
comic presence and, in so doing, succeed in embodying the mysticism
of the body politic to legitimate his power. By pardoning Aumerle
before her entrance, Henry has demonstrated his absolute power over
the natural bodies of his subjects, but the audience has already seen
his willingness to exercise this very power *without* due authority in
ordering the summary executions of Bushy and Green in 3.1. Henry's
problem is clearly not one of power but of legitimation. Leonard
Tennenhouse has argued that in the history plays "[t]he popular
energy embodied in carnival legitimizes authority, provided that
energy can be incorporated in the political body of the state" (79).
As the beggar who rules the king, the duchess embodies the forces
of carnival but resists incorporation within the body politic as defined
by Henry by virtue of her identification with the mystical power

inherent in genealogy. After detailing the aspects of carnival associated with Bolingbroke in acts 1 and 2, Tennenhouse concludes:

> It is especially significant that Bullingbroke embody these features as he rescues the principle of inheritance which underwrites Richard's right to wear the crown. Bullingbroke repeats his uncle's words as he lays claim to a title and, with it, to the authority of the blood, "Wherefore was I born? / If that my cousin king be King in England, / It must be granted I am Duke of Lancaster" (II.iii.122–4). (80)

What Tennenhouse fails to recognize is that once Henry himself betrays the principle of genealogy, the figures of carnival abandon him. After taking his cousin-king's patrimony in addition to his own, Henry finds the figures of carnival aligned against him, first with the duchess of York as she pleads for Aumerle (who, we must recall, merely sought to restore Richard to *his* title) and later with Hotspur (who supported the arguably superior claim of Mortimer). Of Falstaff—Shakespeare's ultimate embodiment of the spirit of carnival—Tennenhouse writes:

> Falstaff frequently anticipates the lawlessness he will enjoy when Hal assumes authority. . . . Upon hearing of Henry IV's death, again (in *Part II*) he looks forward to the dissolution of the state: "I know the young king is sick for me. Let us take any man's horses, the laws of England are at my commandment" (V.iii.135–7). Thus Shakespeare uses the figures of carnival to represent a source of power contrary to that power inhering in genealogy. (83)

However, in following Hal in expectation of preferment, Falstaff is no more opposed to the "power inhering in genealogy" than Hotspur's rebels. He merely shares Hal's own attitude toward the crown, expressed in his last interview with his father, "You won it, wore it, kept it, gave it me; / Then plain and right must my possession be" (*2 Henry IV* 4.5.221–22).

Throughout the tetralogy, Shakespeare never lets us forget that Henry IV, having betrayed the principle of genealogy in deposing Richard II, could not make that claim. The duchess, though cast in the comic role of beggar, represents the concepts of natural order and lineal descent which, of course, were the traditional bulwarks defending the rights of kings. The visual contrast between the duchess's age and Henry's youth helps us remember that the principles of natural order and genealogy have been undermined in this transition of power: though Henry was old enough to be Richard's heir, Richard was too young to be his father (3.3.204–05). The violation of natural order transforms the comic force of procreation and genealogy into tragic ideas, leading to a reign marked by civil strife. In the scene before her intercession for Aumerle's life, the duchess emphasizes the naturalness of her love for her offspring, arguing:

> Hadst thou groan'd for him
> As I have done, thou wouldst be more pitiful.
> But now I know thy mind, thou dost suspect
> That I have been disloyal to thy bed,
> And that he is a bastard, not thy son.
> Sweet York, sweet husband, be not of that mind,
> He is as like thee as a man may be,
> Not like to me, or any of my kin,
> And yet I love him.
>
> (5.2.102–10)

The conventionally comic denial of cuckoldry turns Aumerle's "likeness" to York into a sign of her loyalty. York's betrayal of his own son amounts to a betrayal of himself, a variation of the aristocratic body's self-betrayal, and a rejection of natural bonds for arbitrary, "political" bonds. Although her husband repeatedly attempts to dismiss her as a "fond mad woman," "unruly woman," and "frantic woman," she has clearly displaced both York and Henry as the representative of natural, lineal descent. As a figure of inversion, the duchess casts a veil of irony over the proceedings of the pardon scene by exposing the fact that it is her husband and Henry—not herself and Aumerle—who have forsaken the principles of order each has outspokenly defended earlier in the play. The contrast may be epitomized in York's wry wordplay on his wife's insistent pleas for pardon: "Speak it in French, King, say *'pardonne moy.'*" That, according to the duchess, amounts to the inversion of setting "the word itself against the word," trading the "natural" sense of the native tongue for an arbitrary and "chopping French" of political expediency. Exposing the neutrality of the sign demystifies all sense of the "natural" legitimation of authority. But Henry chooses the "native" English pronunciation in this scene with his aunt.

In pardoning Aumerle but not his co-conspirators, Henry, according to Tennenhouse, "shows both sides of the coin of power: he vows to use unlimited force in the interest of the state, and he displays generosity in the interest of the blood" (81). In light of the subsequent scene in which Exeter reveals Henry's desire for Richard's death, perhaps Aumerle's pardon should be interpreted not as generosity in the interest of the blood but as an attempt to manipulate its symbolic power to legitimate his new authority. However, as a mother pleading for her son's life, the duchess embodies a more natural and more consistent representation of genealogy and prevents Henry from wielding the metaphysics of blood for his own purposes. The importance—and economy—of "The Beggar and the King" lies in Shakespeare's use of the comic treatment of the pardon to expose that betrayal through the comic inversions of his unruly duchess in the very scene in which Henry attempts to stage his generosity to the principle of blood. Lulled by the comic relief the scene provides, the audience may not recognize the importance of the duchess's role as the moral gauge until, shocked by another abrupt change of tone, they reevaluate Henry's "generosity" in light of Exeter's determination to fulfill Henry's wish by murdering Richard.

The comic re-staging of the pardon scene after the duchess's entrance explores the boundaries between tragedy and comedy and examines common assumptions about the nature of similarity and difference. Many critical accounts of the play contrast Richard's deficiency and Henry's capability; comparing the play's comic pardon scene with Sagudino's account reveals instead two types of failure: Richard's powerlessness to back symbol with substance and Henry's inability to legitimate his power with the metaphysics of blood.[13] Both men undergo changes of identity that serve to demystify the legitimating function of royal identity: "'The case is altered,' quoth Plowden." At his deposition, Richard condemned himself for consenting "'T' undeck the pompous body of a king." But faced with the comedy of "The Beggar and the King," Henry is incapable of reactivating the metaphysics of the body politic to legitimate his new identity.[14] As a result, he determines to commit the same offense that led to Richard's demise and urges the murder of a prince of the blood. The importance of this offense should not be minimized; it is, after all, the principle of blood that maintained the necessary legitimizing difference between sovereign and subject while providing the conceptual similarity between sovereign and successor. More than any other single scene, the comic pardon scene damages Henry's credibility when the inversions orchestrated by the duchess expose his guilt in deposing Richard as at least equal to Aumerle's for wishing to restore him. The comic insistence of the duchess leaves Henry little choice but to say, "I pardon him as God shall pardon me."

As a succession play, *Richard II* defied the normal Elizabethan practices of typological interpretation (Campbell, Axton). Shakespeare shifts the force of the figure to highlight not the expected similarities between Richard and Elizabeth but the similarities between Richard and *Henry*. Robert Ornstein catalogues some of the similarities Shakespeare used to draw the comparison: "Like Richard in the opening scene, Henry in the closing scene must pretend to judge a henchman for a crime in which he is complicit. . . . Like Richard he has shed a kinsman's blood; like Richard he fears rebellious subjects; and like Richard he banishes the follower who was his hangman" (124). One more overlooked similarity must be added: Richard had pardoned Mowbray for conspiring against him (1.1.137–41) just as Henry pardons Aumerle. Instead of using his chosen historical material to draw any of the usual "lessons" for contemporary politics in which polemicists cast Richard either as tyrant or martyr, Henry as hero or usurper in order to support a preferred candidate for the succession, Shakespeare exposes the hollowness of the rhetorical strategies by demonstrating instead the similarities between Richard and Henry. The political realism of Shakespeare's characterizations of the two cousins shifts the locus of similitude from a diachronic to a synchronic parallel; by displaying the abuses of both men against the crown they wore, he limits their usefulness as precedents for individual candidates for the throne, shifting the focus away from personalities to the underlying issues of the succession debate.

If *Richard II* can be read as a succession play which avoids the dangers of identifying contemporary figures with historical characters while exposing the self-serving use of historical analogy for what it was, then evaluation of its success in achieving a lack of referentiality must be qualified by a pivotal historical fact: the followers of the earl of Essex arranged for its performance on the eve of their uprising. While the players were exonerated from association with the treasonous incident, unlike the less fortunate author of *The First Part of the Life and Raigne of King Henrie IIII,* the play itself seems in some way guilty. Though Elizabeth knew which role she was intended to play, unlike Richard II she was unwilling to do what force would have her do, even in her old age.[15] We will probably never know whether Essex or his followers ever actually identified him with Henry IV or not; apparently, however, enough of his contemporaries drew that conclusion to make it necessary for Henry Leigh, an agent of Essex and Lord Mountjoy, to reassure James "that Essex had no thought of the English throne for himself" (Wilson 150). Rather than indulging in such identifications, Essex's supporters may simply have recognized in Shakespeare's play an implicit support for James's superior genealogical claim to the succession, a claim which Essex was actively promoting in a power bid for himself against Cecil. Part of Essex's plan included asking James to send an ambassador to London by the first of February, promising him that "You shall . . . be declared and acknowledged the certain and undoubted successor to this Crown and shall command the services and lives of as many of us as undertake this great work" (qtd. in Wilson 152). James hesitated and did not send his ambassadors until he knew Essex had failed (Neale 17, McManaway 220).

How other conspirators saw themselves we do not know, but it is wonderfully apt that Shakespeare's friend and patron, the earl of Southampton, had his death sentence commuted after his mother, like Shakespeare's duchess of York, successfully interceded on his behalf to the queen.

II

Lucio sets the central conflict of *Measure for Measure* into motion at the end of the first act by urging Isabella to play the beggar's role and seek a pardon for her brother Claudio.

> Go to Lord Angelo,
> And let him learn to know, when maidens sue,
> Men give like gods; but when they weep and kneel,
> All their petitions are as freely theirs
> As they themselves would owe them.
>
>   (1.4.79–83)

In the final act, Isabella again kneels to beg a pardon, this time from Duke Vincentio for Angelo himself. Lucio is wrong, of course; unlike the dowager countess of Southampton and Shakespeare's duchess of York, Isabella is an absolute failure as an intercessor.[16] What she would have is offered to her, but only at the price of her much-valued virginity. If she cheats by participating in the bed-trick, so does Angelo by reneging on Claudio's pardon. In the final analysis, her efforts to achieve her brother's pardon by fair means or foul are futile. For that matter, her last-act appeal to Duke Vincentio on Angelo's behalf is equally unsuccessful; though she kneels a second time, the duke dismisses her plea without explanation, saying only "Your suit's unprofitable; stand up, I say" (5.1.455).

What is Shakespeare's intent in so drastically rewriting the scene of pardon, the interlude of "The Beggar and the King"? Is it simply a rejection of the power of the beggar-maid to control the king, a celebration, even, of the accession of a male monarch after decades of rule by a maiden queen? Perhaps; but Isabella is not the only "beggar" in *Measure for Measure*. In the comically slanderous meeting between Lucio and the disguised duke in the third act, Lucio twice associates the "absent" duke with beggars. First, he complains that "It was a mad fantastical trick of him to steal from the state, and usurp the beggary he was never born to. Lord Angelo dukes it well in his absence; he puts transgression to't"; later he accuses the duke of the very transgressions Angelo prosecutes in his absence, confiding that although "He's now past it, yet (and I say to thee) he would mouth with a beggar, though she smelt brown bread and garlic. Say that I said so" (3.2.91–95, 182–84). However reliable Lucio's gossip may or may not be, by tying the duke to beggars he associates the potential role-inversions of the topos with the play's thematic interests in substitute authority, illicit sexuality, and royal surveillance.

Lucio's double exposure of the duke's "beggary," first in the slander cited above and later by removing the duke's disguise as a mendicant friar, reveals a troublesome facet of the duke's personality: he is, essentially, a "fantastical" trickster quite capable of—even insistent upon—playing both beggar and king. Vincentio denies Isabella's suit because, like Lucio's interference, it is ill timed; he will not grant Angelo a pardon before his *coup de théâtre,* his final trick: the revelation that Claudio is still alive, spared from the execution ordered

by Angelo by a last-minute reprieve written by the duke himself. Like
the king at the conclusion of *All's Well That Ends Well,* the duke
seems ready to step forward and deliver an epilogue exposing his
dual identity as the beggar-king, player-duke seeking applause for his
efforts.

The similarities between Vincentio's theatrical pardon scene and
James's spectacular last-minute pardon of the Bye conspirators have
often been noted in discussions of *Measure for Measure.*[17] Looking
once again at letters representing the historical scene emphasizes two
aspects of James's control of events which may help explain why
Shakespeare rewrote the beggar and king topos as he did, making so
explicit the theatrical basis of its potential role inversions. First, the
letters reveal an even keener awareness of the theatricality of the
royal pardon scene than is recoverable from Sagudino's account of
Henry VIII's 1517 pardon. More importantly, they place great emphasis on James's personal direction of the scene. In Sagudino's letter,
Wolsey's role as beggar is as critical to the scene as Henry's role as
king; James, unlike Henry, did not even appear in public (his disguise
of absence was more foolproof than Vincentio's), yet he shares the
spotlight with no one in the letters describing his spectacular pardon
of the conspirators.

Much like the Essex rebels, the Bye conspirators apparently planned
to seize the king and dictate an alteration of government which would
secure the toleration of religion. The trials and ensuing executions
generated widespread interest. On 27 November 1603 Sir Dudley
Carleton detained one of John Chamberlain's servants overnight "to
have time to discourse unto you these tragical Proceedings" (*Cobbett's
State Trials* 2: 47). Carleton's letter includes considerable detail concerning Ralegh's trial, observing that "Sir Walter Ralegh served for a
whole act, and played all the parts himself" (47). The conclusion of
what Carleton clearly recognized as a drama of state was, however,
left in doubt:

We cannot yet judge what will become of him [Grey] or the rest; for all are
not like to go one way. Cobham is of the surest side, for he is thought least
dangerous. . . . They say the priests shall lead the dance tomorrow; and
Brooke the next after: for he proves to be the knot that tied together the
three conspiracies; the rest hang indifferent betwixt mercy and justice,
wherein the king hath now subject to practise himself. (50)

In a second letter, written 11 December, Carleton continues to describe the theatrical dimensions of the king's justice; he writes, "I may as well leap in where I left, when I wrote to you by your man, and proceed in order by narration; since this was a part of the same play, and that other acts came betwixt, to make up a tragical comedy" (51). The tragic acts contained, as expected, the executions of the two priests and Brooke. Carleton relates that the two priests "were very bloodily handled by the executioner, for after they had been turned off they were both cut down alive" (51). Later Carleton tells us that when the executioner held up Brooke's head and cried "God save the King," no one seconded him but the sheriff.

I have quoted at length from Carleton's account of the executions because they set the stage for what was recognized at the time as an extraordinarily theatrical pardon scene a few days later. As Carleton notes, "A fouler day could hardly have been picked out, or fitter for such a tragedy." He goes on to describe in detail how Sir Griffin Markham and Lord Grey were each brought to the scaffold and taken through the usual pre-execution rituals only to be sent back, the first told that "since he was so ill prepared, he should yet have two hours respite," the second that the sheriff had received orders from the king to change the order of the executions. Carleton tells us that "neither could any man yet dive into the mystery of this strange proceeding." He continues:

The Lord Cobham, who was now to play his part, and by his former actions promised nothing but *matiere pour rire,* did much cozen the world; for he came to the scaffold with good assurance, and contempt of death. . . . Some few words he used, to express his sorrow for his offence to the king, and craved pardon of him and world . . . and with those words would have taken a short farewell of the world, with that constancy and boldness, that we might see by him, it is an easier matter to die well than live well. (51)

Cobham, too, was interrupted and told that he was to be confronted with some other of the prisoners. Grey and Markham were brought back to the scaffold, and according to Carleton, the three men looked at one another "like men beheaded, and met again in the other world." Finally came the denouement:

Now all the actors being together on the stage (as use is at the end of play), the sheriff made a short speech unto them, by way of the . . . heinousness of their offences, the justness of their trials, their lawful condemnation, and due execution there to be performed; to all which they consented; then saith the sheriff, see the mercy of your prince, who, of himself, hath sent hither to countermand, and given you your lives. There was then no need to beg a *plaudite* of the audience, for it was given with such hues and cries, that it went from the castle into the town, and there began afresh. . . . (51)

James had "no need" of an applause-begging epilogue.

A second letter, published within weeks of the event, has received less attention from critics of the play than Carleton's letter, in spite of its wider availability to contemporary playgoers. This letter marvels at both the theatrical nature of the affair and James's controlling role in it:

In the meane time, while the Court was full of uariety of discourse, some speaking out of probabilitie, others arguing out of desire, what was like to be the fortune of all, or of any of the Offendours, his majestie hauing concluded onely in his own secret heart (which is the true oracle of grace and knowledge) in what manner to proceed; and that without asking counsel of any earthly person it pleased him to resolue betweene God and himselfe, that their execution should be stayed, euen at the instant when the axe should be layde to the trees rootes. For the secret and orderly carriage whereof, his majestie was careful to preuent all cause or colour of suspicion, of that judicious, royall, and vnexpected course which followed. . . . [M]y relation may rather seeme to be a description of some ancient History, expressed in a well-acted comedy, than that it was euer possible for any other man to represent, at one time, in a matter of this consequence, so many liuely figures of justice and mercy in a king, of terror and penitence in offenders, and of so great admiration and applause in all others, as appeared in this action, carried only and wholly by his majesties owne direction. (*Cobbett's State Trials* 2: 66, 68)

To this anonymous author, James excelled as a playwright, presenting in a "well-acted comedy" as "liuely figures of justice and mercy in a king, of terror and penitence in offenders" than "it was euer possible for any other man to represent." It is tempting to view this statement as a gauntlet thrown to challenge the less royal playwrights who, in response, rushed onto the boards their own versions of secretive, disguise-loving magistrates in the early years of James's reign.

The correspondent is also impressed by the fact that the action was "carried only and wholly by his majesties owne direction"; in other words, James, as Carleton had earlier said of Ralegh, played all the parts himself. Like Vincentio, James had scripted a pardon scene which was intended to play without an intercessor, without a beggar. Carleton tells us that:

> The lords of the council joined in opinion and advice to the king, now in the beginning of his reign to shew as well examples of mercy as severity, and gain the title of Clemens, as well as Justus. . . . The king held himself upright betwixt two waters; and first let the lords know, that since the law had passed upon the prisoners, and that they themselves had been their judges, it became not them to be petitioners for that, but rather to press for execution of their own ordinances. (52)

Like Isabella's, the lords' suit was unprofitable. The severity of the law was due to the lords' own judgment, "their own ordinances." James, like Vincentio, allows them to "strike home" in the "ambush of [his] name" only to reverse their sentences in the final act. James was careful to distinguish between the law's capacity and his own; it is within the power of the law to pass sentence, but only the king could pardon. It was this vital distinction between capacities, as noted earlier, that led the French kings to use the power of pardon to extend their prerogative rights (Davis 52, 58); even at this early point in his reign, James is alert to maintain his prerogative powers over against the common law.

The theatricality of Vincentio's actions provided the ideal format for a "play of mind" exploring the relationship between common law and equity.[18] As Leonard Tennenhouse observes, "Angelo is unable to distinguish between kinds of fornication and thus proves incapable of making legal distinctions" (157). Nor is he able to distinguish between the heads of Claudio and Ragozine or the maidenheads of Isabella and Mariana—at least, not in the dark. But because of the play's multiple substitutions and duplications, his confusion is understandable. Common law's dependency upon precedent leads to a proliferation of analogies and substitutions that can make a mockery of justice; capable of seeing only similarity, as the agent of common law Angelo sends Juliet to the same cell as common prostitutes and condemns Claudio to death with a confessed murderer. If the lords of James's court were reluctant "to press for execution of their own ordinances," it was no doubt because they were aware of the excesses justice without mercy could inflict; to borrow Lucio's phrase, the rigor of the law allowed a man's head to stand "so tickle on [his] shoulders that a milkmaid, if she be in love, [might] sigh it off" (1.2.171–73). The only remedy for the situation was an appeal to a higher authority not limited to acting on the similarities of precedent but capable of recognizing the crucial differences between present cases and past precedents—capable, that is, of exercising equity.

The conflict between justice and equity played a significant role in Ralegh's trial, which was itself recorded in the form of a playscript. One exchange between Ralegh and the Lord Chief Justice captures the legal distinctions between common law and equity essential to understanding the legal conflict at the heart of *Measure for Measure:*

Ralegh: The king at his coronation is sworn *In omnibus Judiciis suis aequi-tatem, non rigorem Leis, observare.* By the rigour and cruelty of the law [Cobham's accusation] may be forcible evidence.
L.C.J.: That is not the rigour of the law, but the justice of the law . . .
Ralegh: Oh my lord, you may use equity.
L.C.J.: That is from the king; you are to have justice from us.
                                        (*Cobbett's State Trials* 2: 16)

The use of equity depended upon the will of the king; if James sought to remove all other actors from his scene of pardon, it was no doubt because he sensed the ability of the exercise of the royal pardon, as a prerogative power, to establish the supremacy and singularity of his authority over that of common law. So, like Vincentio, James avoids scripting a part for a beggar at his scene of pardon, neatly avoiding any distractions from his supreme role as royal pardoner.

However, as Mary Ellen Lamb's recent study of the play explains, *Measure for Measure* is, if anything, too conscious of the roles it presents to its characters:

Role-playing in *Measure for Measure* poses the question of the relationship between our "roles" and our "selves." Is there one basic "self" underlying a series of roles? Or is identity made up only of a succession of roles? At what point does role-playing help us to discover a "self," a previously unacknowledged aspect of our being, and at what point does role-playing work to destroy a "self," making all roles relative and arbitrary? (140)

In urging his subjects into duplicate and duplicitous roles and in subsuming the two logically necessary and distinct roles of beggar and king in his own person, Vincentio's spectacle undermines the source of his power to pardon. Equity, as a prerogative power, depended upon the person of the king. By destabilizing his own identity, Vincentio also destabilizes his authority. If the duke's duplications and substitutions have led Angelo, the play's representative of common law, astray, they have also created a situation that portrays the basis of the common lawyer's suspicions of the king's prerogative courts. As John Selden's aphorism expresses it,

Equity is a roguish thing. For law we have a measure . . . equity is according to the conscience of him that is chancellor, and as that is larger or narrower, so is equity. 'Tis all one as if they should make the standard for the measure a Chancellor's foot. (Holdsworth 1: 467–68)

It is no wonder the blanket pardons are as disturbing as Angelo's blanket condemnation; they are meant to be. There is no measure to equity if in one moment the duke appoints as a deputy the inconstant Angelo "Who may, in th' ambush of [his] name, strike home" (1.3.41), and in the next personally pardons all offenders; it becomes quite impossible to tell whether one is dealing with the criminal or the judge, the beggar or the king.

If in the final analysis *Measure for Measure* leaves little upon which to base a choice between the respective judicial approaches of Angelo and the duke, that fact had also been presaged by an exchange between Attorney General Edward Coke, spokesperson for common law, and Sir Walter Ralegh, supplicant to the king's equity:

Att.: Thou art the most vile and execrable Traitor that ever lived.
Ralegh: You speak indiscreetly, barbarously and uncivilly.
Att.: I want words sufficient to express thy viperous Treasons.
Ralegh: I think you want words indeed, for you have spoken one thing half a dozen times.
Att.: Thou art an odious fellow, thy name is hateful to all the realm of England for thy pride.
Ralegh: It will go near to prove a measuring cast between you and me, Mr. Attorney.

(*Cobbett's State Trials* 2: 26)

As the play's embodiment of comic irreverence, Lucio would have felt right at home slinging slanderous remarks and witty insults with

Coke and Ralegh. If he is the only one not pardoned for his lechery, it is not so much for his slander as for its levity, its playfulness. In exposing the duke's disguise, revealing Vincentio to be the beggar-king, Lucio exposes the role-playing that *is* the duke's identity at the very moment that he disrupts the duke's finale. John D. Cox sees Lucio's role as "joker" as "akin to the topsy-turvy world of carnival" and finds it intriguing that Shakespeare should add this role to his source play, George Whetstone's *Promos and Cassandra,* in light of Whetstone's insistence upon a decorously "strict social separation of styles and subjects" (152–53). Once again, what Shakespeare adds to the scene of pardon is the comedy.

As Mary Ellen Lamb has noted (131–36), Lucio provides an alternative locus for the theatrical principle in the play. Lucio has directed Isabella's first interview with Angelo in a proleptic version of the final act; if he contests the duke's direction of that act to secure a role for himself in it, it is because he is reasserting his right to speak, to act. Though he cannot make the friar-duke's claim to absolute autonomy—that "His subject am I not"—Lucio represents the "masterless man" of the other end of the social spectrum. Like Aumerle, Lucio merely seeks to take back what authority itself had usurped: in this case, "the beggary he [the duke] was never born to." The duke's withdrawals and disguises were intended to conceal the theatrical basis of his control over the affairs of Venice; by preventing the friar-duke from withdrawing and by revealing his true identity, Lucio demonstrates that the place of the trial—outside the town's gates—is coterminous with the place of the stage.[19]

Historical royal pardon scenes were intended to display royal power and contain the last vestiges of unrest. The comic treatment these rituals receive in plays like *Richard II* and *Measure for Measure* exposes the theatrical basis of those state spectacles, demystifying the royal display of mercy intended to win subjects' loving obedience. By using the duchess and Lucio to reclaim the theatricality the state had borrowed from the stage and made its own, Shakespeare asserts the ancient right of wandering minstrels and masterless men—of all those who earn a living begging for applause—to play.

Notes

1. On the use of the bodies of execution victims as signs of power, see Foucault 48–49, 55, and Scarry 27–59.

2. I am indebted to Rebecca Bushnell for several insightful comments concerning the staging of conflict in tragicomedy and the multiple layers of power at work in obtaining royal pardons.

3. Because of the prevalence of forfeiture penalties, virtually anyone in need of a pardon was, technically, a commoner. In cases of treason, special parliamentary or royal action was necessary to rehabilitate an attainted title.

4. Nor is Shakespeare the only dramatist to find humor in the "comic" resolution of the pardon scene; *The Spanish Tragedy, The Book of Sir Thomas More, The Revenger's Tragedy,* and perhaps other contemporary dramas as well all give the ceremony of pardon an irreverently comic staging.

5. On the players' stubborn defense of their right to perform, see Mullaney 26–47.

6. On the dating, censorship, and revisions of *The Book of Sir Thomas More,* see McMillin. It is interesting that McMillin argues for a composition date for *The Book of Sir Thomas More* that would place it near the likely composition date for *Richard II* and a revision date that would place renewed interest in it near the composition of *Measure for Measure.*

7. A narrative example of the comic treatment of pardon may be found in Sir John Harington's *The Metamorphosis of Ajax.* After telling one anecdote demonstrating More's wit while in the Tower, Harington continues with another: "[F]or after this, one coming to him as of good will, to tell him he must prepare him to die, for he could not live: he called for his urinall, and having made water in it, he cast it, & viewed it (as Physicians do) a pretie while; at last he sware soberly, that he saw nothing in that mans water, but that he might live, if it pleased the King; a pretie saying, both to note his own innocencie, and move the Prince to mercie: and it is like, if this tale had bin as frendly told the King, as the other perhaps was unfrendly enforced against him, sure the King had pardoned him" (101). Harington follows this anecdote with one about how Sir John Heywood "scaped hanging with his mirth, the King being graciously and (as I thinke) truely perswaded, that a man that wrate so pleasant and harmlesse verses, could not have any harmfull conceit against his procedings" (102).

8. The comedy of these scenes includes the double entendre of the wife who "craves" to be executed before her husband, pleading that "you knowe not what a comforte you shall bring / to my poore hart to dye before my husband" and the response, "Bring her to death, she shall haue her desire" (7.643–45). The one execution that is staged is accompanied by fairly lame examples of gallows humor spoken by the clown; for example, he observes, "Wold I weare so farre on my iurney. The first stretche is the worste me thinks" (7.638–41, marginal addition).

Other examples of confusion over pardons which receive comic treatments in Renaissance plays include Pedringano's false hopes of reprieve in *The Spanish Tragedy* 3.6 and the duke's pardon of his own son Lussurioso instead of his stepson, a pardon which left the stepson in prison to become the victim of an execution order his brothers hoped to use against Lussurioso, in *The Revenger's Tragedy* 2.3 and 3.1-4, 3.6.

John Bellamy's study of Tudor treason law provides examples of several condemned traitors who were offered last-minute pardons upon the condition that they would comply with the king's wishes. His examples include Bishop John Fisher, who was executed only days before More, and four Elizabethan priests who also refused to accept the queen's conditions and were executed. Bellamy suggests that the possibility of such eleventh-hour reprieves may help explain the cooperative scaffold behavior of the condemned (200–201).

9. Aumerle's conspiracy received a strong comic staging in the 1987 Royal Shakespeare Company production directed by Barry Kyle, which featured Michael Kitchen as Henry IV, Bernard Horsfall as York, Rosalind Boxall as the duchess, and Paul Venables as Aumerle.

The farcical dimension of the conspiracy has been noted by Biggins, Zitner, and Black. Although my analysis of the ultimate effect of the comedy is closer to Zitner's, I agree with Black that the nature of the comedy owes much to the medieval cycles of Richard's own day (see Black 110–12).

10. For a discussion of the dramatic background of judgment scenes, see Ide.

11. Shakespeare refers to this ballad on four other occasions: *Love's Labor's Lost* 1.2.110, 4.1.66; *Romeo and Juliet* 2.1.14; and *2 Henry IV* 5.3.101.

12. At the conclusion of *All's Well That Ends Well* the king steps forward to deliver the epilogue and begins by recalling the theatricality of his role as king: "The king's a beggar, now the play is done" (Ep.1). In the immediate context, of course, the "king" is a "beggar" simply because he is asking the audience to lend him their "gentle hands." In the broader context, however, he is reminding the audience that the world-as-stage metaphor is not perfectly reversible; when the play is done, the asymmetry between his social status and that of a king is restored. See Jean Howard's essay on *Much Ado about Nothing* for an analysis of similar contradictions in staging rank and gender.

Stephen Greenblatt discusses the leveling effect of commonplace explications of the player-king in More's English works, published in 1557. While More's application invokes the leveling stroke of death to erase the asymmetry of status almost as quickly as his reader has absorbed it, Greenblatt finds that the theatrical metaphor "has a leveling effect even without the invocation of death, for to conceive of kingship as a dramatic part, an expensive costume and some well-rehearsed lines, is potentially at least to demystify it, to reduce its sacral symbolism to tinsel" (*Self-Fashioning* 27).

13. Critics for whom the pardon scene is either not comic or merely "comic relief" between the deposition and murder scenes tend to read *Richard II* as a deliberate contrast between the deposed Richard and the usurping Bolingbroke:

"The contrast between Bolingbroke as an efficient ruler and Richard as an unwise one contributes to the play's structure and helps to balance the last phase against the first" (Ure lxxv).

"*Richard II* thus illustrates the failure of a weak king. . . . But Henry has the public virtues which Richard lacks, and these make him successful in spite of the dubious legality of his title" (Ribner 165).

"The crisis of Richard's incompetence ends with his deposition. . . . By the time the deposition scene has ended, there is no doubt of Henry's political qualities—he is strong, determined, shrewd, and ruthless, not particularly attractive but eminently capable" (Ornstein 121–22).

"Another occasion for Henry to display his authority occurs when Aumerle, his conspiracy discovered, begs forgiveness, and Henry grants it. With this, Shakespeare completes the contrast between Richard and Henry. Richard lacks the power of generosity as well as the capacity for ruthlessness. Henry possesses both and can manifest either power in extreme as he so chooses" (Tennenhouse 81).

14. Both before and after his coronation, Henry differs from Richard in knowing how to deal with *force,* how to use it himself. At Flint, Richard concedes, "What you will have, I'll give, and willing too, / For do we must what force will have us do" (3.3.206–07). In the pardon scene, Henry willingly concedes what his aunt will have, for *he* must do what *farce* will have him do. Henry's worst defeats always occur on the comedic fields of the farcical, here with his beggar-aunt and later with "that old white-bearded Satan," Falstaff. Shakespeare refers to the ballad of the Beggar and the King once more in the tetralogy: when Falstaff learns of the death of Henry IV. Calling himself King Cophetua, Falstaff prepares to rush to Hal's side; like the figures in the ballad, Falstaff confuses the roles of beggar and king, boasting, "I know the young king is sick for me. Let us take any man's horses, the laws of England are at my commandement" (*2 Henry IV* 5.3.101, 135–36). Unlike his father, however, Henry V has learned how to maintain his own identity as king in the presence of beggars.

15. See Ure lvii–lxii for a concise explanation of the relationship between *Richard II* and Hayward's history.

16. See Ide (113–18) on the relationship between *Measure for Measure*'s pardon scenes and the Parliament of Heaven scenario.

17. See Lever xlviii–li; Bennett; Stevenson; Goldberg 231–39; Tennenhouse 154–59; and Greenblatt, *Negotiations* 136–37.

18. See Altman's discussion in *The Tudor Play of Mind.*

19. The topographical connection between the duke's trial scene and the public theaters of London is made by both Leah Marcus and Steven Mullaney in their discussions of *Measure for Measure.*

Works Cited

Altman, Joel B. *The Tudor Play of Mind: Rhetorical Inquiry and the Development of Elizabethan Drama.* Berkeley: U of California P, 1984.

Axton, Marie. *The Queen's Two Bodies: Drama and the Elizabethan Succession.* London: Royal Historical Soc., 1977.

Bellamy, John. *The Tudor Law of Treason: An Introduction.* London: Routledge, 1979.

Bennett, Josephine Waters. Measure for Measure *as Royal Entertainment.* New York: Columbia UP, 1966.

Biggins, D. "Very Tragical Mirth: Some Odd Uses of Comedy in Shakespeare." *Southern Review: Literary and Interdisciplinary Essays* (Adelaide, Australia) 12 (1978): 24–37.

Black, James. "The Interlude of the Beggar and the King in *Richard II.*" *Pageantry in the Shakespearean Theater.* Ed. David M. Bergeron. Athens: U of Georgia P, 1985. 104–13.

The Book of Sir Thomas More. Ed. W. W. Greg. London: Malone Soc., 1911.

Campbell, Lily B. "The Use of Historical Patterns in the Reign of Elizabeth." *Huntington Library Quarterly* 1 (1937–38): 135–67.

Cobbett's Complete Collection of State Trials. Ed. T. B. Howell. 2 vols. London, 1809.

Cox, John D. *Shakespeare and the Dramaturgy of Power.* Princeton: Princeton UP, 1989.

Davis, Natalie Zemon. *Fiction in the Archives: Pardon Tales and Their Tellers in Sixteenth-Century France.* Stanford: Stanford UP, 1987.

Fletcher, John. "To the Reader." *The Faithful Shepherdess.* Ed. Cyrus Hoy. *The Dramatic Works in the Beaumont and Fletcher Canon.* Ed. Fredson Bowers. Cambridge: Cambridge UP, 1976. 3: 497.

Foucault, Michel. *Discipline and Punish: The Birth of the Prison.* Trans. Alan Sheridan. London: Lane, 1977.

Goldberg, Jonathan. *James I and the Politics of Literature: Jonson, Shakespeare, Donne, and Their Contemporaries.* Baltimore: Johns Hopkins UP, 1983.

Greenblatt, Stephen. *Renaissance Self-Fashioning: From More to Shakespeare.* Chicago: U of Chicago P, 1980.

———. *Shakespearean Negotiations: The Circulation of Social Energy in Renaissance England.* Oxford: Clarendon, 1988.

Harington, Sir John. *A New Discourse of a Stale Subject, Called The Metamorphosis of Ajax.* Ed. Elizabeth Story Donno. London: Routledge, 1962.

Holdsworth, W. S. *A History of English Law.* 8 vols. London: Methuen, 1924.

Howard, Jean E. "Renaissance Antitheatricality and the Politics of Gender and Rank in *Much Ado about Nothing.*" *Shakespeare Reproduced: The Text in History and Ideology.* Ed. Jean E. Howard and Marion F. O'Connor. London: Methuen, 1987. 163–87.

Ide, Richard S. "Shakespeare's Revisionism: Homiletic Tragicomedy and the Ending of *Measure for Measure.*" *Shakespeare Studies* 20 (1988): 105–27.

James, Mervyn. *Society, Politics, and Culture: Studies in Early Modern England.* Cambridge: Cambridge UP, 1986.

Kantorowicz, Ernst H. *The King's Two Bodies: A Study in Mediaeval Political Theology.* Princeton: Princeton UP, 1957.

Kyd, Thomas. *The Spanish Tragedy.* Ed. J. R. Mulryne. New Mermaids. London: Benn, 1983.

Lamb, Mary Ellen. "Shakespeare's 'Theatrics': Ambivalence toward Theater in *Measure for Measure.*" *Shakespeare Studies* 20 (1988): 129–46.

Letters and Papers. Henry VIII. Public Record Office.

Lever, J. W., ed. *Measure for Measure.* The Arden Shakespeare. 1965. London: Methuen, 1986.

Levy, F. J. *Tudor Historical Thought.* San Marino, CA: Huntington Library, 1967.

McManaway, James. "Elizabeth, Essex, and James." *Elizabethan and Jacobean Studies: Presented to Frank Percy Wilson.* Oxford: Clarendon, 1959. 219–30.

McMillin, Scott. *The Elizabethan Theatre and* The Book of Sir Thomas More. Ithaca: Cornell UP, 1987.

Marcus, Leah S. *Puzzling Shakespeare: Local Reading and Its Discontents.* Berkeley: U of California P, 1988.

Montrose, Louis. "Renaissance Literary Studies and the Subject of History." *English Literary Renaissance* 16 (1986): 5–12.

Mullaney, Steven. *The Place of the Stage: License, Play, and Power in Renaissance England.* Chicago: U of Chicago P, 1988.

Neale, John Ernest. *Elizabeth I and Her Parliaments.* 3 vols. New York: St. Martin's, 1953–57.

Ornstein, Robert. *A Kingdom for a Stage: The Achievement of Shakespeare's History Plays.* Cambridge: Harvard UP, 1972.

Ribner, Irving. *The English History Play in the Age of Shakespeare.* Princeton: Princeton UP, 1957.

Richard II. By William Shakespeare. Dir. Barry Kyle. With Jeremy Irons. Theatre Royal, Newcastle-upon-Tyne. 12 Feb. 1987.

Scarry, Elaine. *The Body in Pain: The Making and Unmaking of the World.* Oxford: Oxford UP, 1985.

Shakespeare, William. *The Riverside Shakespeare.* Gnl. ed. G. Blakemore Evans. Boston: Houghton, 1974.

Stevenson, David Lloyd. *The Achievement of Shakespeare's* Measure for Measure. Ithaca: Cornell UP, 1966.

Tennenhouse, Leonard. *Power on Display: The Politics of Shakespeare's Genres.* New York: Methuen, 1986.

Tourneur, Cyril. *The Revenger's Tragedy.* Ed. Lawrence J. Ross. Lincoln: U of Nebraska P, 1966.

Ure, Peter, ed. *King Richard II.* By William Shakespeare. 4th Arden ed. Cambridge: Harvard UP, 1956.

Willson, David Harris. *King James VI and I.* London: Cape, 1956.

Zitner, Sheldon P. "Aumerle's Conspiracy." *Studies in English Literature, 1500–1900* 14 (1974): 239–70.

Wales, Ireland, and 1 Henry IV

CHRISTOPHER HIGHLEY

IN MAY OF 1603, several weeks after the death of Queen Elizabeth, and following his surrender to Lord Mountjoy, the Irish rebel chieftain Hugh O'Neill, earl of Tyrone, traveled to London to receive his pardon from the new king. Part of Tyrone's journey led through Wales, where he was greeted by the enraged women of that country, who, as Fynes Moryson relates, flung "durt and stones at the Earle as he passed, and . . . revil[ed] him with bitter words." Historians have accepted Moryson's own reading of the encounter, assuring us that in this act of scapegoating the women were avenging themselves upon Tyrone for the "Husbands and Children" they had lost in the recent wars and expressing their solidarity with the English cause (Moryson 336).[1] But it is equally conceivable that the attack was motivated by a different set of loyalties, and that the women targeted Tyrone not because they were sharing in English hostility but because they looked upon him as the failed and discredited leader of a cause they had themselves supported.

Although Moryson does not censure the women's action, his account registers a certain unease with their lack of respect for Lord Mountjoy, in whose company Tyrone travels. Unlike Moryson, who suppresses the potentially ambiguous motives behind the attack, other writers were convinced that the common people of Wales were sympathetic toward and in collusion with the Irish rebels. This was cer-

91

tainly the view of a group of loyal Welsh gentry who in January 1599 wrote to the Privy Council about Tyrone's local popularity and of a sympathetic bond uniting the subject people of Wales and Ireland. "No Welshmen," they warned, "should be used in service against the Irishmen, because they were not to be trusted" (*C.S.P. Ireland 1598–99* 461–62).[2]

English suspicions of complicity between the lower orders of Wales and the Irish rebels may have been a logical outgrowth of the general identification of the two countries. In the sixteenth century, such a link was routinely established by invoking the English conquest and settlement of Wales as an example to guide and justify current colonial policy in Ireland. English officials there treated this earlier conquest as a model to be imitated, and urged that the policies used in subduing the Welsh be revived in Ireland. Applauding the appointment of Sir Henry Sidney as Lord Deputy in Ireland, and punning on his previous title of Lord President of the council in the marches of Wales, William Gerard told the Privy Council that "A better president [precedent] . . . colde not be founde then to imitate the course that reformed Walles" (qtd. in Penry Williams 31).[3]

The association of Ireland and Wales, however, was not simply based on a recognition of the similar struggle each country had waged against English rule. Conceptually, the English organized their Celtic neighbors through a network of flexible and shifting relationships that allowed the English to both distinguish and, where appropriate, make strategic connections between them. While the respective genealogies of the Irish and Welsh distinguished them on the basis of ethnicity, the two peoples were conflated in the English mind by the perceived affinities between their languages. Hotspur's claim in *1 Henry IV,* that he would "rather hear Lady, my brach [i.e., bitch], howl in Irish," than "the lady sing in Welsh" (ed. Bevington, 3.1.230–31), is a virulently misogynist variation on the commonplace identification of Welsh and Irish as equally bestial languages.[4]

Hotspur's gibe is one of several allusions to Ireland in a play that coincides with a critical juncture in Elizabeth's Irish campaign. While it cannot be dated precisely, *1 Henry IV* was most likely written and first performed between August 1596 and 25 February 1598, when it was entered in the Stationers' Register (Bevington, *Henry IV, Part 1* 8–9). It was at this time that reports of the imminent collapse of

English rule in Ireland became more frequent and shrill. In February 1597, for example, Maurice Kyffin reported that Elizabeth's army was in a state of disarray, and the country approaching anarchy: "our soldiers die wretchedly in the open streets and highways; the native subjects spoiled and brought to extreme beggary; no service in war performed; no military discipline or civil justice exercised; briefly, the whole kingdom ruined and foraged" (*C.S.P. Ireland 1596–97* 233). With the proliferation of newsletters and the circulation of political gossip, a general—if not necessarily accurate—awareness of events and conditions in Ireland spread beyond the council chamber to a much broader audience.[5] That Shakespeare was himself familiar with these conditions is suggested by the compelling affinities between the "pitiful rascals" impressed by Falstaff in both parts of *Henry IV,* and the wretched state of Elizabeth's malnourished, largely conscript, army in Ireland (Part 1, 4.2.61).[6]

Underlying the crisis was an escalation in Irish resistance to English rule. Earlier in the century, Irish opposition to the private plantation schemes of English adventurers had generally been local and uncoordinated.[7] In Ulster, traditionally the most intractable and rebellious province, the maintenance of English control had since 1567 hinged upon the cooperation of Hugh O'Neill, second earl of Tyrone. But after his provocative decision to accept the outlawed Gaelic title of The O'Neill in 1595, Tyrone's usefulness and loyalty to the crown became increasingly vexed and uncertain.[8] Following his first direct attack upon English forces, Tyrone was declared a traitor in June 1595. Although he was to reassert his loyalty to the crown and to receive a temporary pardon a year later, Tyrone had now set upon a course of galvanizing native resistance to the English and transforming it into a nationalist struggle for independence (Hayes-McCoy 121).[9]

In their letter of January 1599 to the Privy Council, the Welsh authors disclosed that the local people had proclaimed Tyrone Prince of Wales and King of Ireland. The authors claimed that "Tyrone had in his service 500 Welshmen" and "that he had friends in Wales, that looked for him, as he was both favourable and bountiful to Welshmen." Furthermore, Tyrone's Welsh sympathizers made the intriguing assertion that their hero was "descended of Owyne Clyne Dore, who had interest both in Ireland and Wales . . . [and] that there was a

prophecy the Earl of Tyrone should prevail against the English nation"
(*C.S.P. Ireland 1598–99* 462). Previously unnoted by critics of *1
Henry IV,* the putative genealogical link between Owyne Clyne Dore
(a variant spelling of Owen Glendower) and Tyrone prompts an interpretation of Glendower and his part in the Percy rebellion as a displaced actualization of Tyrone's contemporaneous rebellion in Ireland.

II

When Glendower informs Hotspur of his education in England—
"I can speak English, lord, as well as you; / For I was trained up in
the English court" (3.1.117–18)—the play's first audiences could have
recalled Tyrone's similar upbringing in England. Sir Henry Sidney had
taken the nine-year-old Hugh as his ward in 1559 and sent him to
England, where he was educated in the reformed faith under the
patronage of Sidney and Leicester in preparation for his later strategic
reinsertion into Irish society. Both Glendower and Tyrone had experienced the "civilizing" effect of English culture and both had served
English authority: Glendower as a follower of Henry Bolingbroke,
Tyrone as an ally of Elizabeth. With both men, though, familiarity
with English ways had only bred a latent resentment, and upon returning to their respective homes they had rebelled against their former
English benefactors and masters.[10]

Biographical affinities between Glendower and Tyrone represent
one straightforward form of topicality. But since Ireland is a pervasive
subtext in *1 Henry IV,* contemporary events and conditions there are
also registered in more diffuse and complex ways.[11] For instance, in
its general configuration the rebel alliance simulates the underlying
structure and dynamics of Irish resistance. The play's rebel alliance
is underwritten by kinship ties just as the rebellion in Ireland was
based upon a coalition of various families and factions. G. A. Hayes-
McCoy observes that, "since the Maguires, O'Donnells, and O'Neills
were interrelated, the developing confederacy of the Ulster lords has
the quality of a family compact" (118). Mortimer's marriage to Glendower's daughter completes a triangular alliance that through the
marriage of Mortimer's sister to Hotspur also includes the powerful
Percy family. To the king, Mortimer's marriage into a rebellious Welsh
family is a provocative crossing of national and racial boundaries that

equips his rival with a power base; to the rebels, on the other hand, it represents an invaluable exogamic alliance that unites the north of the realm with both the west and Wales in a bond of consanguinity against the king.

In order to prevent the formation of larger groupings against their rule in Ireland, the English promoted competition and hostility between and within the clans and septs that constituted tribal society. Edmund Spenser recalled how the English had originally "set up" Tyrone, "then called Baron of Dongannon," to "beard" his rival and predecessor "Turlagh Lenagh." But the plan backfired when Tyrone turned the power invested in him by Elizabeth against the English (Spenser 113). Unlike his predecessors, Tyrone largely succeeded in foiling the English strategy of divide and conquer, and through cultivating connections with other families he was able to establish a nearly unified front of opposition: "All Ulster," declared an English tract of 1598, "is now joined together in Rebellion against the Quene, saving the Countie of Louth . . . all the Captens of Countries are bound to the Earle of Tyrone, either by Affinitie or Consanguinitie or duetie" (Hogan 33). During the parley between Tyrone and an English delegation in December 1597, the latter were taken aback by Tyrone's willingness to push demands on behalf of other septs and Gaelic leaders. Thomas Jones, the English recorder of the interviews, saw in Tyrone's audacity an attempt by the "crafty traitor" to enlarge his constituency by adopting the grievances of groups he had previously ignored: "His demand made now for the Moores and Connors, and for Edmund Gerald [Kavanagh], of whom he made no mention in his treaty with Sir John Norreys, may induce us to think that, the longer he is suffered, the further will he extend his power" (*C.S.P. Ireland 1596–97* 488–89). Even more alarming to the English delegation was Tyrone's demand for liberty of religion, a claim he made, according to Jones, in order "to become popular amongst this idolatrous people" (490). By December 1597, then, the English faced in Tyrone a rebel leader of national standing whose aspirations must have appeared uncannily similar to those of his precursor Glendower some two centuries earlier.[12]

Tyrone's status as the single unrivaled head of Irish resistance certainly does not correspond with the place of Glendower in the structure of the play's rebel alliance. Glendower is one component of a remarkably heterogeneous rebellion that brings together an array of groups that were each capable in their own right of challenging or destabilizing the authority of the Tudor state. Ranged against the king by the end of act 1 are the Welsh, the Scots (who as mercenaries fought alongside Tyrone in Ireland), a dissident group of clergy, and a rebellious fraction of the English aristocracy. Shakespeare thus accentuates the threat from the Celtic fringe by compounding it with these other threats, particularly the internal threat of a factious nobility led by the Percies.[13] The Percies of *1 Henry IV* are the ancestors of Thomas Percy, seventh earl of Northumberland, who in 1572 had been executed for the leading part he had played in the abortive Northern Rebellion, a regional uprising that had aimed at restoring Catholicism and establishing Mary Stuart as Elizabeth's successor (Neale ch. 11). Thomas's brother Henry had pursued the same objectives, and in 1585 he died in the Tower, suspected of plotting against Elizabeth's life (*DNB*). In reviving memories of an independent recusant family, the Percy presence in *1 Henry IV* helps foreground the continuing struggle between crown and aristocracy. The Northern Rebellion may have been the last of the great feudal uprisings against the crown, but its failure did not signal the demise of the "overmighty subject" whose private armies and fortified houses continued throughout Elizabeth's reign to deny the crown a monopoly on either violence or allegiance.

Glendower is Tyrone's main analogue in the play, but he is not the only character that the first audiences might have identified with the Irish "arch-traitor" (*C.S.P. Ireland 1598–99* 162). In the early seventeenth century, the attorney-general for Ireland, Sir John Davies, invoked Mortimer as an equivalent figure to Tyrone.[14] Offering parallels to Tyrone from England's own past, Davies observed that

when England was full of tenants-at-will our barons were then like the mere Irish lords, and were able to raise armies against the crown; and as this man was O'Neal in Ulster, so the Earl of Warwick was O'Nevill in Yorkshire, and the Bishopric and Mortimer was the like in the Marches of Wales. (qtd. in Canny, "The Ideology of English Colonization" 591)

Mortimer, in fact, sets off a series of topical resonances in relation to Ireland. In particular, his marriage to Glendower's daughter brings to the surface a collection of cultural anxieties about the attraction of native society for English settlers in Ireland. Mortimer's obscure capitulation to Glendower replays the process of "going native" whereby English colonists in Ireland were assimilated to Gaelic society. The earliest Old English settlers were the group most associated with this lapse from civility. Discussing them in *A View of the Present State of Ireland* (1596), Spenser noted that, through intermarriage and promiscuous contact generally, they had "degenerated and grown almost mere Irish, yea and more malicious to the English than the very Irish themselves" (48). Significantly, Spenser includes among the Old English families who "have degendered from their ancient dignities," "the great Mortimer, who forgetting how great he was once in England, or English at all, is now become the most barbarous of them all, and is called Macnemarra" (66). In his search for support from all available quarters, Tyrone had appealed successfully to the Old English "'gentlemen of Munster' to join the Ulster confederacy and to 'make war with us'" (Hayes-McCoy 123). The Glendower-Mortimer bond, by refiguring the much-feared collusion between England's Gaelic and Old English enemies in Ireland, contributes yet another dimension to the topical nuances of the play's rebel alliance.

If we accept the king's view in 1.2 that Mortimer has defected to the enemy voluntarily, then we can also connect him with the English soldiers and officers who deserted to the Irish, and who in some cases are reported to have helped train Tyrone's army (Canny, "Permissive Frontier" 23–24; Rowse 417). Also, as a regional commander who starts out loyal to his monarch but later turns traitor, Mortimer conveys the unease with which Elizabeth and her government viewed the post of Lord Deputy in Ireland, a post that was notoriously sensitive and dangerous for both parties. For Elizabeth, investing power in regional commanders was always a calculated gamble because that power could readily be abused and possibly turned against a vulnerable central government. This problem was especially acute in Ireland, where the local administration was always out of sight—if never out of mind—of the queen and her advisers, and in touch with the court via slow and unreliable lines of communication. Elizabeth complained repeatedly of the lack of regular and reliable news from the wars; a "regular postal service to Ireland" was not established until late 1598 (Falls, *Elizabeth's Irish Wars* 228).

It was not uncommon for Elizabeth's Lord Deputies to be accused of exploiting their office for personal gain, but on occasion more serious charges of the kind the king levels at Mortimer were also made (1.3.77–92). In 1592, for instance, after his return to England, Sir John Perrot was tried for high treason. Perrot, it seems, was guilty of little more than slandering the queen; but through the efforts of his rivals he was also charged with conspiring with the Spanish to overthrow Elizabeth. These charges may have proven unduly alarming to the government because of the fact that Perrot was reputed to be Henry VIII's bastard son and half-brother to Elizabeth; in *1 Henry IV,* Mortimer is a blood relation of the king and pretender to the throne (Spenser 109, Schwind 51–52, *DNB*).

In the process of unraveling its dense and overlapping webs of topical significance, we need to consider how the play works upon these materials for ideological purposes. Whether we speak of Shake-speare's deliberate intentions or of the play's "political unconscious," *1 Henry IV* constitutes an intervention in the discursive field of Anglo-Irish relations. In both reproducing and critically reshaping prevailing cultural and political realities, the play undertakes a form of "social *work.*"[15] As part of its ideological design, the play handles Glendower in a way designed radically to curtail the anxiety-causing potential of the Celtic chieftain and of Tyrone in particular. To this end, the play initially sets up an image of Glendower as both hostile and admirable, an image that is fully congruent with ambivalent English depictions of Tyrone and his fellow Irish chiefs.[16]

The descriptions of Glendower that precede his appearance at 3.1 characterize him as a figure of formidable power. Westmorland sees Glendower as "irregular and wild," an uncivilized outlaw whose "rude hands" have defeated and taken Mortimer captive (1.1.40–41). For Hotspur, he is the "great Glendower," a "valiant combatant" in his fight with Mortimer (1.3.101,107). Sounding a more sinister note, the king ascribes Glendower's strength not to physical valor but to witchcraft. Henry calls him "that great magician, damned Glen-dower" (1.3.83), epithets that resonate suggestively with Tyrone's reputation as "the Great Divill" (qtd. in O'Faolain 182).[17] Through a similar collection of tropes, Tyrone was constructed as a potent adver-sary of English rule and transformed into something of a mythical entity, more animal or demon than mortal man. The assorted labels applied to him by Lord Deputy Burgh—the Running Beast, the Great Bear, the Northern Lucifer, and Beelzebub—collectively suggest a strange blend of elusiveness, boldness, and inscrutable evil (O'Faolain 191).

In the only scene in which he actually appears, however, Glendower turns out to bear little resemblance either to the early descriptions of him in the play or to those in Shakespeare's main sources. Glendower acts as courteous host to his fellow rebel-lords, boasts of his proficiency in English and musical composition, shows a civilized self-restraint, and even yields to Hotspur over the issue of land distribution (3.1.131). But even as Shakespeare domesticates Glendower, invalidating his frightening reputation, he turns the chieftain into a figure of ridicule. Falstaff's satirical vignette of Glendower mastering the forces of Hell (2.4.326) lays the ground for Hotspur's demystification of Glendower's prodigious self-image and magical pretensions. The exposure of Glendower as a hoax is all the more devastating precisely because his principal accuser is one of Glendower's own allies. And behind Glendower's preoccupation with prophecies and astrological signs we can perhaps detect a more general disdain for the superstitions that Protestant Englishmen associated with the popular Catholicism of both Wales and Ireland.

After his humiliation by Hotspur, Glendower does not appear again. The disarming of Glendower seems complete when, discouraged by unfavorable prophecies, he fails to appear for the crucial battle (4.1.125–27, 4.4.16–18). Shakespeare emphasizes Glendower's absence by evacuating the Welsh altogether from the battle of Shrewsbury. In this, he follows his source in Daniel and not Holinshed, for whom "Welshmen" are present although Glendower himself is not (Holinshed 25). The particular explanation for Glendower's absence is Shakespeare's own invention, and its inclusion has the effect of nullifying Glendower's alleged "magic"—transforming it from a potential source of opposition to the state into a rationale for inaction (Zitner 145).

Glendower's fate, moreover, is extended to the rebel alliance as a whole, which dissolves before its full military impact is felt. After a planning session marked by personal rivalries and arguments over the distribution of land, the rebel alliance unravels internally and spontaneously as if in confirmation of the continuing trust placed by the

English in the policy of undermining the cohesion of the Irish forces. Despite Tyrone's acknowledged success at bonding the native community, one English observer remained confident that "many [Irish families], which now shadow themselves under the cloak of Tyrone's villainies, will yield great means, and plot good courses for Tyrone's ruin and overthrow, if they might see Her Majesty fully resolved to prosecute war against them" (*C.S.P. Ireland 1598–99* 169).

In the deterioration of Glendower from a principal scourge of the English to charlatan and palpable absence—and in the parallel fate of the alliance generally—the play can be seen as disempowering the figure of the Celtic chieftain by literally wishing him away. Theatrical magic imaginatively assuages English anxieties about his modern counterparts in Ireland. *Henry IV, Part 1* was not unique in offering this kind of wish-fulfillment. Between 1596 and 1597, at the same time the Chamberlain's Men were playing *1 Henry IV,* the Admiral's Men at the Rose were performing *The History of the Life and Death of Captain Thomas Stuckeley,* a play that directly confronts the issue of Irish rebellion by setting an early scene in Ireland at the time of Shane O'Neill's revolt. The murder of Shane by his own Scottish associates and the spectacle of his severed head offered vicarious satisfaction to all who sought the overthrow of the present O'Neill (Simpson 207–09).

III

In one of the more curious metaphors imposed on Tyrone by the English, Lord Deputy Burgh, notifying Robert Cecil in July 1597 of his plans to march against and defeat Tyrone, vowed "to 'beat the Diana' in the proud traitor's fort, which he hath made upon the ford" (*C.S.P. Ireland 1596–97* 340). On the surface, Burgh's analogy can be taken as a commonplace attempt to disarm Tyrone by effeminizing him, just as Hotspur emasculates Glendower by likening the Welshman's garrulousness to that of "a railing wife" (3.1.155). But the analogy, which rests upon the association of Tyrone and Diana as forest dwellers, also demonizes Tyrone by linking him to a goddess whom the Renaissance portrayed from one perspective as a dangerous and uncontained figure, an Amazon who existed outside and in defiance of established, male, power structures.[18]

Burgh's assimilation of Tyrone to this figure of female misrule alerts us to the part played by women in both the Irish rebellion and in the Welsh rebellion of *1 Henry IV.* Glendower's daughter is the only Welshwoman to appear in the play but not the only one mentioned. Mortimer, in fact, only falls into her hands after first coming perilously close to other, less gentle, ones. In the play's opening scene, Westmorland tells the king how

> the noble Mortimer,
> Leading the men of Herefordshire to fight
> Against the irregular and wild Glendower,
> Was by the rude hands of that Welshman taken,
> A thousand of his people butcherèd—
> Upon whose dead corpse there was such misuse,
> Such beastly shameless transformation
> By those Welshwomen done as may not be
> Without much shame retold or spoken of.
>
> (1.1.38–46)

This, the play's only allusion to the incident, is a teasing hint of an account contained in Shakespeare's principal source, Holinshed's *Chronicles.* When Holinshed confronts the incident he is just as reticent as Westmorland, and refuses to relate it fully lest the "honest eares" and "continent toongs" of the decorous English readers be scandalized (20). Only when the women repeat their atrocity after a later battle does Abraham Fleming, the editor of the second (1587) edition of the *Chronicles,* add a less inhibited account.[19]

The dead bodies of the Englishmen, being above a thousand lieng upon the ground imbrued in their owne bloud, was a sight (a man would thinke) greevous to looke upon, and so farre from exciting and stirring up affections of crueltie; that it should rather have mooved the beholders to commiseration and mercie: yet did the women of Wales cut off their privities, and put one part thereof into the mouthes of everie dead man, in such sort that the cullions [testicles] hoong downe to their chins; and not so contented, they did cut off their noses and thrust them into their tailes as they laie on the ground mangled and defaced. (34)

Since England's Celtic borderlands could be cognitively mapped along one axis as symbolically continuous and interchangeable, it follows that in their wider provenance the castrating energies of

Fleming/Shakespeare's Welshwomen evoke the dangers of native, Celtic women generally. In fact, the Welshwomen's atrocities have their counterparts in reports from Ireland that deal with the fate of English settlers and soldiers there, reports that were more an index to what the English wished to believe than to what had actually occurred. In October 1598, for example, the Chief Justice of Munster, William Saxey, told Robert Cecil about the mutilations inflicted by the rebels on the English dead: "some with their tongues cut out of their heads, others with their noses cut off" (*C.S.P. Ireland 1598–99* 300). And the first earl of Essex alleged that it was the practice of the rebels "to cut off their [English victims'] privy parts, set up their heads and put them in their mouths" (qtd. in Canny, *Elizabethan Conquest* 139).

Both play and social text, then, imagine the threat from the Celtic fringe in terms of the overthrow of a masculine English identity through castration. Spenser, likewise, referred to the Old English settlers who had turned native as having "degendered," a term that implied both general devolution and sterility (Hamilton 527).[20] Fleming's uncensored version of the atrocity presents the Welshwomen's violence as a kind of ritual performance that turns the human body into a text upon which gender and power relations are symbolically contested. First the soldier is castrated and the "privities" stuffed in his mouth; then the nose—a surrogate phallus—is removed and stuffed in the anus. By cutting and transposing the soldiers' noses and "privities" the Welshwomen invert and parody an "official" notion of bodily integrity and hierarchy, conflating and joining in carnivalesque fashion the lower regions with the higher. The gesture of blocking the mouth is both an expression of gender conflict—it symbolically transfers to men the stipulation of silence enjoined by society upon women—and an evocation and rejection of English attempts to impose their language upon the people of Wales and Ireland.

If the acts of cutting and gagging related by Fleming and Essex are familiar components in an imaginary repertoire of colonial violence constructed by the English, Fleming's account of the sodomizing of the soldiers, on the other hand, has no apparent precedent. The women consummate their performance with what the Renaissance regarded as the ultimate sexual transgression. Penetrating the soldiers with their victims' own noses, the women assume the kind of sexual dominance that the culture reserved for men while making it appear as if their male victims are sodomizing themselves. In short, the women's act of silent ventriloquism destroys the soldiers' last vestigial claims to manhood.

Although the atrocities in Fleming/Shakespeare have a basis in contemporary allegations of Irish brutality, those same allegations do not specifically ascribe the atrocities to women. Fleming/Shakespeare's identification of the crimes as female-specific can be taken as symptomatic of the period's drive to criminalize women, a process that was most marked on the fringes of the nation-state and that tended to focus on the most vulnerable and powerless kinds of women. Christina Larner argues in her study of the relations between Scottish state-building and witch-hunting in the sixteenth century that masterless or lower-class women were typically constructed and targeted as the final embodiments of resistance to the expansionist and "civilizing" thrust of the nation-state (199). As Fynes Moryson's account of the Welshwomen's attack on Tyrone suggests, English ethnographic knowledge of the Welsh also tended to identify women as most adept at avoiding containment or moral cleansing. This assumption persisted in Wales long after the Renaissance, for when a royal inquiry was conducted into the state of education and manners in Wales in the mid-nineteenth century, it was "the backwardness and immorality" of the women that the commissioners singled out for censure (Morgan 92).

But Fleming/Shakespeare's castrating women are also conceived in response to the specific anxieties aroused by Celtic, and especially Irish, women. A particularly well-documented anxiety concerned their role as wet nurses to the children of Old English settlers. Like many of the English, Spenser believed that in taking the nurse's milk, the child internalized her "nature and disposition," thus subverting its potential to achieve a civilized English identity (Spenser 67–68, Greenblatt 185). In general, the Irishwoman was supposedly unimpressed by patriarchal authority and the other institutional props of the "godly" society. This was adduced from her indifference to the proscriptions that banned English and other "civilized" women from war. The scandalous appearance of Shakespeare's Welshwomen on the field of battle, in fact, recalls the English claim that Irishwomen played a crucial part in promoting rebellion. Among his neighbors

and allies Tyrone numbered "O'Donnell's Ineen Duv—she whom the
Four Masters describe as a woman 'like the mother of Machabees who
joined a man's heart to a woman's thought'" (O'Faolain 121). Another
Irish Amazon was the legendary Grace O'Malley, "a great feminine
sea captain" of Connaught, as Sir Henry Sidney called her in 1583
(qtd. in Schwind 45). At times cooperating with the English, at times
defying them, she was, according to Lord Justice Drury, "a woman
that hath impudently passed the part of womanhood and been a great
spoiler, and chief commander and director of thieves and murderers
at sea," while in 1593 Sir Richard Bingham characterized her as that
"notable traitoress and nurse to all rebellions in the province for forty
years" (qtd. in Chambers 93, Schwind 43).

Not all rebel women were as conspicuous and individually powerful
as Grace O'Malley. Sir Geoffrey Fenton complained in January 1601
of "the witches of that country (which aboundeth with witches),
[who] are all set on work to cross the service [English campaign] by
extraordinary unseasonable weather" (qtd. in Rowse 417). Support
for the rebels was also forthcoming, as Humphrey Gilbert pointed
out, from the "churls and 'Calliackes' [*cailleacha,* old women], or
women who milked their [the rebels'] 'Creates' [*creacha,* herds] and
provided their victuals and other necessaries." Therefore, reasoned
Gilbert, "the killing of [the women] by the sword was the way to
kill the men of war by famine" (qtd. in Quinn 127).

Henry IV, Part 1 also presents two distinct classes of Celtic women.
Glendower's daughter is clearly of a different social standing from
her sister Welshwomen, whose collective action marks them as an
all-female version of the many-headed monster so feared by the prop-
ertied and privileged of Tudor England. What she shares with them,
though, is a desire to enter male space and cross gender boundaries:
"She'll be a soldier too, she'll to the wars," is how Glendower trans-
lates his daughter's Welsh words as the rebels prepare to leave for
battle (3.1.190). Together, Glendower's daughter and her plebeian
Welsh sisters exemplify the double-construction of the native woman
within English colonial discourse as eroticized enchantress and/or
fierce Amazon. Contemporary writing on Ireland typically alternates
between eroticizing and demonizing native women, offering them as
objects for voyeuristic inspection and degrading them as hags, can-
nibals, or infanticides. The English traveler Luke Gernon neatly encap-
sulates this binary vision in his remark that the women of Ireland

"are wemen at thirteene, and olde wives at thirty. I never saw fayrer wenches nor fowler calliots, so we call the olde wemen" (357).

The central danger embodied in Glendower's daughter is her ability to entrap male onlookers. She is described as "Charming [Mortimer's] blood with pleasing heaviness" (3.1.212), effectively overpowering the English war lord with her bewitching—and unintelligible—Welsh words and songs. And her obscure attraction is confirmed in the revealing wish of the anti-lover Hotspur to occupy "the Welsh lady's bed" (3.1.237). Seduction was a form of symbolic castration also feared by the English in Ireland. When direct means failed, the rebels allegedly employed the wiles of native women to entrap the settlers. During the siege of an English town in Limerick, for example, the Irish earl of Desmond "sent a fair young harlot as a present to the [English] constable, by whose means he hoped to get the house; but the constable, learning from whence she came, threw her . . . with a stone about her neck, into the river" (qtd. in Greenlaw et al. 174).

IV

In *1 Henry IV,* our encounter with the castrating Welshwomen could hardly be more fleeting. Textually, the women are twice removed or doubly mediated, since Westmorland's report of the atrocity to the king is based on the prior report made to Westmorland by a "post from Wales" (1.1.37). The very brevity of Westmorland's report and the king's puzzling failure to respond to it seem designed to minimize the transgressive import of the incident. Yet the result of such reticence is to make the incident more enigmatic and disturbing. The surrounding narrative in Fleming's account at least provides a context for the violence by offering precedents of female cruelty from antiquity, whereas in the play its very obscurity is a cause for speculation. The Welshwomen's violation seems to be raised only to be immediately repressed, but as I shall argue, it remains in the play's memory as a problem that must be returned to and later resolved.

Responsibility for symbolically overcoming or canceling this violation falls to Prince Hal. His pivotal role in the recovery of a masculine English identity that has been specifically lost to women depends upon his own conspicuous insulation from them. As Peter

Erickson sees it, the essential characteristic of the Englishman in such Shakespearean figures as Talbot (*1 Henry VI*) and Henry V is an "approved image of manhood based on resistance to women and on allegiance to men" (125). Hal's possession of what Erickson calls "self-contained masculine purity" (124) effectively denies the determining and contaminating power of women over men, the kind of power readily associated with the nursing and fostering roles of Irishwomen.

Prince Hal's combat with "this northern youth" (3.2.145) Hotspur thus becomes a pivotal moment in the play's rehearsal of the subversion and recovery of a masculine and militant English identity. Their confrontation in the Welsh borderlands recalls us to the scene of an earlier heroic encounter

> When on the gentle Severn's sedgy bank,
> In single opposition, hand to hand,
> [Mortimer] did confound the best part of an hour
> In changing hardiment with great Glendower.
>   (1.3.98–101)

The later fight effects a substitution of one set of "valiant combatants" (1.3.107) for another, projecting onto Hotspur the oppositional energies originally invested in Glendower. Hotspur becomes a final attenuated image of Tyrone in the play, the scapegoat who must bear off Tyrone's residual danger. In Hal's single combat with Hotspur, Shakespeare triumphantly re-presents the protracted and inconclusive warfare in Ireland as a chivalrous conflict that is simple, direct, and final.

Against his great rival, Hal asserts and achieves a vigorous male sexuality. Vernon's famous description of Hal in battle dress evokes the energy of the prince and his company in specifically sexual terms and likens Hal's skill at horsemanship—he "vaulted with such ease into his seat" (4.1.108)—to sexual mastery over women. As the battle of Shrewsbury approaches, images of sexual vitality and erection turn into a kind of phallic competitiveness between Hal and Hotspur. Before the battle, Hotspur imagines their imminent encounter as a blend of homoerotic camaraderie and violence: "I will embrace him with a soldier's arm, / That he shall shrink under my courtesy"; but afterward it is Hal who proclaims victoriously over Hotspur's corpse "how much art thou shrunk" (5.2.73–74, 5.4.85–86). Similarly, the struggle between Tyrone and his English male adversaries was represented in terms of a genital rivalry. In his "Happy Farewell to the fortunate and forward most Noble Earle of Esex," Thomas Churchyard wrote,

> When *Mars* shal march, with shining sword in hand,
> A craven cock cries creak, and hangs down wing,
>   Will run about the shraep and daer not stand.
> When cocks of gaem coms in to give a bloe,
>   So false *Tyroen* may faint when he would fight,
> Thogh now alowd on dunghill duth he croe.
>
> (Nichols 434)

Churchyard's put-down of Tyrone as flaccid and impotent works by simply contradicting the pervasive English recognition of the earl's enviable strength and virility: "He is the best man of war of his nation, having had his education in our discipline, and being naturally valiant," thought Sir George Carewe (*C.S.P. Ireland 1592–96* 231). Hal's desire to kill Hotspur, while capturing and internalizing his rival's accumulated stock of personal chivalric capital, offers a way of channeling the opposed impulses of hatred and admiration that the English felt for Tyrone.

As we have already noted, the play's climactic showdown returns us to the same liminal space between two realms in which Mortimer is captured and the Welshwomen commit their atrocity. More precisely, the final battle takes place on the outskirts of Shrewsbury, a town strategically situated on the margins of English territory in the marches of Wales. Forming a corridor of land on either side of the English-Welsh border, the marches of Wales had traditionally been divided into a series of miniature principalities, each governed by its own marcher lord. Equipped with their own private armies and observing only their own laws, these local magnates were synonymous with political autonomy and resistance to the crown. It was only with the shiring of the marches and the introduction of English legal and administrative procedures in 1536 as part of the first Act of Union that the crown finally curtailed the anomalous powers of these magnates and so took control of the region (Penry Williams 20–21, Glanmor Williams ch. 11). Yet long after their pacification and political incorporation the Welsh borderlands were still perceived as a locus of disorder and instability on the fringes of the nation-state.[21] At the same time, the whole of Gaelic Ireland beyond the English pale was also referred to as an extended march or borderland. The pale itself, as J. H. Andrews argues, was thought of not so much as a fixed physical area but as "a moving 'colonial' frontier" (182). To enlarge its extent was a major goal of English officials, who hoped thereby to convert the Gaelic borderland into civil shire ground.

The victory of the king's forces over the rebels in this highly charged territory, then, signifies an act of boundary-marking in which the political center of the nation physically and symbolically asserts control over its volatile and vulnerable borders. And in resecuring the border between England and Wales, Hal enacts the metaphorical reintegration of the corpses of the English soldiers. For as Mary Douglas argues, in a variety of cultures "the body is a model which can stand for any bounded system. Its boundaries can represent any boundaries which are threatened or precarious" (115).

Writing with the benefit of hindsight and from a later position of English security in Ireland, Sir John Davies argued that Ireland's systemic problems could be attributed to "the absence of our Kings, three of them only since the Norman conquest have made royal journeys into this land" (166). For Davies, Edward III's success in governing Ireland was due to the "personal presence of the King's son as a concurrent cause of this Reformation, because the people of this land, both English and Irish, out of a natural pride, did ever love and desire to be governed by great persons" (165). *Henry IV, Part 1* offers the fantasy-remedy outlined by Davies of an activist male heir visiting the fringes of the realm and virtually single-handedly banishing rebellion. What made the fantasy both more compelling and more hollow, however, was the reality it belied of an aging woman ruler, who had never set foot in Ireland, and who stubbornly resisted all discussion of a successor.

While Hal is conceived on the one hand as an antidote to Elizabeth's inadequacies and failures, he is also drawn as an ideal successor to the long parade of men whom Elizabeth had appointed to govern in Ireland. At a later stage in Hal's career, Shakespeare explicitly likens Henry V on his victorious return from France to Elizabeth's own "General" returning from Ireland with "rebellion broachèd on his sword" (*Henry V,* ed. Taylor, 5.0.25–35). Critics have almost unanimously taken these lines to be a reference to the earl of Essex, Elizabeth's penultimate and ill-fated Lord Deputy in Ireland, yet the "General" in question could conceivably be his successor, Lord Mountjoy (Bevington, *Tudor Drama* 290). Although *1 Henry IV* dates from the time when the young and charismatic Essex was first being linked with the Irish post, there is no reason to assume that Hal represents anything more than a general pattern of the kind of decisive and single-minded leadership required in Ireland.[22] Between 1596 and March 1599 the Irish command was in a state of flux, with two Lord Deputies and three interim justices in turn occupying the chief position (Ellis 330). The arrival of the aggressive Thomas, Lord Burgh, as deputy in May 1597 had occasioned considerable confidence that Tyrone would soon be defeated, but less than five months later Burgh was dead of typhus (Hayes-McCoy 123–24).

When Hal pronounces Hotspur's epitaph and observes the "fair rites of tenderness" (5.4.97) toward Hotspur's corpse, he reconstitutes a code of battlefield honor that the Welshwomen had so outrageously violated in this same territory. Yet even after Hal's consummation of his victory, the memory of that initial act of female castration still haunts the action. In a gesture that critics have long puzzled over, Falstaff, acting out his own genital rivalry with Hotspur ("Why may not he rise as well as I?" [5.4.123–24]), mutilates the corpse by stabbing it in the thigh. With that strategically placed blow, the repressed returns, disrupting the play's mechanisms of reintegration and resolution.[23] In the last lines of the play, a second eruption follows, when the king announces his plan to march "towards Wales, / To fight with Glendower and the Earl of March" (5.5.39–40). The sudden re-intrusion of Glendower and Mortimer transforms the effect of closure from a reassuring completion into a postponement, the deferral of a threat apparently dismissed earlier.

That the play's ideological design should finally falter is hardly surprising, for in Ireland at this time Tyrone remained threatening and uncontained. "He is now become impotent to contayne himself within his bounds; but Seeketh to Usurpe the whole province," declared an exasperated English observer in 1598 (Hogan 33). Only in December 1601 at the decisive battle of Kinsale were Tyrone's forces finally routed. In the meantime, Elizabeth's commanders argued about Tyrone's intentions and how to deal with them. Unable to fix on a consistent course of action, the English first declared him a traitor, then pardoned him and parleyed with him, then attacked him and tried to trick him with such "shiftes and subtelties," as the Privy Council put it, "tyll tyme serve to use more forcible meanes to reduce him to other manner of obedience" (Dasent 422).

Notes

An earlier version of this paper which I delivered at "The Unmaking of Margins" conference at the University of Toronto (10-11 March 1989) has since appeared in pre-publication (mimeographed) form in *Comparative Literature in Canada / La littérature comparée au Canada: The Unmaking of Margins / Défaire les marges* 20 (Fall 1989). I wish to thank the Stanford Humanities Center, where this essay was begun, as well as Susan Kneedler and Stephen Orgel for their many suggestions.

1. For modern references see Glanmor Williams 368; Falls, *Mountjoy* 209; and O'Faolain 271–72.

2. When quoting the Irish state papers I have mostly relied on the printed calendar, although in some instances I have consulted the original manuscripts in the Public Record Office, London (P.R.O.). From 1585 on, as Cyril Falls notes, the calendars are virtually complete transcriptions of the originals (*Elizabeth's Irish Wars* 347–48).

3. Also see Canny, *Elizabethan Conquest* 97–99, on the utility of the Welsh analogy and Sir Henry Sidney's policy of establishing Welsh-style provincial presidencies in Ireland.

4. On the issue of language, Ann Rosalind Jones mentions Thomas Coryat's ironic coupling of "the Welch and the Irish" as among "the best and most learned languages of the world" (Coryat, qtd. in Jones 113).

5. See Bennett on the early development of a news service in Elizabethan England (220–47).

6. For a vivid account of these conditions that also mentions their pertinence to both parts of *Henry IV* and to *Henry V,* see O'Faolain 154–59. Paul A. Jorgensen speculates that John of Lancaster's deception of his opponents in the Gaultree Forest incident of *2 Henry IV* is indicative of the increasingly "treacherous" tactics (and the Smerwick massacre in particular) employed by the English against Irish rebels (490–91).

7. The major exception to this was the Munster rebellion led by James Fitzmaurice Fitzgerald in 1569. As Nicholas P. Canny explains, "from the beginning Fitzmaurice's rebellion assumed a wider dimension than any of the others as he identified with the Counter-Reformation against the heretic English" (*Elizabethan Conquest* 147).

8. Originally Baron Dungannon, Tyrone was elevated to the peerage as the second earl of Tyrone in 1585 (Hayes-McCoy 117–18).

9. Tyrone drifted into indirect opposition to the English by first supporting the disturbances of his kinsmen and allies (Hayes-McCoy 118–22). The period between June 1595 and June 1598, when open hostilities resumed, was generally one of sporadic

fighting, treaties, pardons, and duplicities on both sides (Falls, *Elizabeth's Irish Wars* chs. 13–14). The first major battle of the rebellion was fought at the Yellow Ford in August 1598, where the English were routed (Hayes-McCoy 124–25; Falls, *Elizabeth's Irish Wars* ch. 15). On the chronology of Tyrone's rebellious career also see Ellis 298–312, esp. 303–07 for Tyrone and a nationalist confederacy.

Basing his findings on a limited body of bardic poetry, Brendan Bradshaw has detected in late sixteenth-century Ireland "the first stages of development of a national political consciousness, and of the creation of an image of the Gaelic dynast as a national rebel leader" (74). His argument is challenged by T. J. Dunne.

10. On Glendower's training and service in England see Fackler 311–12 and Lloyd.

11. Some of the problems associated with an older historicism that I have tried to avoid are set forth by David Bevington (*Tudor Drama* esp. 1–26), while the sort of multilayered topical approach I have attempted is positively laid out by Leah S. Marcus (esp. 32–43).

12. Sean O'Faolain discusses the parley of December 1597; he sees Tyrone's demands as effectively formulating the rights of "an emergent Irish nation" (196). See Lloyd on the Glendower rebellion.

13. I have found Jonathan Dollimore and Alan Sinfield's discussion of these various threats as they appear in *Henry V* to be especially helpful (215–27).

14. Shakespeare, like Holinshed before him, confuses Sir Edmund de Mortimer with his nephew Edmund Mortimer, the fifth earl of March (Bevington, *Henry IV, Part 1* 287–88).

15. This is a phrase Jean E. Howard uses in her lucid account of the methodologies and practice of so-called new historicist Renaissance critics (35).

16. Patricia Fumerton (256) and David B. Quinn (61) discuss a more general English ambivalence toward Ireland which oscillates between admiration and revulsion.

17. And compare "the great Devil of the North" (*C.S.P. Ireland 1598–99* 505). At 2.4.357 Falstaff calls him "that devil Glendower."

18. This version of Diana can be found in Richard Beacon's *Solon His Follie* (Oxford, 1594), 3–4, as well as in the first of Spenser's *Two Cantos of Mutabilitie* (c. 1596).

19. Also see the discussion in Rackin 172–73.

20. The fiction of national identity as male and virile made much of the Saxon origins of the English people because the Saxons were considered the masculine race *par excellence*. A rhetoric of Saxon-Englishness in the sixteenth century is especially marked in works arguing for the vigorous independence of England from Continental hegemony (see, for example, John Aylmer, *An harborowe for faithfull and trewe subjectes, agaynst the late blowne blaste concerninge the governmēt of wemen* [London, 1559]) and in patriotic celebrations of English overseas expansion (Shakespeare's *Henry V*).

21. Dramatic representations helped perpetuate this view of the marches as lawless territory. *1 Sir John Oldcastle* (1599), for example, opens with an affray between Lords Herbert and Powis and their followers in the border town of Hereford.

Recent work by Steven Mullaney and Leah S. Marcus has explored the symbolic connotations of urban boundaries in the early modern period, emphasizing the process by which communal fears were projected into the Liberties and suburbs of Elizabethan and Jacobean London.

22. The allusion to Essex in *Henry V* only occurs in the Folio version of the play. See Patterson for a persuasive reading of the differences between the Folio and First Quarto texts that integrates textual and historicist methods.

23. Gayle Whittier has a helpful discussion of Falstaff's stabbing of Hotspur. She sees it as symbolically replicating the assault "wrought by the barbaric Welshwomen upon dead warriors' bodies," and as an indication of Falstaff's submerged androgyny (32–33).

Works Cited

Andrews, J. H. "Geography and Government in Elizabethan Ireland." *Irish Geographical Studies.* Ed. Nicholas Stephens and Robin E. Glasscock. Belfast: Queen's U of Belfast, 1970. 178–91.

Andrews, K. R., N. P. Canny, and P. E. H. Hair, eds. *The Westward Enterprise: English Activities in Ireland, the Atlantic, and America, 1480–1650.* Liverpool: Liverpool UP, 1978.

Bennett, H. S. *English Books and Readers, 1558–1603: Being a Study in the History of the Book Trade in the Reign of Elizabeth I.* Cambridge: Cambridge UP, 1965.

Bevington, David, ed. *Henry IV, Part 1.* The Oxford Shakespeare. Oxford: Clarendon, 1987.

———. *Tudor Drama and Politics: A Critical Approach to Topical Meaning.* Cambridge: Harvard UP, 1968.

Bradshaw, Brendan. "Native Reaction to the Westward Enterprise: A Case-Study in Gaelic Ideology." Andrews, Canny, and Hair 65–80.

Calendar of State Papers Relating to Ireland, of the Reigns of Henry VIII, Edward VI, Mary, and Elizabeth. Ed. Hans Claude Hamilton et al. 11 vols. London, 1860–1912.

Canny, Nicholas P. *The Elizabethan Conquest of Ireland: A Pattern Established, 1565–76.* Hassocks: Harvester, 1976.

———. "Identity Formation in Ireland: The Emergence of the Anglo-Irish." *Colonial Identity in the Atlantic World, 1500—1800.* Ed. Nicholas Canny and Anthony Pagden. Princeton: Princeton UP, 1987. 159–212.

———. "The Ideology of English Colonization: From Ireland to America." *William and Mary Quarterly* 3rd ser. 30 (1973): 574–98.

———. "The Permissive Frontier: The Problem of Social Control in English Settlements in Ireland and Virginia, 1550–1650." Andrews, Canny, and Hair 17–44.

Chambers, Anne. *Granuaile: The Life and Times of Grace O'Malley, c. 1530–1603.* Dublin: Wolfhound, 1979.

Dasent, J. R., ed. *Acts of the Privy Council of England, 1596–97.* ns vol. 26. London, 1902.

Davies, Sir John. "A Discovery of the True Causes Why Ireland Was Never Entirely Subdued, Nor Brought under Obedience of the Crown of England, until the Beginning of His Majesty's Happy Reign" (1612). *Elizabethan Ireland: A Selection of Writings by Elizabethan Writers on Ireland.* Ed. James P. Myers, Jr. Hamden, CT: Archon, 1983. 146–84.

Dictionary of National Biography (DNB). Ed. Sidney Lee and Leslie Stephen. 63 vols. New York: Macmillan, 1885–1900.

Dollimore, Jonathan, and Alan Sinfield. "History and Ideology: The Instance of *Henry V.*" *Alternative Shakespeares*. Ed. John Drakakis. London: Methuen, 1985. 206–27.

Douglas, Mary. *Purity and Danger: An Analysis of the Concepts of Pollution and Taboo*. London: Ark, 1985.

Dunne, T. J. "The Gaelic Response to Conquest and Colonisation: The Evidence of the Poetry." *Studia Hibernica* 20 (1980): 7–30.

Ellis, Steven G. *Tudor Ireland: Crown, Community, and the Conflict of Cultures, 1470–1603*. London: Longman, 1985.

Erickson, Peter. "Fathers, Sons, and Brothers in *Henry V.*" *William Shakespeare's* Henry V. Ed. Harold Bloom. New York: Chelsea, 1988. 111–33.

Fackler, Herbert V. "Shakespeare's 'Irregular and Wild' Glendower: The Dramatic Use of Source Materials." *Discourse: A Review of the Liberal Arts* 13 (1970): 306–14.

Falls, Cyril Bentham. *Elizabeth's Irish Wars*. London: Methuen, 1950.

———. *Mountjoy: Elizabethan General*. London: Odhams, 1955.

Fumerton, Patricia. "Exchanging Gifts: The Elizabethan Currency of Children and Poetry." *ELH* 53 (1986): 241–78.

Gernon, Luke. "A Discourse of Ireland, Anno 1620." *Illustrations of Irish History and Topography, Mainly of the Seventeenth Century*. Ed. C. Litton Falkiner. London: Longmans, 1904. 345–62.

Greenblatt, Stephen. *Renaissance Self-Fashioning: From More to Shakespeare*. Chicago: U of Chicago P, 1980.

Greenlaw, Edwin, et al., eds. *The Works of Edmund Spenser: A Variorum Edition*. 10 vols. Baltimore: Johns Hopkins UP, 1932–49. Vol. 5. 1936.

Hamilton, A. C., ed. *The Faerie Qveene*. By Edmund Spenser. London: Longman, 1977.

Hayes-McCoy, G. A. "The Completion of the Tudor Conquest, and the Advance of the Counter-Reformation, 1571–1603." *A New History of Ireland*. 9 vols. Ed. T. W. Moody, F. X. Martin, and F. J. Byrne. Oxford: Clarendon, 1976. 3: 94–141.

Hogan, Edmund, ed. *The Description of Ireland . . . in Anno 1598*. London, 1878.

Holinshed, Raphael. *Holinshed's Chronicles of England, Scotland, and Ireland*. 6 vols. 1587. London, 1807–08. Vol. 3.

Howard, Jean E. "The New Historicism in Renaissance Studies." *English Literary Renaissance* 16 (1986): 13–43.

Jones, Ann Rosalind. "Italians and Others: Venice and the Irish in *Coryat's Crudities* and *The White Devil.*" *Renaissance Drama* ns 18 (1987): 101–19.

Jorgensen, Paul A. "The 'Dastardly Treachery' of Prince John of Lancaster." *PMLA* 76 (1961): 488–92.

Larner, Christina. *Enemies of God: The Witch-Hunt in Scotland*. London: Chatto, 1981.

Lloyd, J. E. *Owen Glendower*. Oxford: Clarendon, 1931.

Marcus, Leah S. *Puzzling Shakespeare: Local Reading and Its Discontents*. Berkeley: U of California P, 1988.

Morgan, Prys. "From a Death to a View: The Hunt for the Welsh Past in the Romantic Period." *The Invention of Tradition*. Ed. Eric Hobsbawm and Terence Ranger. Cambridge: Cambridge UP, 1983. 43–100.

Moryson, Fynes. *The Itinerary of Fynes Moryson.* 4 vols. Glasgow: MacLehose, 1908. Vol. 3.

Mullaney, Steven. *The Place of the Stage: License, Play, and Power in Renaissance England.* Chicago: U of Chicago P, 1988.

Neale, J. E. *Queen Elizabeth I.* New York: Doubleday-Anchor, 1957.

Nichols, John, ed. *The Progresses and Public Processions of Queen Elizabeth.* 3 vols. London, 1823. Vol. 3.

O'Faolain, Sean. *The Great O'Neill: A Biography of Hugh O'Neill, Earl of Tyrone, 1550–1616.* London: Longmans, 1942.

Patterson, Annabel. "Back by Popular Demand: The Two Versions of *Henry V.*" *Renaissance Drama* ns 19 (1988): 29–62.

Quinn, David B. *The Elizabethans and the Irish.* Ithaca: Cornell UP, 1966.

Rackin, Phyllis. *Stages of History: Shakespeare's English Chronicles.* Ithaca: Cornell UP, 1990.

Rowse, A. L. *The Expansion of Elizabethan England.* London: Macmillan, 1955.

Schwind, Mona L. "'Nurse to All Rebellions': Grace O'Malley and Sixteenth-Century Connacht." *Eire-Ireland* 131 (1978): 40–61.

Simpson, Richard, ed. *The School of Shakspere.* 2 vols. New York: Bouton, 1878. Vol. 1.

Spenser, Edmund. *A View of the Present State of Ireland.* Ed. W. L. Renwick. Oxford: Clarendon, 1970.

Taylor, Gary, ed. *Henry V.* The Oxford Shakespeare. Oxford: Clarendon, 1982.

Whittier, Gayle. "Falstaff as a Welshwoman: Uncomic Androgyny." *Ball State University Forum* 20 (1979): 23–35.

Williams, Glanmor. *Recovery, Reorientation, and Reformation: Wales, c. 1415–1642.* Oxford: Clarendon, 1987.

Williams, Penry. "The Welsh Borderland under Queen Elizabeth." *Welsh History Review* 1 (1960): 19–36.

Zitner, S. P. "Staging the Occult in *1 Henry IV.*" *Mirror up to Shakespeare: Essays in Honour of G. R. Hibbard.* Ed. J. C. Gray. Toronto: U of Toronto P, 1984. 138–48.

Sovereignty, Disorder, and Fetishism in *Marlowe's* Edward II

DAVID H. THURN

A POLOGISTS AND DETRACTORS alike seem to agree that *Edward II* produces a complex modulation and splitting of affect: our powers of identification are under sharp strain as the play distributes, divides, directs, and reverses our sympathies before the halting, somewhat tortuous spectacle of deposition.[1] Uncertainty is our characteristic stance as we witness the at times puzzling movement in Mortimer (from indignant patriot to scheming Machiavellian), in the queen (from patiently suffering wife to conspiring adulteress), in the favorites Spencer and Baldock (from parasitic sycophants to loyal supporters courageous in death), in Kent (who switches his allegiance more than once in the play), and in Edward himself (from weak, indulgent, impetuous *rex inutilis,* to a heroic king triumphant in battle, and finally to the broken and weary ruler who elicits our pity as we witness the last traces of regal dignity struggling vainly against despair[2]). The tumultuous historical period at issue, from the accession of Edward II in 1307 to the execution of Mortimer in 1330, would seem to require a complex response, for it presents the divisions within a realm threatened with the possibility of deposition. The

115

central dilemma, presented to Marlowe by his sources (primarily Holinshed, but also Fabyan and Stowe [Ribner 128]), involved the patent
inadequacies of the king and a group of disaffected barons whose
constitutional position was not clearly defined and therefore whose
theoretical grounds for the deposition were shaky (Peters 236–45).
The anxious uncertainty surrounding the issue of deposition finds its
way into the English history plays of the early 1590s. In the anonymous *Woodstock,* in Marlowe's *Edward II,* and in Shakespeare's
Richard II, it is never resolved: whether a monarch may be justifiably
deposed remains uncertain.[3] These plays raised disturbing questions
about the legitimacy of royal power in even rightful successors to
the throne.

Marlowe's play is framed by news of the death of one king (Gaveston
reads the letter that opens the play: "'My father is deceased; come
Gaveston . . .'" [1.1.1]), and the somewhat tentative emergence of
another. What falls in between is a spectacle of internecine wars,
civil broils, and marital strife resulting, according to the rhetoric of
the play, from Edward's attachment to Gaveston. In permitting Gaveston's return, the death of Edward's father precipitates a division of
the realm ("'. . . come Gaveston, / And share the kingdom with thy
dearest friend'") and an ongoing conflict in the relations of power
among monarchy, nobility, and commons. Critics often point out that
this conflict is triggered not primarily by the erotic passion that links
Edward and Gaveston, but by the violation of class structure represented by Edward's patronage of his lowborn minion.[4] But I think it
would be a mistake to ignore the way in which the play, even as it
refuses to stigmatize Edward's desire for Gaveston in the terms of
Christian teaching, allows the spectator to recognize the effects of
an insidious, because partially concealed, entanglement of sexual and
political proprieties. Drawing a structural parallel between Edward's
love for Gaveston and Mortimer's dangerous alliance with Isabella,
Marlowe undermines any attempt to distinguish homosexual from
heterosexual desire on moral grounds. Still, the play asks us to witness
and to recognize as familiar the sometimes barely perceptible slippage
from the political to the sexual spheres in the representation of transgression. In Edward's disavowal of the queen, enacted onstage as she
is time and again displaced by the "Greekish strumpet" Gaveston, or
in Isabella's treacherous inconstancy, disorders of desire are revealed

to be the shadow of political disorder.[5] A confusion at the level of sexuality seems to accompany disturbances in the body politic, and in the field of representation itself: the play refuses to organize itself into a dramatic spectacle that would allow us to take up stable positions of sympathy. Unlike Marlowe's earlier plays, *Edward II* does not present a single charismatic figure whose drive for mastery represents itself in compelling visual moments of (illusory) totality and identity: whereas Tamburlaine's sights of power, Faustus's spectacles of magic, and Barabas's scenes of reckoning extend and stabilize the movement of mastery, Edward's scenes of embrace represent precisely the abdication of power, the loss of mastery. In these earlier plays specular structures tend to validate the hero's narcissistic desire for unity and totality and to obscure its failure, whereas in *Edward II* they work rather differently, by *thematizing* this failure: the lovers' exchange of pictures, for example, while it is a gesture designed to console, finally serves only to define the separation: "Here take my picture and let me wear thine; / O, might I keep thee here as I do this, / Happy were I, but now most miserable" (1.4.127–29). *Edward II* makes explicit the failure of the narcissistic moment which sustains an imaginary unity, identity, and totality in a structure of reflection. Violent strife cuts across the forms designed to fix a specular illusion, both at the level of sexual desire and at the level of state. Although Edward, in addressing Gaveston on his return from exile, calls himself "Thy friend, thy self, another Gaveston" (1.1.142), and takes joy in his sight (1.1.150), Gaveston remains for the most part "divorced from King Edward's eyes" (2.5.3). The spectacles of sovereignty, furthermore, have degenerated into "idle triumphs, masques, lascivious shows / And prodigal gifts bestowed on Gaveston" (2.2.157–58), while "Libels are cast against [King Edward] in the street, / Ballads and rhymes made of [his] overthrow" (2.2.177–78), and even the nobles in Edward's own court produce only "rancorous" heraldic devices for the king's "stately triumph" (2.2.12, 33). The play stages the consequences of a breakdown in the imaginary constructions that maintain self and state: something disturbs the lines of sight by which they constitute themselves.[6]

Spectacle and power are central issues in Marlowe's English history play. Stephen Orgel, of course, established the clear relation of these terms in *The Illusion of Power,* where he demonstrates the symbolic mediation of power in the Stuart court that occurs by means of theatrical spectacle staged with reference to the king's ideal perspectival position. And Stephen Greenblatt has extended this work in *Renaissance Self-Fashioning,* where he focuses on the symbolic practices of the Tudor period by which the state managed to represent, but also (and therefore) to contain subversion within "orthodox" discursive forms.[7] His discussion of Holbein's painting *The Ambassadors* elegantly articulates the idea (17–27): an illegible anamorphic blur hovers in the center foreground of a canvas otherwise composed, in exemplary fashion, according to conventional laws of perspective.[8] Depicting two impressive figures surrounded by the emblems and instruments of an intellectual mastery of the world, striking in its self-sufficient balance, the painting is traversed and disturbed by another, eccentric line of perspective: only by taking a position to the side of the painting, and thereby pressing the rest of the work out of focus, does the illegible blur reveal itself as a skull. The effect is to challenge our conventional representations of the world, to reveal "the power of human shaping affirmed everywhere else in the painting": "In the same artistic moment, the moment of passage from the center of the painting to the periphery, life is effaced by death, representation by artifice" (20, 21). Jacques Lacan had earlier discussed the Holbein painting, in the seminars represented in *The Four Fundamental Concepts of Psycho-Analysis,* as an illustration of how distortions in the field of vision work to disrupt the position of the subject fixed in a specular relation to its objects, to what it takes to be reality (85–90). "Vision," he writes, "is ordered according to a mode that may generally be called the function of images. This function is defined by a point-by-point correspondence of two unities in space. Whatever optical intermediaries may be used to establish their relation, whether their image is virtual, or real, the point-by-point correspondence is essential" (86). The anamorphic blur collapses the correspondence, giving rise to "a partial dimension in the field of the gaze, a dimension that has nothing to do with vision as such" because you apprehend the form only "by walking out of the room" (88). The emergence of the death's-head thematizes the dissolution or loss of the imaginary subject required to order the field of vision. But beyond the level of content, the Holbein painting reveals an instability in the structure of specularity: it is both the site of the subject's ongoing attempt to maintain its unity in imaginary fictions and the sign of the elusive relation, even barrier, between the subject and its objects.[9]

What I am interested in here is the dual function of specular structures as they work both to support and undermine the imaginary fictions of self and state. I would like to suggest that the instability of affect before the spectacle of deposition in *Edward II* is directly related to this paradoxical function. Marlowe stages a kind of discomfiting anamorphic spectacle of sovereign power struggling fitfully to maintain itself and increasingly unable to conceal its imaginary stays. The effect is to provoke in the spectator a recognition not only of the means by which the state constitutes and consolidates its power in the field of vision, but also of the strategies by which dramatic narrative shapes an audience's response to the materials of chronicle history. Marlowe stages the events of the chronicles in anamorphic perspective, revealing "History" to be the sphere in which mutually exclusive possibilities are contested and sometimes held in exquisite tension.[10] The representation of history, Marlowe seems to suggest, must enable us to glimpse both the real events toward which it points and the devices of rhetoric upon which it invariably depends. According to *Edward II,* history is the realm where the apprehension of a coherent and purposive sequence of events must fail. More fundamentally, the play uncovers in the field of the gaze a conflict between the subject's struggle to establish order by positing as counterpart an imaginary unity and the disavowal or exclusion which this effort requires.

The central terms of my reading appear within the first two hundred lines of the play. Just disembarked as the play opens, Gaveston meets three poor men seeking position. He treats them with arrogant indifference, preferring instead to surround himself with "wanton poets, pleasant wits, / Musicians, that with touching of a string / May draw the pliant king which way I please." He knows that "Music and poetry is [the king's] delight," and imagines the entertainments that he will provide in a speech which is as calculating as it is seductive:

> Therefore I'll have Italian masques by night,
> Sweet speeches, comedies and pleasing shows,
> And in the day when he shall walk abroad,

> Like sylvan nymphs my pages shall be clad,
> My men like satyrs grazing on the lawns
> Shall with their goat feet dance an antic hay;
> Sometime a lovely boy in Dian's shape,
> With hair that gilds the water as it glides,
> Crownets of pearl about his naked arms,
> And in his sportful hands an olive-tree
> To hide those parts that men delight to see,
> Shall bathe him in a spring, and there hard by
> One like Actaeon peeping through the grove
> Shall by the angry goddess be transformed,
> And running in the likeness of an hart,
> By yelping hounds pulled down and seem to die;
> Such things as these best please his majesty.
>   (1.1.49–70)

Gaveston conceives the king's delight in the language of Ovidian transformation: the figures of this speech blur the distinctions between the animal, the human, and the divine (sylvan nymphs, men like satyrs, and boys in the shapes of Diana and Actaeon), between actors and spectators, active and passive (the daytime spectacle seems to include Edward as participant, while Actaeon appears himself as a spectator in a scene which ends with the hunter becoming the hunted), and between the masculine and the feminine: the lovely boy who takes Diana's shape holds "an olive-tree / To hide those parts that men delight to see."[11] Critics have long noticed the sexual ambiguity of "those parts that men delight to see": it is unclear whether we are meant to postulate masculine or feminine sexual "parts." The difficulty of fixing the terms of sexual difference here, of marking sexual proprieties with confidence, is of course one of the central representational problems of the Elizabethan stage and its all-male acting companies.[12] But what is striking about these lines in particular is that they present a spectacle which, in sustaining the sexual ambiguity, operates according to the logic of the fetish. According to Freud ("Fetishism"), the fetish strikes a compromise for the boy confronted with the anatomical difference he refuses to accept, allowing him (and Freud himself) to theorize the presence of the thing he also perceives to be lacking. The fetish is a substitute for a perceived lack which wards off the implied threat of the spectator's own castration by rendering the perceptual problem of sexual difference undecidable:

"What had happened, therefore, was that the boy had refused to take cognizance of the fact perceived by him that a woman has no penis. No, that cannot be true, for if a woman can be castrated then his own penis is in danger; and against that there rebels part of his narcissism which Nature has providentially attached to this particular organ" (215). The fetish is a specular (and speculative) construction which, by an oscillating logic, both preserves and denies the threat posed by the perceived absence. Curiously, Freud suggests in the next sentence that the scenario of the boy's panicked response to his problem of perception may have some explanatory value within the political realm as well: "In later life grown men may experience a similar panic, perhaps when the cry goes up that throne and altar are in danger" (215). Freud's fiction allows us to shift our attention from the troubled relationship between sight and sexual difference to the equally troubled relationship between sight and the political threat of deposition already imminent in the opening scene of the play, where altar and throne seem near collapse: Edward humiliates the bishop of Coventry for being the cause of Gaveston's exile by stripping him of his "golden mitre," "rend[ing] his stole," and committing him to the Tower; and Lancaster has demanded that Edward send Gaveston back into exile, "Or look to see the throne where you should sit / To float in blood and at thy wanton head / The glozing head of thy base minion thrown" (see 1.1.130–32, 186–99). In dramatizing the contest between the king and his barons, and controlling its political threat only precariously (even at the end with the installation of Edward III), the play itself functions according to the logic of the fetish: the spectacle of deposition becomes "the vehicle both of denying and asseverating" (Freud 218) the absence of sovereign power.

In presenting a scenario of threatened deposition, *Edward II* stages the panic and violence that results when the investments of royal subjects in a construct of sovereignty are no longer supported by it, or reflected in it. The crown, the symbol of sovereign power, is revealed to be a sign related to the king not by natural necessity, but only by arbitrary compact. Consequently, the audience, the barons, and Edward himself can no longer position themselves with any stability before the crown and the political order it sanctions. The image of the crown, of the king, no longer has the power to mediate and stabilize the threat within the political realm, and therefore to sustain an illusion of natural order within it. Kent remembers when times were different:

> I do remember in my father's days,
> Lord Percy of the North being highly moved
> Braved Mowbery in presence of the king,
> For which, had not his highness loved him well,
> He should have lost his head, but with his look
> The undaunted spirit of Percy was appeased,
> And Mowbery and he were reconciled. . . .
>   (1.1.108–14)

Edward, however, cannot command the look that appeases and must opt for what is, according to Kent, the only alternative. In the midst of violent battle with rebels who "do confront and countermand their king" (3.3.4), Edward vows vengeance, promising that "ere long their heads shall satisfy, / T'appease the wrath of their offended king" (3.3.24–25). It is the decapitated head and not the king's "look" that appeases. Threats of decapitation appear throughout in the heated exchanges of political confrontation. To behead is to empower: decapitation, according to the rhetoric of the play, is the means by which disputes of privilege and power may be resolved. The play's central conflict is positively driven by threats and counterthreats of decapitation. Kent urges Edward to revenge himself upon the barons, "and let these their heads / Preach upon poles for trespass of their tongues" (1.1.116–17). The implication of treason enrages them and sets off bitter contention that puts heads at hazard: "Cousin," warns Mortimer, "our hands I hope shall fence our heads / And strike off his that makes you threaten us" (1.1.122–23). The decapitated head is repeatedly presented as the sign of power over one's enemies (see, e.g., 2.5.53, 3.2.53–55).

The play reminds us, as Kent reminds Edward in the opening scene, that the act of decapitation is properly a means by which sovereignty may assert its right by claiming paternal authority. Rising to a pitch of patriotic fervor, the young Spencer reminds the disheartened Edward, about to engage the rebels in battle, of his noble ancestry in a speech which will inspire the king to victory:

> Were I King Edward, England's sovereign,
> Son to the lovely Eleanor of Spain,
> Great Edward Longshanks' issue, would I bear
> These braves, this rage, and suffer uncontrolled
> These barons thus to beard me in my land,
> In mine own realm? my lord, pardon my speech.
> Did you retain your father's magnanimity,
> Did you regard the honour of your name,
> You would not suffer thus your majesty
> Be counterbuffed of your nobility.
> Strike off their heads and let them preach on poles;
> No doubt such lessons they will teach the rest,
> As by their preachments they will profit much
> And learn obedience to their lawful king.
>   (3.2.10–23)

And in lines that recall the violent fury of Tamburlaine, Edward tells us he will use the blood of headless trunks to institute his immortal right against "traitorous progeny":

> If I be England's king, in lakes of gore
> Your headless trunks, your bodies will I trail,
> That you may drink your fill and quaff in blood,
> And stain my royal standard with the same,
> That so my bloody colours may suggest
> Remembrance of revenge immortally
> On your accursed traitorous progeny,
> You villains that have slain my Gaveston.
>   (3.2.135–42)

The association of paternal authority and decapitation appears again in explicit terms at the end of the play, when Edward's son, now confirmed as king, emerges from the council chamber and, claiming his father's authority and even his very speech, accuses Mortimer of killing the king: "Traitor, in me my loving father speaks / And plainly saith 'twas thou that murderedst him" (5.6.41–42). The last two acts have portrayed the young prince's gradual, if tentative, assumption of sovereign authority as he prepares to "step into his father's regiment" (3.3.85). And it is his ritual offering of Mortimer's head to his father's hearse that finally confirms this authority in the last scene. This gruesome rite receives considerable attention, and may be seen in some sense to complete the funeral ceremony for Edward I, whose "exequies" the bishop of Coventry was about to celebrate when interrupted by Edward and Gaveston in the opening scene (see 1.1.175). The play ends with the lords presenting the head to the king, who calls for his father's coffin and his funeral robes, and then addresses the head directly:

> Go fetch my father's hearse where it shall lie
> And bring my funeral robes. Accursed head,
> Could I have ruled thee then as I do now
> Thou hadst not hatched this monstrous treachery.
> Here comes the hearse, help me to mourn, my lords.
> Sweet father, here unto thy murdered ghost
> I offer up this wicked traitor's head. . . .
>
> (5.6.94–100)

The ritual image that ends the play marks the formal resolution of the strife that follows the death of the father (the words "'My father is deceased . . .'" open the play) and consequent violation of the paternal demand that Gaveston not return to England: "Mine uncle here," declares Mortimer, "this Earl, and I myself, / Were sworn to your father at his death / That he should ne'er return into the realm" (1.1.81–83). It is only when the young king, becoming the vehicle of his father's voice, charges Mortimer and orders his decapitation that the play symbolically restores proper relations among the three Edwards.

The political scenario of the play, then, draws together the claim to sovereignty, paternal authority, and the prerogative of decapitation. The play's implication that, by presenting the decapitated head of an enemy, one can assert and preserve political (and paternal) power, needs more detailed attention. The head becomes the "witness" and guarantor of rightful power, and therefore offers symbolic protection against treason, rebellion; it speaks or "preaches upon poles" (see 1.1.117, 3.2.20, 4.6.93, 112) the lessons of submission, obedience to the one who claims sovereignty. The sight of the horrifying decapitated head that also, paradoxically, has the power to assure, to stabilize, recalls of course the logic of the fetish, and more specifically here, Freud's short analysis of the Medusa's head.[13] The Medusa's head, for Freud, manages to "isolate" horrifying and reassuring effects, and therefore has what Freud calls apotropaic power: "What arouses horror in oneself will produce the same effect upon the enemy against whom one is seeking to defend oneself" (213). Freud's discussion thus provides an explanation both of the affect of horror and of its transformation. The symbol of the Medusa's head, according to Freud's reading, in concentrating both phobic and counterphobic associations, manages to structure an otherwise threatening scenario: it organizes the anxiety over a perceived lack by linking the perception to an explanation of that lack, a theory by which the spectator can preserve his own integrity and power.[14] The decapitated heads in Marlowe's play seem to have a similar organizing force: they inspire an unsettling fear but also, by "preaching upon poles," provide an explanation of how they came to be that way, and therefore have the effect of stabilizing the political order. We find a rather neat illustration when Edward, imprisoned and anguished, anticipates for the first time having to resign the crown to Mortimer and imagines his crown in the aspect of a Medusa's head. He hopes it will,

> . . . like the snaky wreath of Tisiphon,
> Engirt the temples of his hateful head;
> So shall not England's vines be perished,
> But Edward's name survives, though Edward dies.
> (5.1.45–48)

Tisiphon, not so incidentally, is one of the three Furies sprung from the blood of Uranus, castrated and deposed by his sons, and is charged with avenging crimes of parricide (Graves 37–38). By imagining his crown "the snaky wreath of Tisiphon," Edward hopes to terrify and destroy his enemy but also to preserve his own name and "England's vines" by investing lost property with an abstract power of preservation.

In dramatizing the effects of threatened deposition, the play reveals that the coherence provided by the crown and an offering of heads is ungrounded: only artificial, it has no basis in a "natural" political order. To sustain an illusion of coherence in the face of imminent deposition, it becomes necessary to construct a theory that will preserve sovereign power even as it acknowledges its loss. Historically, this is precisely what the barons did: in order to justify a transfer of power and maintain an image of order, they carefully drew up charges against Edward that included as much of thirteenth-century deposition theory as possible (Peters 241). Theory intervenes as reassurance within a disturbing political scenario. Marlowe's play may be seen to do the same thing to the extent that it relies increasingly upon morality conventions (the emblematic figures of the mower and Lightborn, the *contemptus mundi* that Edward exhibits in prison, Mortimer's sudden emergence as a Machiavel and stage Vice, and his rather frequent recourse to the image of "Fortune's wheel," etc.) to provide the spectacle of deposition with an abstract coherence. But the real impact of the play comes, I think, in its exposure of both the arbitrariness of the terms designed to ensure an abstract coherence, thereby to prop up an illusion of natural order, and the threat of violence they attempt to resolve. Marlowe gives considerable attention to the role of titles, names, claims of birth and of "right" within the political arena, very nearly making them laughable even as he reveals the devastating effects of their collapse upon body and realm.

The tenuous and arbitrary character of political schemes of order appears from the beginning, when Gaveston's contemptuous farewell to "base stooping" before the "lordly peers" in the opening soliloquy (1.1.18) is shortly ratified as Edward, having for the first time greeted Gaveston only moments before, bestows political titles upon him with frivolous abandon: "I here create thee Lord High Chamberlain, / Chief Secretary to the State and me, / Earl of Cornwall, King and Lord of Man" (1.1.153–55). Within forty lines, Gaveston will also become "lord bishop" (1.1.193). The barons will later acknowledge Gaveston's position only jeeringly, an affront to the king, who has already taken offense at their initial failure to greet his friend:

> EDWARD
> Will none of you salute my Gaveston?
> LANCASTER
> Salute him? yes; welcome Lord Chamberlain.
> MORTIMER JUNIOR
> Welcome is the good Earl of Cornwall.
> WARWICK
> Welcome Lord Governor of the Isle of Man.
> PEMBROKE
> Welcome Master Secretary.
>
> (2.2.64–68)

Their bitter mockery is hardly surprising in light of the impulsive, at times reckless, offhandedness that Edward displays in his delegations of political office, which seem to be little more than gestures of momentary gratitude, anger, or mollification (see 1.4.65–69, 353–55; 3.2.49, 146). That royal titles under Edward do not reflect a realm unified by hierarchical order is clear when Edward suggests that his barons "Make several kingdoms of this monarchy / And share it equally amongst you all" (1.4.70–71). But we have already seen that the titles Edward confers on Gaveston, with whom he will "share" his kingdom, are an instrument not of effective corporatist rule but of dangerous division.

Gaveston provokes an upset in claims of birth as well, as he is openly contemptuous of the "Base leaden earls that glory in [their] birth," refusing to "creep so low, / As to bestow a look" on them (2.2.74, 76–77). And the feeling is mutual. From the beginning the barons take deep offense at the "upstart pride" (1.4.41) of Gaveston, the "base peasant," "creeping ant," and "ignoble vassal" who presumes to "talk . . . of a king" although he is "hardly . . . a gentleman by birth" (1.4.6ff.). Mortimer Senior recoils in disgust when he sees Gaveston occupying the queen's throne at Edward's side ("What man of noble birth can brook this sight?" [1.4.12]), while Warwick admonishes the king to fulfill his princely station by ridding himself of Gaveston ("You that are princely-born should shake him off" [1.4.81]). In an unexpected reversal, Edward considers the barons "rude and savage-minded men" (1.4.78), and seems to prefer men like the low-born Gaveston, and the scholar Baldock, whose gentry is "fetched from Oxford, not from heraldry" (2.2.243). Marlowe's omission of all reference to the divine right of kings (Ribner 132), and his lowering of the class status of Gaveston, Baldock, and Spencer from that of their models in Holinshed,[15] only emphasizes the arbitrary, even whimsical basis for political power in the world of the play.

As the dramatic action hollows out the signs of political entitlement, the cries of "right" become equally meaningless, ringing out from either party with almost ludicrous facility (e.g., 3.2.38, 3.3.5, 4.5.28–29). The movement by which the play undoes the imaginary supports of sovereign power and the hierarchical order it requires culminates, of course, in the scenes of terrifying debasement that end the play, where Edward, filled with "strange despairing thoughts," and "endless torments" of mind, is violently torn between regal determination and anguished submission, his body and his realm on the edge of disintegration as he fitfully prepares to relinquish the "wished right" of head and crown (5.1.62–63, 79–80). Before returning to the last act, I would like to consider more specifically the effect of Gaveston on the mapping of political space in the play.

The stability of the realm depends, it is clear from the vows sworn to Edward's father at his death, upon Gaveston's continued exile. The presence of Gaveston and the existence of political order, according to the barons, are mutually exclusive conditions. "If you love us, my lord," old Mortimer declares with utter simplicity in the first scene, "hate Gaveston" (1.1.79). The bishop of Canterbury is more specific about the political entailment in his own ultimatum: "Either banish him . . . / Or I will presently discharge these lords / Of duty and allegiance due to thee" (1.4.60–62; cf. 1.1.104–05, 2.2.208–11). On the other hand, Gaveston's banishment threatens Edward's own stability. The king, "whose eyes are fixed on none but Gaveston" (2.4.62), makes the connection explicit in a simple declaration of fact after being coerced to sign "the form of Gaveston's exile": "Thou from this land, I from my self am banished" (1.4.1, 118). In either case, the same mechanism is at work, for while the barons depend for their identity upon the expulsion of Gaveston, Edward preserves his own only by banishing queen, realm, everything else, "So [he] may have some nook or corner left / To frolic with [his] dearest Gaveston" (1.4.73–74). Self and state both appear to rely upon gestures of expulsion and inclusion to sustain an illusion of identity, to constitute and maintain an imaginary position of unity and totality. The basic logic here emerges during the charged argument among the barons over Mortimer's suggestion that Gaveston's exile be repealed yet once more: "Fie Mortimer, dishonour not thy self," says the "inexorable" Lancaster,

> Can this be true 'twas good to banish him,
> And is this true to call him home again?
> Such reasons make white black and dark night day.
>
> .   .   .   .
>
> In no respect can contraries be true.
>
> (1.4.244–49)

Lancaster's confidence in language which is either true or false reflects an investment in fixed identity, in the clear marking of differences, without which stable political order becomes impossible. And it is precisely this principle of identity that Gaveston threatens to subvert: he is, in the eyes of the contentious barons, no mere rival cast in their own image, but a "Monster of men," who "like the Greekish strumpet" has drawn the nation into "bloody wars" (2.5.14–16). Resembling the figures in his "pleasing shows," Gaveston represents the collapse, the murking of the distinctions that ward off threats to identity. Indeed, the thing that the young Mortimer finds most disturbing about Gaveston is precisely his apparent lack of fixity, as he explains to Mortimer Senior, who has tried to calm his hotheaded nephew:

> He wears a lord's revenue on his back,
> And Midas-like he jets it in the court,
> With base outlandish cullions at his heels,
> Whose proud fantastic liveries make such show,
> As if that Proteus, god of shapes, appeared;
> I have not seen a dapper jack so brisk.
> He wears a short Italian hooded cloak
> Larded with pearl, and in his Tuscan cap
> A jewel of more value than the crown. . . .
>   (1.4.406–14)

Fascination and contempt alike fire Mortimer's indignant description of the fantastic opulence and ostentation in the dress of Gaveston and his retinue. By adopting the apparel that belongs properly to his hereditary superiors, Gaveston presumptuously flouts the sumptuary regulations designed to help enforce class distinctions.[16] But only in the next lines, as description gives way to explanation in the rhetoric of the speech, do we fully understand the bitterness that runs through Mortimer's response:

> While others walk below, the king and he
> From out a window laugh at such as we
> And flout our train and jest at our attire.
> Uncle, 'tis this that makes me impatient.
>   (1.4.415–18)

Mortimer is angry because Edward and Gaveston laugh at the appearance of the nobles: in the same way that Mortimer here mocks Gaveston, he says they "flout our train and jest at our attire." This might well prove deeply unsettling, for it raises the specter of a resemblance that undermines the noble claims of natural privilege. The figure of Gaveston, with all of his extravagant adornments, including "a jewel of more value than the crown," may suggest that the trappings of royal power are themselves nothing more than stage contrivances invested with illusory authority. Even early on, Edward implies as much in his choice of verb when, in a moment of impetuous sobriety, he says he will make Warwick his "chiefest counsellor," and promises that his "silver hairs will more adorn [the] court, / Than gaudy silks or rich embroidery" (1.4.344–46). Edward's minion is the more threatening because he presents the barons, despite their refusal to recognize it, with a kind of mirror image, exposing the ungrounded character of sovereign order. Echoing the charges brought against Gaveston, Edward will later call the queen "unnatural" and refer to the nobles themselves as "inhuman creatures," as "monsters" for seeking to depose him (5.1.17, 71, 74).

Gaveston disturbs the spectacle of state, undoing sexual, political, and (I will suggest in a moment) linguistic proprieties. The mutual gaze in which Edward and Gaveston hold each other—Edward's "eyes are fixed on none but Gaveston," who in turn longs for Edward, "in whose gracious looks / The blessedness of Gaveston remains" (2.4.62, 1.4.120–21)—has a disconcerting effect on the entire court. Lancaster complains of the lovers walking "arm in arm" (1.2.20), Warwick of Gaveston "leaning on the shoulder of the king" (1.2.23), and the queen of being forsaken, unregarded, as Edward "dotes upon the love of Gaveston" (1.2.50). The same verb describes both Edward's association with Gaveston, to whom, as he says, "our soul was knit" (3.3.42), and the scene of slaughter it provokes, "when force to force is knit" in "civil broils" (4.4.5, 6). The spectacle of sovereignty breaks down as Edward turns away from the queen's "embracements" (2.4.16), substituting Gaveston on the queen's throne, and as "idle triumphs, masques, [and] lascivious shows" come to replace the images of power that both produce and reflect the normative structure of absolutist monarchy. The play's most energetically detailed and dire portrait of political disarray in England, following Edward's refusal to ransom the elder Mortimer (in 2.2), points again and again to failures in the representation of sovereignty. Young Mortimer's complaint about Edward's idle triumphs leads Lancaster to blunt admonition:

> Look for rebellion, look to be deposed.
> Thy garrisons are beaten out of France
> And lame and poor lie groaning at the gates;
> The wild O'Neil, with swarms of Irish kerns,
> Lives uncontrolled within the English pale;
> Unto the walls of York the Scots made road,
> And unresisted drave away rich spoils.
>   (2.2.161–67)

The "haughty Dane" controls the seas, the "northern borderers" are in revolt, the queen forsaken, the court ignored by foreign ambassadors and "naked, being bereft of [the peers] / That make a king seem glorious to the world." "Libels are cast against [the king] in the street, / Ballads and rhymes made of [his] overthrow," and disgraceful jigs composed by "the fleering Scots" (2.2.168ff.). The one time the king displayed his banner in the field, his "soldiers marched like players, / With garish robes, not armour," while Edward himself, "Bedaubed with gold, rode laughing at the rest, / Nodding and shaking of [his] spangled crest, / Where women's favours hung like labels down" (2.2.183–87). Frivolous and feminine, Edward fails to project the image of a king: his appearance is repugnant to the nobility and disastrous for the realm. And it is, as Kent points out, Edward's association with Gaveston that is responsible: "My lord, I see your love to Gaveston / Will be the ruin of the realm and you" (2.2.208–09). In capturing the king's eye, Gaveston disturbs the representation of sovereignty upon which the realm depends for its identity. Defining a second, conflicting specular structure, Gaveston diverts the sovereign gaze, undoes the ideal image of the king. The ambiguous, protean figure of Gaveston introduces, in effect, an anamorphic blur that works to expose the artifice of sovereign power.

Drawing the pliant king which way he pleases, Gaveston reveals how precarious are the signs, the nomenclature of sovereignty. Gaveston represents a threat to fixed reference, a force of fluidity and displacement that undermines crown and country alike. Only very

tenuously does the symbol of the crown retain its stabilizing power
as the rebellious barons "seek to make a new-elected king" (5.1.78;
cf. 1.4.54–55): it has become a shifting token of sovereign power
sanctioned only by the violence that underwrites possession. Under
Gaveston's sway, Edward casts even the geographical identity of England in provisional terms. "And sooner shall the sea o'erwhelm my
land," he promises his minion, "Than bear the ship that shall transport
thee hence" (1.1.151–52). In a later moment of inventive exaggeration, Edward imagines the island coming unmoored and floating into
unknown regions of the world: "Ere my sweet Gaveston shall part
from me / This isle shall fleet upon the ocean / And wander to the
unfrequented Ind" (1.4.48–50). Gaveston disturbs the customs of
identity that compose and organize the state even as he assures
Edward of his own identity by providing him with a mirror reflection:
Edward is "another Gaveston" whose narcissistic gaze protects him
from self-banishment by fixing him in specular relation with an identical other. Still, the play reveals that the narcissistic effort to organize
and control alterity (the subject tries to fix itself by postulating objects
of permanence and identity in the world) is bound to fail. Through
most of their careers, Tamburlaine, Barabas, and even Faustus (in
spite of his moments of tormented wavering) appear quite able to
sustain enterprises driven by the narcissistic desire to possess self
and world, to appropriate otherness by rendering it a function of self.
Edward, on the other hand, rarely achieves even a moment of stable
possession. Gaveston complicates Edward's gestures of identification
and self-possession because his fluid, protean nature undermines the
very possibility of stable reference that such gestures assume. Frequently associated with water, with the sea and its creatures—Mortimer Junior calls him "that vile torpedo," a dangerous stinging fish
"Which being caught, strikes him that takes it dead" (1.4.221ff.),
while Lancaster represents him in his heraldic device as "a flying-
fish / Which all the other fishes deadly hate" (2.2.23–24; cf. 2.4.37)—
Gaveston is linked with a thematic pattern of language that suggests
precisely the loss of stability and order, the destruction of the forms
of identity. The sites of subversion seem frequently to have a fluid
aspect. The civil wars bring "lakes of gore," "channels [that] overflow
with blood" (3.2.135, 4.4.12); channel water is a real or imagined
instrument of humiliation, in the "baptism" of the bishop, and the

roadside shaving of the king (1.1.187, 5.3); the sea is the site of violent storm and shipwreck, as well as the avenue of rebel forces; and the "lake," "the mire and puddle" where Edward stands "up to the knees in water," water dripping from his "tattered robes," is the scene of the king's final torture and disintegration (5.5). Finally, Mortimer, the most dangerous threat to the kingdom, states that his name derives etymologically from the "dead sea" (see 2.3.21–26).

The figure of Gaveston introduces into the realm a force that cannot be assimilated into a political system that depends upon a hierarchy of fixed differences. When Edward recalls Gaveston from exile, he violates the paternal law that authorizes the political order, replacing a principle of symbolic identity with the possibility of displacement and volatile fluidity. Gaveston is himself displaced immediately after the king learns of his death, disappearing from the play after the first lines of act 3 and replaced in Edward's affections by the young Spencer in the next scene (3.2.143–47). The disruptive force embodied by Gaveston extends beyond the boundaries of character to define the political space of most of the play's five acts. The stage, as the space of our possible identifications, is as shifting and unstable a sight as is Gaveston. Gaveston is the anamorphic figure that disturbs the fixed position of the viewer (audience and aristocrats both) before the spectacle of sovereignty and its illusion of "natural" order: he makes us aware of the arbitrariness of the paternal law that institutes fixed differences in gender, political position, and language regulated by contraries that can in no respect be true. The rejection of paternal law defines the major part of the play's action, which is framed by the letter bearing news of the death of one king (Edward's father) and the letter responsible for the death of another (Edward himself). This last letter, which Mortimer has had written in "unpointed" (unpunctuated) Latin, enacts on the textual level the division of the realm dramatized by the plot:

> The king must die or Mortimer goes down;
> The commons now begin to pity him,
> Yet he that is the cause of Edward's death
> Is sure to pay for it when his son is of age,
> And therefore will I do it cunningly.
> This letter written by a friend of ours
> Contains his death yet bids them save his life.

> "*Edwardum occidere nolite timere bonum est*":
> "Fear not to kill the king, 'tis good he die."
> But read it thus, and that's another sense:
> "*Edwardum occidere nolite timere bonum est*":
> "Kill not the king, 'tis good to fear the worst."
> Unpointed as it is, thus shall it go.
>
> $\qquad\qquad\qquad\qquad\qquad\qquad\qquad$ (5.4.1–13)

The equivocating letter installs in the very text a kind of semiotic impropriety, a compromise structure that, like the fetish, allows the perceiver to have it both ways: the text of the letter permits contraries to be true.[17]

Gaveston having undone the bonds of monarchical authority, the political space of the play is marked by division, by the loss of the illusions which give the kingdom an artificial coherence, allowing monarch and subjects alike to position themselves within a stable structure of recognition. With the failure of the fictions of sovereignty comes an extended series of desperate and violent attempts to maintain, restore, or appropriate the authority that would reinvest the divided realm with the value of unity. Once Lancaster and Warwick have been executed, it is Mortimer who emerges to oppose Edward, and it is in the staging of their irreconcilable claims in the last scenes that we get the most devastating vision of the panic and violence that, as the cry goes up against the crown, tears sharply at body and realm. No longer able to command in his own name (cf. 1.1.168), Edward is vulnerable to being "wound[ed] . . . with the name of Mortimer, / That bloody man" (4.6.38–39). In a striking moment of symbolic retaliation for the violent assault Mortimer's name makes upon his heart, Edward will tear the piece of paper that bears the dreaded name:

> By Mortimer, whose name is written here;
> Well may I rent his name that rends my heart.
> $\qquad\qquad\qquad$ [*Tears the paper*]
> This poor revenge hath something eased my mind,
> So may his limbs be torn as is this paper.
>
> $\qquad\qquad\qquad\qquad\qquad\qquad\qquad$ (5.1.139–42)

Both Edward and his rival seek to retain the name of king, but while Mortimer conspires to have his power "under-writ" with "a king's name" (5.2.14) and boasts that "All tremble at [his] name" (5.6.13), he does appear to fall victim to Edward's curse when he is sent in the final scene to be dismembered and beheaded. Edward, on the other hand, recoils in grief when he reminds himself in prison that he is yet king: "oh, at that name / I feel a hell of grief" (5.5.88–89). Names have themselves become the sites of division and violent anguish. The equivocating letter and the tearing of the name both dramatize a strife that reaches into the very fabric of the play's language.

Edward II presents the scene of history largely deprived of its theoretical supports: in its scattered, shifting focus, the play keeps the spectator's eye moving as it seeks out stable sites of identification. The emergence of Edward III in the last scene only partially compensates for the devastating vision, in the last acts, of a realm split by the claims of two kings—Edward becomes the victim of his own recognition that "Two kings in England cannot reign at once" (5.1.58)—and two "courts," the dungeon where Edward lies in abject misery, and the court "where Lord Mortimer remains" (see 5.3.59, 61). The order of sovereignty gives way as Edward struggles vainly to preserve his name as king, grasping in violent agitation at the crown that he feels slipping away, hoping to find some last moments of comfort. He pleads to be "king till night, / That [he] may gaze upon this glittering crown," and so allow his eyes to "receive their last content" before crown and head must relinquish their "wished right" (5.1.59–63). As Edward edges fitfully toward deposition, his speeches exhibit the desperate plunges and violent turns and reversals of a mind in torment as it strains to hold onto an illusion of sovereign identity: "must I now resign my crown . . . ?"; "And needs I must resign my wished crown"; "I'll not resign"; "here receive my crown; / Receive it? no . . ."; "Take it"; "Yet stay . . ."; "Here, here! [*Resigns the crown*]" (5.1.36ff.). When he later reels in recognition that the crown is gone, he seems amazed that he still lives at all: "where is my crown? / Gone, gone! and do I remain alive?" (5.5.89–90). Always precarious in Edward's realm as a sign of sovereign identity and power, the crown fails to give the realm even an artificial coherence and very nearly becomes the sign of its absence. The scene of state has been displaced by a scene of sordid despair and disintegration, by the dungeon where Edward is imprisoned, "the sink / Wherein the filth of all the castle falls" (5.5.55–56). Here the king's joints shake, convulsive sobs nearly "[rent] the closet of [his] heart," and "foul excrements" soil his body (see 5.3, 5.5). Curiously, the language Edward had earlier used to describe the effects of his longing for Gaveston echoes strangely here, in the play's account of his final torture and terrifying murder. Gaveston returned into exile, Edward's pain had given rise to extravagant comparison:

> My heart is as an anvil unto sorrow,
> Which beats upon it like the Cyclops' hammers,
> And with the noise turns up my giddy brain,
> And makes me frantic for my Gaveston;
> Ah, had some bloodless Fury rose from hell,
> And with my kingly sceptre struck me dead,
> When I was forced to leave my Gaveston.
>   (1.4.311–17)

Now in the final scenes confined to a "vault up to the knees in water" (5.5.2), Edward appears to repeat some of the same experience: his body numbed, his mind distempered by one who "plays continually upon a drum," he will confront the bloodless Fury in the figure of the demonic Lightborn, who will strike the king dead with the brutal thrust of a "red-hot" spit, taking care to leave no visible signs of assassination. The obverse of Tamburlaine's conquering sword, Lightborn's spit produces not the bloody images of triumph, the sights of power that represent absolute sovereignty, but a perverse allegory of homosexual rape, carried out in secret, in the dark. Whatever sense of archaic "justice" Lightborn might produce in the audience as he prepares to kill Edward is immediately diminished by the fierce savagery of his action. Even so, the execution reintroduces an implication that Edward has violated sexual as well as political proprieties: panic arises in the realm when the normative structures of sexual and sovereign identity are in danger, and it blurs the distinction between them. In the traces of allegory that characterize the scene, we recognize both the efficacy and the emptiness of the moral fictions used to transform and manage that panic. Finally, the sight of Edward's body, wracked and lifeless, deprives these fictions of their force: the corpse represents the collapse of the imaginary order in which self and state are founded. But when the young prince emerges from the council chamber and steps into his father's regiment, the crown will again assert its precarious hold over the panic and violence that underlies the imaginary scenario, and present an image of sovereignty underwritten by the name of king and an order of decapitation.

Notes

1. Marlowe's *Edward II* has been praised for its indications of "maturity" and its moving portrayal of the personal suffering of a king (Leech, Levin, Cole). (Recent appreciations include Baines; Deats, "Androgyny"; Donaldson; Summers; and Tyler. Despite differences in subject and emphasis, these essays all take a primarily thematic approach to the conflicts enacted in the play, offering analyses of character and plot which are driven implicitly by the critical assumptions of ego psychology. I think this approach is unable to account for the way in which the play both invests in and exposes the limitations of the fictions of character and plot which make historiography possible.) But it has also been rather frequently maligned by the critics, who fault both structure and style: the play lacks "a central feeling or theme" (Bradbrook 161); it has a "thin and drab style" and is preoccupied with "pettiness, impotence, and confusion" (Steane 206, 207); the play shows a "strange moral indeterminacy. . . . It is as if the concerns which, in the first place, directed [Marlowe's] attention to this reign—the weak homosexual king, the sensational violence of his death, the Machiavellian ambition of a Mortimer—take charge of his pen; and when their momentum is spent, he is obliged to trace meaningless patterns on the paper till the imaginative fit seizes him again" (Sanders 121, 125); "*Edward II* presents fragmentary, contradictory emotions in moving but confusing passages amid a numbing deluge of often repetitive events" (Manheim 53). For these readers, Marlowe's style seems to have lost its magnificence, and the dramatic spectacle its focus in *Edward II*. Tucker Brooke reminds us that this play, unlike *Tamburlaine, Doctor Faustus,* and *The Jew of Malta,* was not produced by Henslowe's acting companies, and therefore could not rely upon Edward Alleyn for the "huffe-snuffe bombast" required by Marlowe's more powerful protagonists: instead, the suggestion goes, Marlowe had to distribute the dramatic focus across a number of parts, thus scattering the force elsewhere organized by the Herculean hero (qtd. in Levin 86–87). While there may be some truth in this, it does not explain Marlowe's particular rendering of the problem of deposition in *Edward II*. For useful discussions of the relation between staging and dramatic form in *Edward II,* see Bevington and Shapiro, and Deats, "Symmetry."

2. Elizabeth S. Donno argues that the play reflects an emerging, non-Aristotelian aesthetic of tragedy, that it elicits "admiration" and "commiseration" rather than the classical terror and pity. The play's generic instability, its structural divisions, and its sudden alterations of character, Donno believes, all become intelligible in terms of this new aesthetic, which, in allowing for what she calls "mixed character" and a "double catastrophe" (involving Edward and Mortimer), extends the range of subjects considered suitable for tragedy beyond Aristotelian prescription. Donno's decision to place *Edward II* in the context of an aesthetics of Elizabethan tragedy is a fruitful one, but

I find the notions of "mixed character" and "double catastrophe" finally inadequate as explanatory models of the play's peculiar treatment of plot and character. These models seem to me to be rather too general, and therefore unable to implement sharp theoretical distinctions between Marlowe's play and, say, Shakespeare's early histories.

3. See Manheim 17. He goes on to explain the effect of the carefully established tension that marks the handling of the issue of deposition in these plays: "Politically sensitive viewers of the 1590s must have been at a point where they could no longer abide the king's enormous inadequacies but at the same time could not go against their deep, quasi-religious commitment to the crown. The contending forces in the plays are the contending forces in the viewer. One of the forces temporarily may get the upper hand, but not sufficiently to outweigh the other permanently. Through the experience of the play, intense feelings about the problem may be drained, but nothing has happened or is suggested to prevent the pressure of those feelings from building once more to intensity. The wound cannot be healed."

4. Boyette offers the most acute treatment of this issue. See also Shepherd 204–06.

5. On homosexuality in Renaissance England, see Bray, who argues that it "was not conceived as part of the created order at all; it was part of its dissolution. And as such it was not a sexuality in its own right, but existed as a potential for confusion and disorder in one undivided sexuality" (25).

6. The play most frequently figures the breakdown of the narcissistic gaze in the terms of mourning. See, for example, 2.4.23–29. Shakespeare, of course, will himself explore the political implications of the complex relationship between sight and grief, seeing and mourning in *Richard II*.

7. For a recent reading of Shakespeare's history plays in this context, see Tennenhouse ch. 2.

8. See also Gilman's reading of the painting (98–104). On anamorphosis in general, see Baltrušaitis.

9. See Rose, who discusses the Holbein painting in these terms (167–97, esp. 192–93). On sexuality and representation, see the title essay in her book (225–33). On the historical value of the concept of anamorphosis for understanding the Elizabethan theater within a symbolic topography of London and its margins, see Mullaney. The "place" of the Elizabethan popular stage, Mullaney argues, "on the horizon or threshold of culture brought it into alignment with much that its own period found strange and unfamiliar, and that alignment provided the stage with an anamorphic point of view: an ability not merely to see its own culture through the glass fashioned and provided by the dominant order, but also to view that order *through* its various cultural Others" (131).

10. In this my argument complements Gilman's discussion of *Richard II* (ch. 4). But I want to argue that the model of anamorphic perspective can serve to illuminate not just a cognitive uncertainty, but a constitutive split in the historical subject, the effects of which, furthermore, appear in both the sexual and political orders. An essay which has just come to my attention offers a probing and suggestive account of this splitting of the subject in strict Lacanian terms, and explores its implications for reading *Edward II:* see Lecercle-Sweet.

11. See also Lecercle-Sweet 126–27.

12. Greenblatt argues that there is an intimate relationship, in the Renaissance, between the transvestite theater and the normative (teleologically male) structure of sexual identity (*Negotiations* 66–93): "a conception of gender that is teleologically male and insists upon a verifiable sign that confirms nature's final cause finds its supreme literary expression in a transvestite theater . . . . One consequence of this conceptual scheme . . . is an apparent homoeroticism in all sexuality" (88, 92). Greenblatt concentrates on Shakespeare's handling of this issue in the comedies (86–93). For a brief consideration of the boy actor and his role in the confusion of sexual identity in *Edward II,* see Jardine 22–24.

13. Freud, "Medusa's Head," esp. 212: "We have not often attempted to interpret individual mythological themes, but an interpretation suggests itself easily in the case of the horrifying decapitated head of Medusa. To decapitate = to castrate. The terror of Medusa is thus a terror of castration that is linked to the sight of something. Numerous analyses have made us familiar with the occasion for this: it occurs when a boy, who has hitherto been unwilling to believe the threat of castration, catches sight of the female genitals, probably those of an adult, surrounded by hair, and essentially those of his mother. The hair upon Medusa's head is frequently represented in works of art in the form of snakes, and these once again are derived from the castration complex. It is a remarkable fact that, however frightening they may be in themselves, they nevertheless serve actually as a mitigation of the horror, for they replace the penis, the absence of which is the cause of the horror. . . . The sight of Medusa's head makes the spectator stiff with terror, turns him to stone. Observe that we have here once again the same origin from the castration complex and the same transformation of affect! For becoming stiff means an erection. Thus in the original situation it offers consolation to the spectator: he is still in possession of a penis, and the stiffening reassures him of the fact."

14. Hertz, esp. 165–67. For a good discussion of Medusa's head as it is interpreted both by Freud and by Renaissance writers, see Garber 97–103.

15. Cohen 233. Cohen argues that Marlowe's decision here reflects the strategies of royal centralization: "Throughout western Europe, royal centralization required the partial exclusion of the titular nobility from political power and its replacement by men of humbler station, whose influence depended entirely on monarchical goodwill" (232–33).

16. For a discussion of sumptuary law and its implications for reading Renaissance drama, see Jardine 141–68.

17. For a discussion of the Renaissance traitor's exploitation of the multiple senses of words (and actions), see Mullaney ch. 5.

Works Cited

Baines, Barbara J. "Sexual Polarity in the Plays of Christopher Marlowe." *Ball State University Forum* 23 (1982): 3–17.

Baltrušaitis, Jurgis. *Anamorphoses, ou perspectives curieuses.* Paris: Perrin, 1955.

Bevington, David, and James Shapiro. "'What are kings, when regiment is gone?': The Decay of Ceremony in *Edward II.*" Friedenreich, Gill, and Kuriyama 263–78.

Boyette, Purvis E. "Wanton Humour and Wanton Poets: Homosexuality in Marlowe's *Edward II.*" *Tulane Studies in English* 22 (1977): 33–50.

Bradbrook, M. C. *Themes and Conventions of Elizabethan Tragedy.* Cambridge: Cambridge UP, 1935.

Bray, Alan. *Homosexuality in Renaissance England.* London: Gay Men's Press, 1982.

Cohen, Walter. *Drama of a Nation: Public Theater in Renaissance England and Spain.* Ithaca: Cornell UP, 1985.

Cole, Douglas. *Suffering and Evil in the Plays of Christopher Marlowe.* Princeton: Princeton UP, 1962.

Deats, Sara Munson. "*Edward II*: A Study in Androgyny." *Ball State University Forum* 22 (1981): 30–41.

———. "Marlowe's Fearful Symmetry in *Edward II.*" Friedenreich, Gill, and Kuriyama 241–62.

Donaldson, Peter S. "Conflict and Coherence: Narcissism and Tragic Structure in Marlowe." *Narcissism and the Text: Studies in Literature and the Psychology of Self.* Ed. Lynne Layton and Barbara Ann Schapiro. New York: New York UP, 1986. 36–63.

Donno, Elizabeth S. "'Admiration' and 'Commiseration' in Marlowe's *Edward II.*" *Neuphilologische Mitteilungen* 79 (1978): 372–83.

Freud, Sigmund. "Fetishism." Trans. Joan Riviere. "Medusa's Head." Trans. James Strachey. *Sexuality and the Psychology of Love.* Ed. Philip Rieff. New York: Macmillan, 1963. 214–19. 212–13.

Friedenreich, Kenneth, Roma Gill, and Constance B. Kuriyama, eds. *"A Poet and a filthy Play-maker": New Essays on Christopher Marlowe.* New York: AMS, 1988.

Garber, Marjorie. *Shakespeare's Ghost Writers: Literature as Uncanny Causality.* New York: Methuen, 1987.

Gilman, Ernest B. *The Curious Perspective: Literary and Pictorial Wit in the Seventeenth Century.* New Haven: Yale UP, 1978.

Graves, Robert. "The Castration of Uranus." *The Greek Myths.* 2 vols. Harmondsworth: Penguin, 1955. 1: 37–38.

Greenblatt, Stephen. *Renaissance Self-Fashioning: From More to Shakespeare.* Chicago: Chicago UP, 1980.

———. *Shakespearean Negotiations: The Circulation of Social Energy in Renaissance England.* Berkeley: U of California P, 1988.

Hertz, Neil. "Medusa's Head: Male Hysteria under Political Pressure." In his *The End of the Line: Essays on Psychoanalysis and the Sublime.* New York: Columbia UP, 1985. 161–93.

Jardine, Lisa. *Still Harping on Daughters: Women and Drama in the Age of Shakespeare.* 2nd ed. New York: Columbia UP, 1989.

Lacan, Jacques. *The Four Fundamental Concepts of Psycho-Analysis.* Ed. Jacques-Alain Miller. Trans. Alan Sheridan. New York: Norton, 1981.

Lecercle-Sweet, Ann. "Conscience et méconnaissance dans *Edward the Second* de Marlowe." *Théâtre et idéologies: Marlowe, Shakespeare*. [*Société Française Shakespeare: Actes Congrès 1981.*] Ed. M. T. Jones-Davies. Paris: Touzot, 1982. 115–31.

Leech, Clifford. "Marlowe's *Edward II*: Power and Suffering." *Critical Quarterly* 1 (1959): 181–96.

Levin, Harry. *The Overreacher: A Study of Christopher Marlowe*. Cambridge: Harvard UP, 1952.

Manheim, Michael. *The Weak King Dilemma in the Shakespearean History Play.* Syracuse: Syracuse UP, 1973.

Marlowe, Christopher. *Edward the Second*. Ed. W. Moelwyn Merchant. New Mermaids. London: Benn, 1967.

Mullaney, Steven. *The Place of the Stage: License, Play, and Power in Renaissance England*. Chicago: U of Chicago P, 1988.

Orgel, Stephen. *The Illusion of Power: Political Theater in the English Renaissance*. Berkeley: U of California P, 1975.

Peters, Edward. *The Shadow King: Rex Inutilis in Medieval Law and Literature, 751– 1327.* New Haven: Yale UP, 1970.

Ribner, Irving. *The English History Play in the Age of Shakespeare*. Princeton: Princeton UP, 1957.

Rose, Jacqueline. *Sexuality in the Field of Vision*. London: Verso, 1986.

Sanders, Wilbur. *The Dramatist and the Received Idea: Studies in the Plays of Marlowe and Shakespeare*. Cambridge: Cambridge UP, 1968.

Shepherd, Simon. *Marlowe and the Politics of Elizabethan Theatre*. Brighton, England: Harvester, 1986.

Steane, J. B. *Marlowe: A Critical Study.* Cambridge: Cambridge UP, 1964.

Summers, Claude J. "Sex, Politics, and Self-Realization in *Edward II.*" Friedenreich, Gill, and Kuriyama 221–40.

Tennenhouse, Leonard. *Power on Display: The Politics of Shakespeare's Genres*. New York: Methuen, 1986. Ch. 2, 72–101.

Tyler, Sharon. "Bedfellows Make Strange Politics: Christopher Marlowe's *Edward II.*" *Drama, Sex, and Politics*. Themes in Drama 7. Ed. James Redmond. Cambridge: Cambridge UP, 1985. 55–68.

Symbolic Capital in the *Spanish* Comedia

GEORGE MARISCAL

IT IS A LITTLE-NOTED FACT of literary history that the handful of early modern Spanish plays allowed into the canon of world literature all contain political violence. The reason this detail continues to escape criticism's selective vision is because traditional readings of these plays have fixed our attention on what are less disturbing and therefore what are thought to be more properly "literary" issues: the presence or absence of "great characters," the *comedia*'s preoccupation with "poetic justice," the persistent concern with something called "honor."

I am thinking in particular of Lope de Vega's *The Sheep's Well* (*Fuente Ovejuna*, 1612–14); Tirso de Molina's *The Trickster of Seville* (*El burlador de Sevilla*, c. 1625); and Calderón de la Barca's *Life Is a Dream* (*La vida es sueño*, 1634–35). For historians of the theater, these plays have functioned as signs of Spanish "religiosity" and "emotional power."[1] But in two of the plays, the spectator sees and hears allusions to nothing less than a full-scale rebellion against established authority: Lope dramatizes the historical events surrounding a peasant uprising in 1476; Calderón stages a less concrete occurrence, a kind of *coup d'état* set in Poland and designed to place the rightful heir back on the throne. And, despite its apparent concern with issues

143

of sexuality figured through one of the earliest representations of Don Juan, Tirso's play is in fact about a violent attack against the entire aristocratic body, the corruption of which makes it a susceptible target for both Don Juan's transgressions and the ethical critique by Tirso the priest-dramatist. Within the field of Hispanism, traditional *comedia* criticism has consistently chosen to push such issues into the background in order to focus on either the issues mentioned above or the construction of thematic typologies.

That these three plays lend themselves to a totalizing and aestheticizing approach cannot be denied. *Life Is a Dream,* in particular, was written at that moment during the reign of Philip IV when Spain's economic and military power in Europe was on the wane. Its underlying epistemological principle that all social reality is a dream places on the stage one of the most extreme forms of the ruling elites' disillusionment. The play's apparent concern with philosophical issues is undoubtedly what has maintained its popularity with those interested in sustaining an idealist version of the Western tradition. With regard to Tirso's Don Juan play, the various forms of violence it represents and its Counter-Reformation *deus ex machina* allowed nineteenth-century critics to transform the protagonist into an icon for the Spanish "national characteristics"—passion and honor. Even the decidedly more historical *Fuente Ovejuna* has been read as the story of an ideal love between individual peasants and, more anachronistically, as an account of the subordinate classes' desire for democratic freedoms. In the hands of the German Romantics and their offspring, all three texts were easily extracted from their original context, depoliticized, and tentatively placed within the confines of "world drama."

It is not my intention in this essay to undertake rereadings of these somewhat better known plays. Rather, I want to focus on three texts that to my knowledge have not been translated into English and indeed have failed to achieve a place in the canon of "classic" Spanish theater. Unlike the canonical pieces mentioned above, these are much less easily converted into organic wholes or vehicles for the expression of universal themes. Lope's *La tragedia del rey Don Sebastián de Portugal y bautismo del príncipe de Marruecos* (c. 1595) and *La vida y muerte del rey Bamba* (1597–98) and Vélez de Guevara's *La serrana de la Vera* (1613) have all been criticized for their dramatic incoherency and lack of structural unity. Under the hegemony of formalist criticism, they were relegated to the level of literary failures and historical curiosities. I am less interested in the formal qualities of these plays than in how they may have functioned within the context in which they were produced. Briefly stated, my argument is that each of these plays represents a member of a socially excluded group as protagonist not merely to assert the hegemony of the dominant class but in order to reinvigorate that class and its increasingly contested ideologies. Put another way, social power is allowed to pass through marginal and subordinate figures (women, peasants, Muslims) so that once on the other side aristocratic power is reasserted in a newly configured and revitalized form. The violent removal of some of these figures is less a representation of summary rejection on the part of ruling groups than it is a sign that the dominant had begun to make modifications in its basic ideological apparatus in order to consolidate its hegemonic position.

What I say about the relationship between theatrical practice, excluded groups, and the construction of the nation in Spain is particularly relevant for the so-called crisis period that began near the end of Philip II's reign (1580s and 1590s) and continued throughout that of Philip III. I want to make a historiographic adjustment, however, and distance my position from those of historians who have perpetuated the idea of the "decline" of Spain in the seventeenth century.[2] Although there can be no doubt that a complicated network of economic shifts (high inflation, epidemics, royal bankruptcies, decreased industrial production) and political reversals (the armadas against England, the failed attempt at a dynastic marriage with the English in 1623) took place in this period, the idea of decline or of a major break in the socioeconomic order effaces more subtle microtransformations on the level of ideology and the realignment of governing elites. José Antonio Maravall, for example, has argued that in the period I am discussing the power of the traditional hereditary aristocracy was slowly being displaced by an emergent oligarchy not founded in its entirety on the symbolics of blood (*Poder* 173ff.). In my opinion, this process cannot be separated from the construction of the modern state, a project whose initial and tentative beginnings were undertaken by Philip II in the 1570s through a series of demographic and ethnographic surveys known as the *Relaciones topo-*

gráficas de los pueblos de España. With regard to theatrical practice, one of the most important developments having to do with new political institutions and groups and the dissemination of ruling values was the formation in the new capital city of Madrid (provisional, 1560; permanent, 1606) of an elaborate bureaucracy situated in close proximity to the space of the *corral* or public theater.[3]

As part of the process by which discursive formations were being rearticulated and refined, an implicit debate took place about how Spain was to be imagined as a collective entity. The complicated network of material changes and ideological shifts problematized notions of "dynastic realm" and "universal monarchy," and began to move tentatively toward what Benedict Anderson has called an "imagined political community" conceived of as "both limited and sovereign."[4] On the Iberian peninsula, the construction of a national identity had already passed through a number of complex stages by the end of the fifteenth century. The political unification realized in 1492 by Isabella and Ferdinand was understood by the intellectual class less as the birth of a new organism than as the reconstitution of the lost totality previously known as Hispania. The modern concept of the nation-state was obviously not yet at work in the early modern period. An emergent variant of it, however, was being produced through a new conjuncture of cultural practices and discourses that had at its center an engagement with specific groups marked as Other. Much recent *comedia* criticism interested in psychoanalytic approaches to culture has employed this category. My use of the term has little to do with the structures of the "human psyche," the gaze between individual subjects, or differences of gender and sexuality (although women constitute one group in my argument) and everything to do with the inferior social position occupied by all groups not marked as male, aristocratic, and Catholic. Alterity, therefore, is not an ontological abstraction; rather, it is a historically constructed category capable of being filled in by a variety of different social types. In a like manner, we must think of dramatic characters not as individuals on the nineteenth-century (and novelistic) model, but rather as signs marking a position within a community or social body constituted by discourses of blood, spirituality, status, and sexual difference. Thus a Jewish man or a *nouveau riche* returnee from America (*indiano*), a male gypsy or a prostitute, could all be constructed as Other and therefore deficient according to the terms established by the dominant culture.[5]

To say that there existed certain groups that were represented as subordinate in cultural texts is to repeat a commonplace about early modern Spanish literature. The point I want to make is a different one. I believe that in a period situated during the reigns of Philip II and Philip III a vast project was being carried out to rethink (invent?) the idea of "Spain." Central to the construction of a Spanish national identity in this period was the symbolic integration of those groups formerly excluded, not in a gesture of democratic openness or even of enlightened absolutism, but rather as a way to reinvigorate the monarchical apparatus and the aristocratic culture that sustained it. In many cases, what were anachronistic values in the new context (chivalric-ascetic virtues) were refunctioned and presented as part of an essential "national character." My hypothesis is that the public playhouse was another site where this ideological project was realized, and characters marked as Other functioned as symbolic capital for the elaboration of that project.

Several years ago, Gilles Deleuze described what he called the Other-as-structure, that is, a relation between social elements that problematizes the concept of society as an undifferentiated whole (Appendix). The totalizing social project of the Castilian elites from the time of Philip II on attempted to produce such wholeness. But in order to do so, the "possible" or alternative worlds represented by heterogeneous groups had to be appropriated or at least made to speak the language of the dominant ideology. Even as power "passed through" marginalized groups, if only temporarily, the coalition of aristocracy and monarchy solidified its status as the embodiment of all Spaniards. In the writing of the period, those figures previously marked as Other, that is, neither Catholic nor aristocratic male, moved to the foreground and in many cases took on the characteristics of the dominant culture even in those texts where early on they are cast as oppositional characters. The eventual violence directed against eccentric subjects on stage was an act of purification not in any simple sense—that is, a reimposition of the status quo—but rather an appropriation of their potential for the reconfiguration and ultimate reanimation of the dominant ideologies.

Although in this scenario the so-called dominant retains its power, it would be mistaken to claim that change did not occur; on the contrary, change was a constant at every level of social and cultural life. As recent theories of hegemony have taught us, society itself must be conceived of not as a fixed totality but rather as a continually reshuffled field of discourses and practices. The dominant is in fact a provisional conjuncture of elements that is engaged in constant negotiations with both emergent and residual ideologies. Because in the period I am discussing the practical problem of dissident and potentially threatening groups at least in theory had been resolved by a series of royal policies—the expulsion and forced conversion of Jews (1492), the elimination of Erasmian and Lutheran-influenced domestic heresies (1530s–40s), the repression (1568–71) and eventual expulsion (1609–12) of Muslim converts to Christianity *(moriscos)*— the project of reconceiving the body politic was carried on in writing, where those cultural spectacles we now call literature played an important role.[6]

II
Redefining Patriarchal Power: The Woman Warrior

The place of women as the centerpiece upon which masculine practices depended was in no way limited to the stage. In his *Relaciones de las cosas sucedidas en la corte de España desde 1599 hasta 1614,* Cabrera de Córdoba relates a number of events that might just have easily been enacted in the Corral del Príncipe. I want to quote one passage in particular in order to convey a feeling for the kind of aristocratic activity that was commonplace throughout the period:

Sucedió jueves 23 del pasado, que el duque de Sesa se salió a media noche con un mulatillo que tañía y cantaba, y un pajecillo a tomar el fresco, y fue a parar a la plazuela de la duquesa de Nájera, y de una ventana pidieron al músico que tañese y cantase; y el Duque se lo mandó, y en esta ocasion llegó el de Maqueda con el de Pastraña y Barcarrota, que venian del Prado, y el de Maqueda se enfadó de la música, porque el conde de Villamor que posa allí, habia dado otras en aquella plazuela; *y como tenga una hermana, le pesaba,* y asi se despidió de los que iban con él, y entró en casa y se armó, y tomó un broquel, y con dos o tres se fue para el que tañía y quebróle la guitarra en la cabeza, y echó mano contra el de Sesa sin conocerle; y

estándose achuchillando se le quebró la espada al de Sesa en el broquel del
contrario y el de Maqueda le dió una grande cuchillada en la cabeza, hacia
el lado izquierdo, y otra en el rostro que le baja por el carrillo de la mesma
parte y le llega a cortar el labio interior. . . .

On Thursday, the 23rd of last month [July 23, 1609] it happened that the
duke of Sesa went out at midnight with a page and a mulatto who played
music and sang, and they wound up in the plaza of the duchess of Nájera,
and from a window someone asked the musician to play and sing, and the
duke ordered it to be done, and just then the duke of Maqueda arrived,
together with the dukes of Pastraña and Barcarrota, who were all returning
from the Prado, and the duke of Maqueda was upset by the music because
the count of Villamor who lives there had played music in that plaza before,
and since he had a sister, he was upset, and so he said goodbye to those
who accompanied him, and went in the house and armed himself, and took
a shield, and with two or three men he went over to the mulatto who was
playing music and broke the guitar on his head, and without recognizing the
duke of Sesa he attacked him, and during the swordfight the duke of Sesa's
sword broke on the shield of his opponent and the duke of Maqueda gave
him a large cut on the head on the left side and another on the face that
went from his left cheek down to his lip. (Cabrera de Córdoba 378; emphasis
added)

At the center of this violent but otherwise slapstick narrative is the
duke of Maqueda's sister, who, not unlike most of the women we
meet in the *comedia,* serves as a pretext for the acting out of masculine codes of aristocratic conduct. The female is positioned as an
apparently passive object who nonetheless is ultimately responsible
for the violence that surrounds her. It is my contention that in the
early decades of the seventeenth century, the figure of the daughter-
sister would be given a more active role in theatrical discourse in
order to reinvigorate the ideology of the ruling class.

My test case is Vélez de Guevara's *La serrana de la Vera* (1613).
It is here that we find one of the most striking examples of the
monstrous daughter and the process through which she is appropriated to do ideological work. Vélez's substantial reworking of Lope's
earlier play by the same title (1590s) replaces a peaceful resolution
with a violent ending designed to purify and strengthen the patriarchal and theocratic order. Gila, the protagonist in a dramatic world
populated by characters ranging from peasants to Ferdinand and Isabella, is at once the traditional *serrana,* or mountain girl of medieval

legend, and the much more threatening figure of a woman who demands the kind of complete autonomy associated in the seventeenth century with heretics and madmen. Gila enters into direct conflict with both her father and even the king, but is eventually recuperated through the discourse of martyrdom.

Early in the play we learn that Gila is the embodiment of those characteristics which defined aristocratic masculinity—warfare, hunting, sports. Gila herself admits that her nature is an aberration:

> MAGDALENA
> Erró la Naturaleza,
> Gila, en no hazerte varón.
> GILA
> ¡Ay, prima!, tienes razón.

> MAGDALENA
> Nature erred, Gila, in not making you a man.
> GILA
> Ah, cousin. You are right.

(1.659–61)

But the reversal of sex-determined roles does not pose a problem until Gila finds herself caught up in a swordfight during which she incurs her father's anger:

> GILA
> Apartaos, padre,
> no os pierda el respeto aquí.
> GIRALDO
> Pondré las manos en ti,
> ¡por el siglo de tu madre!
> quebraréte este bordón
> en la cabeza.

> GILA
> Get away, father, if I am not to lose respect for you here.
> GIRALDO
> I'll lay hands on you. I swear on your mother's grave, I'll break this staff over your head.

(1.815–20)

Gila's mannish behavior, which had earlier been a source of Giraldo's pride, is now converted by the dramatist into uncontrolled arrogance. In a particularly striking scene in act 2 in which her father announces to Gila that she has been betrothed, her attitude calls into question the entire patriarchal structure that positioned some women and numerous other groups as subordinate:

> No me quiero casar, padre, que creo
> que mientras no me caso que soy onbre.
> No quiero ver que nadie me sujete,
> no quiero que ninguno se imagine
> dueño de mí; la libertad pretendo.

I do not wish to marry, father, for I believe that as long as I do not marry I am a man. I do not wish to see anyone subject me nor think that they are my lord; I aspire to freedom.

(2.1584–88)

This kind of disruption of conventional social relations accelerates Gila's depravity and ultimately leads to her murdering of several innocent men and her aiming a rifle at King Ferdinand himself in act 3. But in Spain resistance to absolutist authority, whether it be framed by the family or the monarchy, could not possibly produce the kind of radical solution (the elimination of a king) that would be played out in England only a few years later. The sovereignty of the male is contained both in Giraldo's staff, with which he threatens to strike his daughter, and to a greater degree in the quasi-religious status of kingship. Gila will not kill Ferdinand, she says, because as monarch he is not a man but God on earth ("el rey es Dios en la tierra"). When Gila is finally captured by a local police force, however, this representative of the divine, Ferdinand, brackets the Christian values of mercy and forgiveness and refuses to stay the execution for "reasons of State" ("razón de Estado").

It is not that Gila had desired to be a man, as Melveena McKendrick claimed in her 1974 study (115ff.). Rather, the character of Gila reveals that agency and even subjectivity itself could only be achieved through the categories of aristocratic masculine conduct. Given this, the attempted appropriation of *libertad* by a member of a group considered to be inferior could not be tolerated for long. As an undecidable figure who at once affirms and contests traditional values, Gila and her singular behavior must be eliminated; she is placed in chains, garroted, and shot through with arrows. For a contemporary public, this ending was by no means tragic or overly violent. The resonances with St. Sebastian precluded the spectator's focusing on any perceived injustice in this case (a twentieth-century view), and Gila's death was most likely received not only as a just punishment but as a desirable one, since it transformed the figure of the manly-woman into that of the womanish-man (St. Sebastian) and ultimately shifted the character onto the spiritual plane of revitalized religious values. The two female witnesses to the offstage execution, Pascuala and Magdalena, stand in for the audience and give voice to their reaction:

> MAGDALENA
> Al palo llegan con ella.
> PASCUALA
> Ya la arriman, ya la atan.
> MAGDALENA
> Pascuala, los cuadrilleros
> se aperciben a tiralla,
> que ya el verdugo le pone
> el garrote a la garganta.
> PASCUALA
> Perdónete Dios, amén.
> MAGDALENA
> Esta fue tu estrella amarga;
> nunca nazieras al mundo.
> PASCUALA
> Mexor fue nazer, pues pasa
> desde aquel palo a una vida
> que eternamente se acaba.
> MAGDALENA
> Ya disparan las saetas
> los cuadrilleros, Pascuala.
> PASCUALA
> A San Sebastián pareze.

> MAGDALENA
>
> They've got her at the stake.
> PASCUALA
>
> Now they're standing her up and tying her.
> MAGDALENA
>
> Pascuala, the archers are taking aim, and now the executioner puts the garrote around her throat.

PASCUALA

God forgive you, amen.

MAGDALENA

This was your bitter fate; would that you had never been born.

PASCUALA

It was better to be born, for she now goes from that stake to a life that goes on for eternity.

MAGDALENA

Now the archers let loose their arrows, Pascuala.

PASCUALA

She seems like St. Sebastian.

(3.3264–78)

Pascuala's response, that Gila will pass directly from the stake to heaven, reveals the contradiction of a dominant ideology that both punishes the transgressors and rewards them in the afterlife. For a female spectator (such as the noblewoman, Jusepa Vaca, to whom Vélez dedicates his play), the efficacy of this scene would have relied heavily on the notion that the severity of social justice is mitigated by a higher power. For those of us who have witnessed the revival of fundamentalist religion in the 1970s and 1980s, it should be evident that martyrdom as a symbolic practice is an indispensable weapon in the arsenal of theocratic states. The figure of the female martyr, in particular, works to "soften" the harshness of a cultural system that in daily practice denies subjectivity to women at every turn.

In the year 1629 it was reported that of the seventy-three buildings in Madrid with religious functions thirty-four of them were dedicated specifically to the Virgin Mary.[7] Nine of these buildings were for the specialized purpose of praising the Immaculate Conception, an idea that had still not been made part of official Church dogma by Rome but in Spain had attained an unusually elevated status by the turn of the century.[8] What is suggestive about this historical detail for my argument is that it reveals how, at all levels of culture, the rearticulation of dominant ideologies was taking place. The large-scale influx of orders of nuns who had formerly resided outside of the capital made Madrid in the 1590s and early 1600s a center for female clerics comparable only to present-day Rome. Benedictines, Carmelites, Capuchins, Franciscans, and other orders professing a rejection of worldly power all participated with increased intensity in what previously had always been the peculiarly bellicose nature of Catholicism under

the Castilian monarchs. The historian Bartolomé Bennassar (89) reminds us that in the same period, there was a virtual explosion in
Spain of christening female children with those names most closely
associated with the Virgin. In a situation analogous to the one I have
described taking place in theatrical practice, the patriarchal power
of the Church upon which each and every one of its discursive practices depended was allowed *to pass through "the feminine"* so that
it could emerge on the other end renewed and increasingly secure
in its hegemony. The figure of the undecidable woman that we have
seen in Vélez's play was only one site in a complex cultural enterprise
that of necessity would also appropriate other groups considered to
be no less foreign to the aristocratic body.

III
Appropriating the Masses: The Peasant Monarch

In *La vida y muerte del rey Bamba,* Lope resuscitates a figure
equal to the amazonian woman in its undecidability: the peasant king.
Set in the final days of Visigothic rule in Spain (seventh century AD),
the play attempts to dramatize both the crowning and eventual murder of the pious *villano* ruler as well as the Moorish invasion of the
Iberian peninsula. Whether or not the representation of a peasant
clearly superior in moral terms to the aristocracy that defeats him is
a sympathetic gesture by the playwright in the direction of the subordinate classes is not my concern here. Ultimately, it is impossible
to reconstruct authorial intention, and in the case of this play Lope's
own position is particularly unclear.[9] What I propose is that within
the larger project of rearticulating the dominant ideologies, the play
presents us with another example of how social power passes through
marginal groups only to emerge with greater vigor and security.

It should be stated at the outset that Bamba, the peasant king, is
marginal only insofar as his class status. As a representative of Visigothic Spain, he would have signified what for Lope's audience continued to be the mythical origins of the Castilian aristocracy and the
moment of their most pristine blood-purity. At the same time, he
embodies in an uncompromised way traditional Catholic values in
the dangerous time of Christian heresies and Islamic expansionism.
The similarities between Bamba's situation (confronted with Berbers,

Pelagians, and Arians) and that of Philip II (engaged with the Turks, the English, and European Protestantism in general) would not have been lost on the sixteenth-century spectator. But despite Bamba's implicit prestige for a sixteenth-century audience it is his position as an outsider to which Lope, with his repeated use of the country vs. court trope *(menosprecio de la corte / alabanza de la aldea),* calls our attention. This process, together with Bamba's exalted spiritual standing, makes him an unusually powerful spokesman for traditional aristocratic values.

In the opening scene of this chronicle play, it is the Virgin Mary who miraculously appears on stage, and we learn that Bamba himself is especially devoted to her. This should surprise no one given what I have said about the centrality of the female figure in the rearticulation of the ideologies of the Spanish elites. The peasant Bamba in fact displays a set of qualities associated with a superior spiritual status and because of them is made king. He defends the poor in two conspicuous scenes, is humble, and unusually sensitive: "Soy tierno de corazón y en mentando la Pasión lloro así; ¿qué os espantáis?" ("I am tender of heart and at even the mention of the Passion I cry. Why does this surprise you?") (309). The act of weeping and the presence of tears might strike the modern spectator as gender-based behavior, but ever since the Middle Ages they had been signs of sanctity; in Spain, they were mandatory elements in many saints' portraits regardless of the subject's sex. Bamba's righteousness is so great that even as he lies dying, he magnanimously passes his crown to his assassin: "Toma, ponte mi corona no dudes, póntela, acaba que siempre una mala obra con otra buena se paga" ("Here, put on my crown, don't hesitate, put it on, for an evil act should always be repaid with a good one") (342).

That all three of the plays I have chosen to discuss draw heavily upon a religious master-code should not divert our attention from other discourses at work in the text, such as blood, class, and, most importantly, the nation. The juxtaposition of a corrupt aristocracy and the "good peasant," that is, a peasant who embodies *lo godo* or "pure Spanishness," is less a consequence of the dramatist's class allegiances than of the fact that in this play the discourse of class is effaced by those of blood and nation. Early in the play, Bamba had shown himself to be both feeling and intolerant at once. In this regard, he functions as a typical representative of early modern Spanish Catholicism. When shown a palace built by Jews, he declares: "No es bueno, porque, aun pintado aborrezco lo judaico" ("It is not beautiful because, even if they are disguised, I abhor all things Jewish") (317). Despite his apparent "softening" through the discourse of spirituality, Bamba, not unlike Gila in *La serrana,* at certain key dramatic moments speaks the dominant ideology more forcefully than any of those socially superior characters against whom he is ostensibly opposed.

What the final result of this antagonism based on national characteristics and spiritual worth might be is only hinted at in the final scene, when the monarchy of Philip II is prophesied. Bamba is dethroned and murdered, but before these events are allowed to occur he must restructure the nation—"Y así, traigo estas medidas para que España se rija" ("And so I bring these measures so that Spain may be put in order") (325)—and establish a monetary system that sets in place a stable infrastructure: "España muy torpe estaba porque gran agravio hacía no sólo aquel que vendía si también el que compraba" ("Spain was very unfinished because great wrongs were committed not only by those who sold but also by those who bought") (326). Thus the initial gestures toward a modern nation-state and a regulated market-economy are represented as the acts of a non-aristocratic character. The government of the peasant king was necessary for the establishment of "Spain," and the violence that removed him initiated a chain of events that would lead to the eventual moral rebirth of the monarchy. For Lope and the aristocratic members of his audience it was clear that the prophesied renewal of the nation had been realized in their own historical moment. In effect, they viewed themselves as presiding over the end of History. From the perspective of the late sixteenth century, all of the violent acts represented on stage were indispensable preconditions for the glorious reign of Philip II and the golden age of the Habsburgs.

The possibility that a play such as this one, once on the public stage and received by a heterogeneous audience, might have potentially subversive consequences was obviously a real one. How would a spectator from the subordinate classes react to the idea of a peasant king and to the representation of the morally corrupt aristocracy that murders him? These are difficult if not impossible questions to answer.

My sense of the problem, given the social processes of early modern Spain which both produced and were produced by theatrical practice, is that whatever "subversion" we find here is a consequence of our own historical appropriation of the text. For a contemporary sixteenth-century audience, the issues of class and moral superiority would have been rapidly recuperated by the ideological power of the monarchy as a utopian construct and as an enduring institution. Not unlike the defusing of the kind of violence produced by social injustice and sexual transgression that we find in Lope's *The Sheep's Well,* in which a peasant uprising is mediated and resolved by Ferdinand and Isabella, the resolution of Lope's Bamba play is accomplished through the invocation of Philip II as the ideal prince and icon of the national identity.

IV
Converting the Threat of Islam:
The Moroccan Christian

It should surprise no one with a passing knowledge of Spanish history that Muslims figure as part of the cultural intertext in all three plays under consideration. Not unlike the way in which Islam continues to function as Other for the resuscitation of U.S. nationalism in the Reagan-Bush era, the cultures of North Africa and the Middle East were one of the primary constructs against which Spain erected its national identity. The subplot of Lope's Bamba play is concerned with the coming invasion from North Africa; Bamba is assassinated with a Moorish poison; the young captain of the opening scene of *La serrana* is on his way to join Ferdinand and Isabella's final attack on Granada, the last Moorish stronghold on the Iberian peninsula. In between these two historical and dramatic poles (the momentous years 711 and 1492) lie nothing less than over seven hundred years of Islamic presence in Spain.

Since the fall of Granada in 1492, it had been no easy task for the Castilian ruling class to accommodate this particular Other, for even the forcibly converted Moriscos remained an isolated and suspect group until their expulsion was decreed in 1609. Not unlike the Spanish *conversos* (former Jews) before them, the Moriscos were thought to be insincere in their Christianity, secret practitioners of the old faith, and in the latter case a potential fifth column for the imperial adventures of the Turks. Given this particular group's resistance to any facile symbolic appropriation, it was with great excitement and fanfare that the prince of Morocco, Mulay Sheik (Muley Xeque), was converted to Catholicism on the third of November 1593.[10]

The significance of this event was not about to be lost on a writer as attuned to the uses of cultural power and spectacle as was Lope de Vega, and just one year after the baptism his *La tragedia del rey Don Sebastián de Portugal y bautismo del príncipe de Marruecos* opened at one of Madrid's foremost public playhouses, the Corral del Príncipe. The powerful trope of conversion was already a commonplace in the mythology of the period. Antonio de León Pinelo in his *Annals of Madrid* records an event for 1593, the same year of the sheik's baptism, that is remarkably similar to Lope's account of the conversion of the Moroccan prince. During a period of severe drought, the Virgin of Atocha was carried through the streets of Madrid in supplication for rain:

Vio un Turco esclavo la santa imagen y sabiendo el intento conque los fieles la sacaban de su casa, le causó risa burlandose de nuestra Fe, como pudieramos de la suya, y . . . dijo que si en aquella ocasion lloviese el se volveria cristiano. . . . Y antes de acabarse la procesion ni llegar la santa imagen a su iglesia de S. Maria donde habia de estar nueve dias ya la lluvia regaba las calles y el cielo prometia copiosas aguas. El Turco, tocado de la divina mano, reconocio su error, y antes de acabarse la procesion se entro en ella manifestando a voces lo que habia dicho y prometia cumplir . . . que habiendo recibido el Santo Bautismo y libertad de su amo, sirvió toda su vida en el Convento de la Sacratisima Virgen de Atocha.

A Turkish slave saw the holy image and upon learning why the faithful had brought it out of the church, he laughed and mocked our Faith, as we might his . . . and he said that if it should rain on that occasion he would become a Christian. . . . And before the procession was finished and before the holy image had arrived at the Church of St. Mary where it was to remain nine days, the rain filled the streets and the heavens poured out copious waters. The Turk, touched by the divine hand, recognized his error, and before the procession ended he entered the church shouting what he had said and what he had promised . . . and having received Holy Baptism and his freedom from his master, he served the rest of his life in the convent of the Most Holy Virgin of Atocha. (Pinelo 150)

The ideological power of such incidents and their subsequent retellings charged the context for Lope's play in unusual ways. The sheik's status as an aristocrat as well as the religious prestige associated in Islam with his title (descendant of the Prophet) made his conversion even more meaningful for a Catholic audience, and the historical immediacy of the performance would have been especially intense since it was most likely attended by the Moroccan prince himself, who was living in Madrid at the time.

In this play, the violence necessary to the purification and reanimation of the monarchy is confined to the first act, in which King Sebastian of Portugal's ill-fated 1578 expedition to North Africa is prefigured in a dream, played out offstage, and recounted by the Moor, Albacarín. The lack of prudence with which Sebastian undertakes the invasion is central to the text's eventual glorification of Spain's Philip II. More importantly, it contributes to the larger issue of how to contain the unrestrained militarism exemplified by the Portuguese king and shared by much of the aristocracy on the peninsula. When late in the play the Moorish woman, Axa, tells her companion who plans to engage Christian troops in battle, "Cuando es sin fruto ¿de qué sirve, Almanzor, perder la vida?" ("When it bears no fruit, Almanzor, what good is it to lose one's life?" [172]), her remark resonates back to Sebastian's irrational decision to ignore his uncle Philip's advice, venture into the Moroccan interior, and eventually be overcome by a much larger force.

Not unlike the ways in which Gila's warrior-like behavior is simultaneously praised and eliminated, Sebastian's folly is rewarded in his final scene. Since the early Christian period, martyrdom had been a particularly useful discursive practice for refunctioning acts that otherwise might have been condemned for being overly passionate and irrational. The situation of the unfortunate king, as he falls on stage riddled with multiple wounds, recalls that of his namesake the saint and points ahead to that of Gila the *serrana:* "¿Yo no soy Sebastián? Si es que estas flechas por el nombre vinieron tan derechas, entro a morir. ¡Valedme, Virgen pura! ¡Por Cristo muero y por su fe!" ("Am I not Sebastian? If these arrows flew so straight because of my name, I exit to my death. Praise me, pure Virgin! I die for Christ and for his religion!") (142).

By the second act, the dramatic focus on military adventurism and martyrdom shifts to the more immediate problem for the Castilian elites in the late sixteenth century of how to integrate (if only on the ideological level) those groups which had been previously excluded from the social body. That the figure of the Moroccan prince was of inestimable symbolic value was lost on no one. As we shall see, even Philip II, who had once refused to be treated by a Morisco herbalist, declaring: "I want no health that comes from such evil people" (qtd. in Porreño 83), understood the importance of the new convert. In Lope's account of the events, the sheik's initial interest in a local Christian festival that would eventually lead to his conversion is incited and defended by a series of female characters who function as corollaries to the central image of the Virgin. Although he is skeptical and claims he wants only to mock Christian law ("Quiero hacer burla y reír esta ley de los cristianos" [153]), the sheik attends the celebration of the Virgin de la Cabeza, falls ill and is cured, and eventually converts, although not until the friar Victoriano has indoctrinated him in the theological function of the Virgin:

JEQUE
Pues ¿cómo se ha de entender?
VIC.
Que por devoción se alcanza
de Dios, que tiene el poder.
JEQUE
Luego ¿no lo hace María?
VIC.
No, que Dios obra por ella
que como sólo Dios cría
sólo Dios obra.

SHEIK
Then, how is one to understand [the images of the Virgin]?
VIC.
Through devotion to them one receives aid from God who has power.
SHEIK
Then Mary does not do it?
VIC.
No, God works through her for since only God creates, only God works.

(161)

Even after the conversion, female figures are used to mitigate the potential violence of masculinist practices, practices which were no less prevalent among non-Spanish male characters.[11] Because they would rather see him dead than a Christian, certain members of the sheik's retinue decide to poison him. Repeatedly, however, the Muslim women urge tolerance. Axa, for example, warns Almanzor: "¡Oh, cómo os cansáis en vano! si el Jeque ha de ser cristiano el cielo todo lo ordena pues mirad cómo podréis resistir a todo el cielo" ("Oh, how you get worked up for nothing! If the Sheik is to be a Christian, heaven must have decreed it. Watch how you try to resist the will of the heavens") (166). It is no coincidence that in the dream-scene staged in act 3 two female figures representing Catholicism and Islam ("la secta africana") struggle over the Moroccan prince's soul. The figure of the woman, then, functions as a multivalent sign representing religion in general but more specifically the discourse of antiviolence attributed by Lope to Catholic ideology; thus women set the stage for the eventual appropriation of the Muslim male. In act 2, the sheik is surrounded by three anonymous Christian women who have come to see the already celebrated foreigner. After a series of flirtations, they engage him in a debate about the relative merits of the two religions, thereby beginning the process through which the Muslim prince will be transformed.

In a wider context, the sheik's conversion signified both the symbolic conquest of Philip II's rivals and their inclusion into the Spanish political and the Catholic mystical body. As the structure of Lope's title suggests, the failed mission of Sebastian is effaced by the baptism of a member of the Moroccan royal family. The historical convert Mulay Sheik was in fact made a member of the quasi-military order of Santiago, the most prestigious in Spain, and granted a series of privileges reserved for the most elite ranks of the Castilian aristocracy. Lope's claim is that the sheik's incorporation into Spanish society is less a testament to his own character than it is a tribute to that of Philip II, who was doubly wise in his recognition of the foolhardiness of Sebastian's enterprise and of the worthiness of the Moroccan prince. This glorification of the Spanish king as the embodiment of the state may in fact be seen as the ultimate ideological message of the entire text. The final scene of the play, set in Philip's tomb-like palace, El Escorial, is framed by Lope's eyewitness account of the baptism and is nothing less than a paean to Philip, the son of Charles the Emperor ("gran hijo de Carlos"), to the elite of the Castilian ruling class, and to the idea of the Catholic monarchy itself.

It is one thing to claim that the appropriation of marginal groups was necessary to the continued hegemony of the ruling class. It is quite another to suggest that the marginal has direct access to its own social power. Lope emphasizes the fact that in Castilian culture those groups marked as Other are merely the temporary conduits through which the dominant exercises its will and is reinvigorated. The inevitable violence directed at those groups reasserts both their marginality and the renewed power of traditional ideologies. It was not coincidental that the former Mulay Sheik, now Prince Philip of Africa, made the decision to leave Spain for Italy in 1609, the year the Moriscos were ordered out of their Spanish homeland. Although his status as a potent nationalist symbol attached to the royal court continued into the reign of Philip III, the Inquisition's insistence on the enforcement of blood-purity statutes (*estatutos de limpieza de sangre*) produced an environment overtly hostile to even the highest-placed person of North African origins. A wide range of social institutions now excluded "any person who is discovered to descend from the Moors, Jews, heretics or those convicted by the Inquisition, even if they possess every conceivable quality of nobility, valor, Christianity, and education" (qtd. in Asín 196). The imaginary participation of marginal groups in Spanish culture to which the *comedia* had contributed its symbolic power had been displaced, at least on the level of official legal discourse, by direct physical violence marshaled by the state against a sector of its subjects. The idea of a heterogeneous "Spain" exploded in the face of political expediency. The structure of otherness, however, would continue to be filled in by new groups who, as they were represented in theatrical practice, functioned as symbolic capital for the projects of the governing elites for decades if not for centuries to come.

Conclusion:
Symbolic Violence and the Remaking of "Spain"

In 1620 the Discalced Carmelite fathers had convinced Philip III and the Church hierarchy that the as yet uncanonized Teresa de Avila ought to be made the second patron saint of Spain, in tandem with Santiago (St. James the Lesser). The opposition to such a move was sufficiently powerful so as to block the co-patronage until the pope could rule on the matter. When Teresa was granted sainthood in March of 1622, the controversy erupted once again, and the new King Philip IV followed the original decision of his father to establish a shared patronage. The forces of tradition reacted even more forcefully against the verdict than before, and by 1627 aristocratic and ecclesiastical circles were overrun with documents opposing Teresa's promotion. The issue was not fully resolved until 1630 when Pope Urban VIII ruled in favor of the single and uncontested patronage of Santiago.

Over a thirteen-year period, emblematic of a longer process of rearticulation that began in the 1590s, the Spanish ruling class argued over whether or not the imagined community marked "Spain" could construct itself simultaneously around the contradictory figures of a mythical male warrior and a female writer-activist. Francisco de Quevedo referred to the debate as a scandal affecting every level of Spanish life: " . . . [S]e ha revuelto España toda; no el vulgo sólo, sino las iglesias y las universidades, y toda la orden de su caballería" ("All of Spain is in an uproar; not only the common people but the churches and universities and the entire order of knighthood").[12] For traditionalists like Quevedo, the scandal resided in the fact that the partisans who endorsed Teresa's inclusion were proposing nothing less than the demasculinization of society. I have avoided the term "feminization" of culture because the process I am mapping refers neither to gender nor sexuality exclusively nor to those qualities considered essential to "femaleness," but rather to a category encompassing all of those groups not marked as aristocratic, male, pure-blooded, and Catholic. Nevertheless, the case of Teresa's patronage alerts us to the ways in which "the feminine" functioned as a particularly powerful modality of otherness. The ideologies which had propelled both the Reconquest (of the peninsula) and the Conquest (of America) were premised upon the exclusion of those groups who represented such alternative discourses and subjectivities, but by the late sixteenth century they reemerged more insistently than ever before. What I have been suggesting is that, despite the protests of conservatives, this struggle within Spanish culture was necessary to the maintenance of established relations of power.

It goes without saying that a vast network of changes at all levels of society worked to bring about this rearticulation. The absolutist state and by extension early modern theatrical practice could not have been produced without the major economic shift that orthodox Marxism has called the transition from feudalism to capitalism. But in order to understand the ways in which the theater contributed to the kind of cultural micro-transformations I have tried to outline in this essay, we need to follow up on a field of investigation that any totalizing narrative of human history tends to undervalue. This is the field of what Michel Foucault and others have called "discourse," that is, the symbolic practices that determine those groups that must be marked as Other and outside of culture as well as those that might be allowed entry according to a meticulous system of internal hierarchies. As both discourse and practice, the debate over the patron saint, the *comedia,* and cultural spectacles in general exercised considerable influence not only over who was to be considered "Spanish" and who was not but also over what meaning the sign "Spain" might have in the new historical situation.

One of the sites within late sixteenth-century *comedia* production central to the elaboration of this project was the representation of marginalized figures in the theater. The effect of the symbolic violence on stage was not necessarily to contain potential social or political disorder. Despite the existence of those very real tensions that always exist in any cultural body, on the surface at least Spain was relatively calm throughout this period. Rebellions originating from the aristocratic estates or the subordinate classes were virtually unheard of in Spain after the 1520s, even though the Habsburgs were all too familiar with peasant rebellions on a massive scale elsewhere in Europe. On the peninsula by the 1550s there was little of the unbridled intellectual critique of traditional values and none of the outright secularization that one found in England and elsewhere. To a great degree, this was the result of Catholicism's ability to efface social contradictions and articulate its own reinvigorated project (after the Councils of Trent) with that of the emerging absolutist state. On the level of official political discourse, then, the function of the Other throughout the 1590s was filled not by heterogeneous groups on the peninsula as much as by the heretical English and later the rebellious Dutch. In both cases, it was the linking of an incipient capitalist mode of production to a rival religious discourse that called into question the most basic principles of traditional Castilian culture.

Still, within the emergent nation-state itself there were group interests that had to be reconciled with one another and with the dominant class in general. As I have suggested, Philip II's totalizing enterprise was a vast and intricate one. Baltasar Porreño records the ways in which the king insisted that marriages be made between the aristocracies of Castile, Catalonia, Portugal, and the Italian possessions so that "haciéndose la sangre una, por la afinidad, lo fuesen las obligaciones, intereses y razones de acudir a esta Monarquía" ("making the blood one, by affinity, the obligations, interests, and motives for relying on this Monarchy would be one as well").[13] In the plays by Lope and Vélez, we have seen three less privileged groups represented in theatrical practice together with the symbolic violence that was a precondition for the erasure of difference and the adjustment of discursive formations. As Anthony Giddens has reminded us (209ff.), by the late sixteenth century sovereignty meant not so much the presence of superior force but rather the capacity of large and diverse populations to manage the images and signs connected with the state, and thus imagine themselves to be part of a broader community. Violence, therefore, was extended from the physical world to the no less material sphere of culture, where one of the sites on which the internal pacification of Spanish society was enacted was the stage of the public playhouse.

In closing, it is my belief that we must begin to look at the *comedia* not as a literary form primarily concerned with metaphysical issues and universal values. This will strike most non-Hispanist readers as a ridiculously obvious assertion, but within English-speaking Hispanism it can still arouse controversy. Even Spanish studies' selective appropriation of contemporary methodologies (Lacan, Girard, and others) has succeeded in safeguarding the Western tradition, the universality of Man, and the aesthetic privilege of drama. I would argue further that José Antonio Maravall's position in his *Culture of the Baroque* (1975)—the *comedia* as propaganda imposed upon the subordinate classes—also diminishes the complexity of the theater in this period. It is my contention that the *comedia* functioned as an ideological ritual aimed in part at the resolution of practical problems which were taking shape *within* the dominant class itself. In the early seventeenth century, the violence represented on stage against figures such as the amazonian woman, the peasant king, or the threat of Islam stood in as a screen-allegory for the pressing issue of how to theorize the new state. This is most apparent in the period I have selected, but it is no less important to an understanding of texts written at later moments, such as Calderón's own conversion play, *El gran príncipe de Fez D. Baltasar de Loyola* (1669). Insofar as the "dominant" is always a fragile conjuncture of contradictory discourses and practices continually forced to realign itself, we can say that the use of symbolic violence in the public playhouse was a constant throughout the early modern period.

We should be on guard, however, against discovering signs of a playwright's "feminism," his "solidarity" with peasants, or his "tolerance" of other religions—all post-Enlightenment categories not likely to be in place in their modern form in Habsburg Spain (or Jacobean England). Even in those dramatic texts in which characters representing subordinate groups seem to gain the upper hand (as in some plays by Lope) or women receive a "sympathetic" portrayal (as in many by Tirso de Molina), in terms of the reshuffling of the relations of power it was more likely than not traditional aristocratic values that were ultimately renewed. In short, an important part of *comedia* production was less a representation of a new flexibility on the part of the ruling class than it was a cultural manifestation of the pragmatic and significant political problem of how to insure the continued hegemony of that class.

Notes

1. To cite a somewhat exaggerated verdict on the *comedia*'s aesthetic value (although symptomatic of anglophone criticism): John Gassner claimed that the theater of the "Spanish Renaissance was, in effect, merely a prelude" to the magnificence of Elizabethan drama (190).

2. Historians continue to argue over the question of whether or not Spain (Castile, in particular) experienced an economic decline in the seventeenth century. The principal positions are summarized in Kamen, *Spain in the Later Seventeenth Century.*

3. Charles Aubrun has written of the *corrales* in this period: "Leur emplacement coïncide avec les quartiers résidentiels récemment bâtis à l'usage des employés des

administrations publiques au sein de l'Etat extraordinairement bureaucratique créé par Philippe II. . . . leur fonction [the bureaucrats] les rends conscients des intérêts de la communauté, de la *res publica*" (2).

4. Anderson 15. Such a process was not peculiar to Spain. Robert Weimann, for example, has demonstrated how a similar enterprise was undertaken in England during the same period (161–69). My use of Anderson's model is limited insofar as the conditions that produced the idea of the modern nation (print-languages, print-capitalism, etc.) were not fully operative in early modern Europe.

5. That the idea of alterity in the early modern period cut across issues of sexuality and ethnicity is revealed most forcefully in seventeenth-century documents arguing that Jewish males experienced menstruation. See Quiñones, for example. The historian Susan Tax Freeman has recently argued for a distinction between structural (e.g., women) and cultural (e.g., gypsies) forms of otherness.

6. This is not to suggest that physical aggression against and harassment of marginalized groups came to an end. Inquisitorial cases against "judaizers," for example, increased from 1615 on, although most of the people tried in the seventeenth century were not of semitic origin. The shifts in the Inquisition's focus are discussed in Kamen, *Inquisition* 183ff. The group that was a constant target of the Inquisitors throughout both centuries was the "pure-blooded" peasant class, its language, "superstitions," and sexual practices.

7. Jerónimo de Quintana, *Historia de la antigüedad, nobleza y grandeza de la Villa de Madrid* (1629). Quoted in Deleito y Piñuela 98.

8. What has been called the "feminization" of Catholicism in the late sixteenth century may be seen as an analogue to the dissemination of Marianism in the twelfth-century Church, although its origins and consequences differed according to the sociocultural context. On the importance of Marian discourse for the *comedia,* see Sullivan.

9. Walter Cohen has discussed the ways in which Lope refunctions his Latin sources and writes a text heavily dependent on the social valences of verse forms. He concludes that in the end "Lope's propeasant bias expresses and serves the interests of the nobility" (239–52).

10. Mawlay Sayj, the son of the former Sultan al-Mutawakkil, was born in 1566. At the death of his father, who fought with Sebastian of Portugal at Alcazarquivir (1578), he was taken under the protection of Philip II and transferred to Spain. The conversion of a high-ranking Muslim aristocrat to Catholicism produced a euphoria among the Castilian ruling class not unlike the reaction of U.S. conservative ideologues to recent events in Eastern Europe.

11. Mulay Sheik (known as Philip of Africa after his conversion) was particularly devoted to the cult of Mary and in 1602 traveled throughout Spain to visit those shrines dedicated to the Virgin. On the relationship between gendered reason and violence in early modern Europe, see Reiss.

12. "Memorial por el patronato de Santiago y por todos los santos naturales˙ de España" (1628) ["Memorandum on the patron-sainthood of St. James and on all of the natural saints of Spain"] in Quevedo 777.

13. Cf. Porreño 114. The desire for a homogeneous, difference-free, Spain has erupted with disastrous consequences throughout Spanish history. General Franco, for example,

often repeated the slogan: "Unidad de los hombres y de las tierras de España" ("Unity of the men and the lands of Spain").

Works Cited

Anderson, Benedict. *Imagined Communities: Reflections on the Origin and Spread of Nationalism*. London: Verso, 1983.

Asín, Jaime Oliver. *Vida de Don Felipe de Africa, príncipe de Fez y Marruecos, 1566–1621*. Madrid-Granada: CSIC, 1955.

Aubrun, Charles V. "Nouveau public, nouvelle comédie a Madrid au XVIIᵉ siècle." Jacquot 1–12.

Bennassar, Bartolomé. *The Spanish Character: Attitudes and Mentalities from the Sixteenth to the Nineteenth Century*. Trans. Benjamin Keen. Berkeley: U of California P, 1979.

Cabrera de Córdoba, Luis. *Relaciones de las cosas sucedidas en la corte de España desde 1599 hasta 1614*. Madrid: J. Martín Alegría, 1857.

Cohen, Walter. *Drama of a Nation: Public Theater in Renaissance England and Spain*. Ithaca: Cornell UP, 1985.

Deleito y Piñuela, José. *Sólo Madrid es corte: La capital de dos mundos bajo Felipe IV*. Madrid: Espasa-Calpe, 1968.

Deleuze, Gilles. "Michel Tournier et le monde sans autrui." In his *Logique du sens*. Paris: Minuit, 1969. 350–72.

Freeman, Susan Tax. "A Cultural Approach to Marginality in Spain." Phillips and Phillips 1–7.

Gassner, John. *Masters of the Drama*. 3rd ed. New York: Random, 1954.

Giddens, Anthony. *The Nation-State and Violence*. Vol. 2 of *A Contemporary Critique of Historical Materialism*. Berkeley: U of California P, 1987.

Jacquot, Jean, ed. *Dramaturgie et société: Rapports entre l'oeuvre théâtrale, son interprétation et son public aux XVIᵉ et XVIIᵉ siècles*. Vol. 1. Paris: Centre national de la recherche scientifique, 1968.

Kamen, Henry. *Inquisition and Society in Spain in the Sixteenth and Seventeenth Centuries*. Bloomington: Indiana UP, 1985.

———. *Spain in the Later Seventeenth Century, 1665–1700*. London: Longman, 1980.

León Pinelo, Antonio de. *Anales de Madrid (desde el año 447 al de 1658)*. Biblioteca de estudios madrileños, vol. 11. Ed. Pedro Fernández Martín. Madrid: Instituto de estudios madrileños, 1971.

Maravall, José Antonio. *La cultura del barroco: Análisis de una estructura histórica*. Barcelona: Ariel, 1975. English translation: *The Culture of the Baroque*. Trans. Terry Cochran. Minneapolis: U of Minnesota P, 1986.

———. *Poder, honor y élites en el siglo XVII*. 2nd ed. Madrid: Siglo Veintiuno, 1984.

McKendrick, Melveena. *Women and Society in the Spanish Drama of the Golden Age: A Study of the "mujer varonil."* Cambridge: Cambridge UP, 1974.

Phillips, William D., and C. R. Phillips, eds. *Marginated Groups in Spanish and Portuguese History: Proceedings of the Seventeenth Annual Meeting of the Society for Spanish and Portuguese Historical Studies (April 1986).* Minneapolis: Soc. for Spanish and Portuguese Historical Studies, 1989.

Porreño, Baltasar. *Dichos y hechos del rey D. Felipe II.* 1628. Ed. A. González Palencia. Madrid: Editorial Saeta, 1942.

Quevedo, Francisco de. *Obras completas.* Vol. 1: *Obras en prosa.* Ed. Felicidad Buendía. 6th ed. Madrid: Aguilar, 1966.

Quiñones, Juan de. "Memorial de Juan de Quiñones dirigido a F. Antonio de Sotomayor, Inquisidor General, sobre el caso de Francisco de Andrada, sospechoso de pertenecer a la raza judía, discutiendo sobre los medios de conocer y perseguir a ella." ("Memorandum of Juan de Quiñones sent to F. Antonio de Sotomayor, Inquisitor General, regarding the case of Francisco de Andrada, suspected of belonging to the Jewish race, discussing the methods by which that race can be recognized and persecuted") [Biblioteca Nacional, Madrid, VE Cᵃ no. 16].

Reiss, Timothy J. "Corneille and Cornelia: Reason, Violence, and the Cultural Status of the Feminine. Or, How a Dominant Discourse Recuperated and Subverted the Advance of Women." *Renaissance Drama* ns 18 (1987): 3–41.

Ruano de la Haza, J. M., ed. *El Mundo del teatro español en su Siglo de Oro: Ensayos dedicados a John E. Varey.* Ottawa Hispanic Studies 3. Ottawa: Dovehouse, 1989.

Sullivan, Henry W. "La misión evangélica de Tirso en el Nuevo Mundo: La Inmaculada Concepción de María y la fundación de los Mercedarios." Ruano de la Haza 249–66.

Vega, Lope de. *La tragedia del rey Don Sebastián de Portugal y bautismo del príncipe de Marruecos.* Biblioteca de autores españoles, vol. 225. Ed. M. Menéndez Pelayo. Madrid: Atlas, 1969.

———. *La vida y muerte del rey Bamba.* Biblioteca de autores españoles, vol. 195. Ed. M. Menéndez Pelayo. Madrid: Atlas, 1966.

Vélez de Guevara, Luis. *La serrana de la Vera.* Ed. Enrique Rodríguez Cepeda. Madrid: Alcalá, 1967.

Weimann, Robert. *Shakespeare and the Popular Tradition in the Theater: Studies in the Social Dimension of Dramatic Form and Function.* Ed. Robert Schwartz. Baltimore: Johns Hopkins UP, 1978.

Husband-Murder and Petty Treason in English Renaissance Tragedy

BETTY S. TRAVITSKY

I N AN ILLUMINATING review essay on the history of crime in late medieval and early modern England, J. A. Sharpe expresses surprise at finding "the continuity of so many . . . themes" since "conventional wisdom on the subject holds that there should be a decisive break at some point between the mid-sixteenth and late seventeenth century . . . [with t]he Tudor and Stuart centuries, in this as in so much else . . . figured as an age of 'transition'" (202–03). Sharpe does note an exception to this continuity in the "tendency to criminalize the less prosperous social strata" (195). Yet the poor were not the only marginalized group to be heavily criminalized in Tudor and Stuart England, and while Sharpe mentions the rise in this period in witchcraft accusations and in infanticide accusations (200), he fails to follow up on the implications of what Christina Larner has called the increased "criminalization of women," a phenomenon that (in varying degrees) affected women of all classes (69–73).

Although it is beyond my intention to *explain* this last phenomenon, I hope in this essay to draw additional attention to portrayals of the crime of husband-murder in English Renaissance drama in order to demonstrate several interrelated points. The first is that these

171

portrayals are connected to hierarchical Renaissance life since they
depict a contemporary category of female criminal, the petty traitor.
Like all Renaissance wives, the "un"wifely petty traitor was so rigidly
defined by her subordination to her husband-master that if she murdered him she was considered to have committed treason. The second
point is that Renaissance interest in this type of female villain[1] was
widespread, as evinced by the large number of broadsides, domestic tragedies, and tragedies in the traditional canon which depict
husband-murder. The third is that while portrayals of the husband-
murderer in English Renaissance tragedy may seem merely to reflect
a transhistorical phenomenon traditionally termed the "dread of
women"[2] and to concentrate on female rebelliousness, insubordination, and lust, they can be correlated with the historical "criminalization of women" that characterized early modern England.
Additionally, widespread interest in the petty traitor may have lain
in what Catherine Belsey has styled her "challenge to the institution
of marriage, itself publicly in crisis in the period . . . [and] the site of
a paradoxical struggle to create a private realm and to take control
of it in the interests of the public good" (*Subject* 130).[3]

I will begin with a brief survey of the law of petty treason and
the position of the English Renaissance wife. I will then consider a
few portrayals of husband-murder in broadsides, domestic tragedies,
and dramas that have received a great deal of critical attention. And
I will end with a brief discussion of two compositions by Elizabeth
Cary, her play, *The Tragedie of Mariam,* and her protodrama, *The
Life, Reign, and Death of Edward II*. Both Cary's compositions present the otherwise unvoiced—and in some ways distinctive—woman
dramatist's point of view on female treason and Renaissance patriarchy. In presenting far from silent women—and in breaking her own
silence—Cary also provides, as Margaret W. Ferguson has recently
noted in an exciting essay on "the effects of discursive modes of
social construction" (96), an "exemplary meditation on the vexed
relationship between female speech and chastity" (105).

The Contemporary Political Discourse on
Wifely Subordination

Sir Edward Coke termed the 1352 statute of treasons, in force in
his time and indeed until 1828, "this blessed act of 25. E[dward]. 3

[sic]" (2). One "manner of treason" described by the statute is petty treason, namely, "when a servant slayeth his master, or a wife her husband, or when a man secular or religious slayeth his prelate to whom he oweth obedience" (*Statutes* 2: 51–52). The statute marked a social hierarchy in which wives were to husbands as servants were to masters, and carried to its ultimate conclusion the plight of the *feme covert* who, for husband-murder, would be subject to harsher punishment than for mere felony murder, while the reverse was not true for a man who had murdered his wife.

The statute of treasons defined the position of women in England in at least one further way, by encoding the "double standard" (Thomas) into English law. For it established that if the consort of the king committed adultery, or intended to, she was guilty of treason, an obviously impossible situation to reverse. The outstanding Renaissance applications of this provision were the cases of Anne Boleyn and Katherine Howard, two of the queens of the notoriously inconstant Henry VIII.[4] The inequity of these cases is well known. For now, it is perhaps enough to note that the double standard was an instrument of patriarchy, buttressed by law, which recognized, in Keith Thomas's words, "the property of men in women . . . whose function was to cater to the needs of men [and whose] first qualification was chastity" (213). In Peter Stallybrass's more recent formulation, it was "the conceptualization of women as land or possession . . . the fenced-in enclosure of the landlord, her father, or husband" (127). In this connection we might note that Shakespeare's *Othello,* discussed so brilliantly by Stallybrass, provides us with the mirror image of the petty traitor, for Iago orchestrates that tragedy by constructing Desdemona within misogynistic discourse, undermining Othello's sense of Desdemona as secure possession and "Othello's assurance as possessor" (139).

The question of female chastity, as we shall see, is central to most of the accounts and portrayals of petty traitors. In part, this is because petty treason was often linked to the desire to escape an unhappy marriage relationship or to legitimize an illicit affair. In part, it reflects the "unstable conceptualization of the woman," noted by Stallybrass (134), expressed as fear of woman's latent lustfulness and the constant reiteration of that primary requisite that she be chaste.[5] As legal records of defamation cases indicate, chastity was conflated with

silence and with obedience.[6] I will return to the subject below, but
I pause to voice Margaret Ferguson's pointed question, directed at
what she terms "the problematic space between literal and figurative
modes of unchastity": "Just how like a penis *is* a woman's tongue?"
(101). To this we might reply quite like, instancing as evidence the
contemporary phrase "chaste, silent, and obedient" made famous by
Suzanne Hull.[7]

The extent of the subordination (or obedience) required of Renaissance English wives was given expression in 1632, when one T. E.
corrected and saw through the press a collection of laws relating to
women which differed from those concerning men. T. E.'s *Lawes
Resolutions* readily shows that the married woman in Renaissance
England was considered to be legally incorporated into the person
of her husband.[8] In T. E.'s words, a husband and wife "are but one
person, & by this a married Woman perhaps may either doubt whether
shee bee either none or no more then halfe a person" (1: 4). When
a wife addressed her husband as her "lord," she was merely stating
a reality, for she had no public rights, no separate legal personality,
and no redress under law for physical, economic, or social brutali-
zation by her husband. In the section he calls "The Baron may beate
his Wife," T. E. states, "if a man beat an outlaw, a traitor, a Pagan,
his villein, or his wife it is dispunishable, because by the Law Common
these persons can have no action: God send Gentle-women better
sport, or better companie" (1: 7, 128; see also 1: B2v–B3v; 3: I8v).

The legal status of women was of course a function of the hierarchical order of Renaissance society, which was heavily concerned
with questions of order and degree. Such concerns led to enunciations
on the subordination of women to men as well as other matters of
authority. In the official homily entitled "An exhortation, concernynge good order & obedience, to rulers and Majestrates," the subordination of the wife to the husband and its link with other
hierarchical arrangements are underlined in the parallelism of the
following remark:

Every degree of people in theyr vocacion, callyng & office, hath appointed
to theym theyr duetie & order. Some are in hyghe degree, some in lowe,
some kynges and prynces, some inferiours and subjectes, pryestes, and lay-
men, maysters and servauntes, fathers and chyldren; husbandes and wyves,

ryche and poore, and every one have nede of other: so that in all thynges is to be lauded and praysed the goodlye ordre of god, without the whych, no house, no Citye, no common wealth, can contynue & indure or last. (Nv–N1)[9]

The completeness with which the ideal of order and degree was realized in the institutions of early modern England and the extent to which it was subverted are currently matters of scholarly debate.[10] As noted above, Belsey has suggested that the institution of marriage was thrown "into crisis" by a "contest for the control of sexuality in the period" (138) that "cannot be isolated from the political struggles which characterize the century between the Reformation and the Revolution" (143). The divorce debate which she discusses at length is but one expression of this "struggle . . . marking the border between private and public, pamphlet and history" (144).

Popular Echoes of the Theme of Subordination

The patriarchal insistence of the homily on degree, order, and obedience was echoed by domestic conduct-books[11] and by literary portrayals of model Grissills[12] and horrifying Valerias (*Greene in Conceipt*). An interesting dramatic example which contains both types is Joshua Cooke's *Pleasant conceited Comedie . . . how a man may chuse*. In this play, Mistress Arthur is a compendium of such virtues as "Constancie, modest humilitie, / . . . patience, and admired temperance" (O4v; no lineation), who refuses even to criticize her husband's unjust harshness towards her: ". . . since it is his pleasure / To use me thus, I am content therewith, / And beare his checks and crosses patiently" (C). It is instructive that her father and father-in-law are powerless to stop Arthur's abuses; his authority over his wife is absolute.[13] After Arthur has tried unsuccessfully to poison his wife, he marries a whore who proves a predictable conflation of lustfulness, disobedience, and disloyalty, and who tries to rid herself of Arthur by accusing him of the murder of his first wife. At this juncture, Mistress Arthur comes out of hiding to present herself at the trial and to save Arthur's life by disproving her alleged murder, describing herself as she ". . . whom heaven hath still kept to be Arthurs wife" (L).[14]

Although most of the broadside ballads and news pamphlets which regaled the English with sensational and contemporary news are no longer extant (Firth 511), the many titles preserved in the Registers of the Stationers' Company[15] serve to indicate the interest and notoriety associated with female crime in Renaissance England. Pamphlets and ballads recorded actual and rare cases of petty treason as fearful examples of female passion and insubordination, appealing to their audiences with titles that illuminate their bias and their repressive intent, such as "A warning for all desperate Women," "A warning for wives," and "The unnaturall Wife."[16] They are replete with such sentiments as the following, attributed to Ulalia Page, a historical woman who remarks that, "lawlesse love hath lucklesse wrought my woe," and who warns other "wives, let not your hands rebell."[17]

However, these records also suggest the great fascination which the woman who had broken out of bounds held for a society with a rigidly ordered hierarchy in which women's subordination to men and their inferiority were axiomatic, for study of the legal records indicates that in actuality "Elizabethan women . . . were less likely to participate in [violent] activity than their men."[18] As James S. Cockburn tells us, the murder of wives by husbands was far more common than that of husbands by wives in Renaissance England ("Nature and Incidence" 56), although the opposite would seem to be indicated by these contemporary writings.[19] These writings therefore can be said to voice what Ferguson has recently termed the "apparently transhistorical discourse of misogyny" (96), more traditionally thought of as an underlying fear of women. When, in the more full-blown dramatic portrayals of the petty traitor, we find the use of bestial imagery and mythological allusions to archetypical villainesses, we are surely in the presence of this discourse traditionally said to emanate from the dread of women—that is, the sense that the devil lurked just beneath the surface in many women, those fearfully dangerous others whom Jung termed the "negative aspect" of the archetype.[20]

Petty Traitors in Domestic Tragedy

Like the broadside ballads and pamphlets, the new genre of domestic tragedy which developed during the Renaissance exploited popular interest in actual and spectacular contemporary crimes like murder, committed by ordinary people rather than by the heroic and mythic protagonists of traditional tragedies, and put these crimes to homiletic uses (Adams, esp. 100–143).[21] Two anonymous domestic tragedies, *The Lamentable and True Tragedie of M. Arden of Faversham* and *A Warning for Faire Women,* are concerned with specific and contemporary cases of petty treason, the events of which had earlier been the subject of broadside literature.[22]

Although *Warning for Faire Women* is the later play, it is a less satisfactory work, weaker than *Arden,* but much closer in time to both the events that it describes and the earlier broadside materials related to it, and it can be accounted for briefly. *Warning* recounts the murder of George Saunders, a London merchant, by George Browne, an Irishman who fell deeply in love with Saunders's wife. It was with the help of Anne Drurie, an unworthy confidante of both the Saunders, and of her servant, "Trustie" Roger, that Browne murdered Saunders, as well as an innocent passerby, as the first step in his plan to marry the newly made widow. This step, however, was also the last to be implemented, for Browne was apprehended, as were Anne Saunders, Anne Drurie, and Roger, and all of them were tried and executed.

Anne Saunders is a very inconsistently and incompletely drawn woman. The motives attributed to this previously chaste and loyal wife (A4, B, and B1v) for acceding to the Browne-Drurie plot are two: momentary pique at her kindly husband, tellingly expressed by her as an inability "to *submit* my selfe" (C4v: emphasis added), and an extreme credulity which lends itself to Drurie's machinations (C3–C5). The somewhat unclear facts are presented consonantly in all the accounts, as in the lines from the ballad in which Saunders states, "I lyncked my selfe in love; / to hatefull bitter bale, / Throughe which my barcke is ouertourn'd / with quyte contrary gale" ("Wofull lamentacon," st. 6), and in two almost identical pamphlet accounts in which her tearful contrition is given at great length (Golding 1573: B4–C1 and D2v–D4; and 1577: A7–B3 and B6–B7). Despite her confession, and despite the ballad's lines, we certainly have no sense of an abandonment on her part to passion, or a strong willingness to comply with the murder-plot, aside from one brief masque, during which she and Browne embrace (D–D2).[23] Rather, her modesty and good character are referred to recurrently.

A modern reader, unimpressed by the haphazard nature of Renaissance legal procedure,[24] is moved to wonder whether she was really guilty, as so strenuously charged and as she finally confessed, of being an accessory both before and after the fact. We are moved less by Mistress Saunders's villainy or sexuality than by her maternity: she is shown early in the play with one child, her lying-in before her trial is reported, and she takes a tearful farewell from all her children at the end of the play (B2v–B3; I2; and K2–K3v).[25]

The more interesting female villain in the piece, even though the play revolves around the crime of petty treason, is the avaricious Anne Drurie, a white witch who tells fortunes and prepares remedies, a deceitful, false friend, and a bawd who is full-bloodedly termed "that instrument of hell / That wicked Drurie" (D–Dv). *Warning,* however, is relatively primitive as theater; it is also redolent of the medieval dramatic tradition, employing such features as the personifications of Chastitie, Murder, Tragedie, and Hystorie; a masque (alluded to above); an induction; and a conclusion.

Arden of Faversham, on the other hand, is a far more consciously artistic, sophisticated, and successful play. It is often considered the inspiration for the composition of *Warning,* and it is the source, apparently, of the unique extant ballad on the crime which was printed in 1633, the year of the third quarto (*Roxburghe* 8: 48). Like *Warning,* it is based on an actual crime, but it was written far later than the events it dramatizes, and it molds its sources, mainly Holinshed's *Chronicles,*[26] into a coherent artistic statement, changing, or at least suppressing facts to fit this end.

The result is a strong female protagonist, often called a "bourgeois Clytemnestra."[27] Self-consciously disloyal to her husband and fully in love with her rather unattractive lover, Alice Arden is capable of such lines as the following: "... Mosby, let me still enjoy thy love, / And happen what will, I am resolute" (sc. 1, lines 218–22). But she is also a complexly drawn creature of her own time, expressing some qualms even before the murder is done (8.59–79), and then, consistently, given lines of contrition after the crime:

> . . . but for thee I had never been strumpet.
> What cannot oaths and protestations do
> When men have opportunity to woo?
> I was too young to sound thy villainies,
> But now I find it and repent too late.
>
> (18.14–19)

In a period in which the wife's "standing improves (though always in subjection to her husband)" the mistakenness of Alice's effort to escape "the chain of bondage which is marriage" (Belsey 144–45) is the root of her tragedy. Alice's notoriety highlights what Belsey calls the troubled Renaissance "politics of gender" and "instability in the meaning of the family" (147).

The play's subtitle states its bias; in it "is shewed the great mallice and discimulation of a wicked woman, the insatiable desire of filthie lust and the shamefull end of all murderers" (t.p., 1592 ed.). And it abounds in lines on the falseness of women (e.g., 1.20 and 207–08; 11.17–30), which, while true to the facts in a sense, nevertheless deemphasize the equal culpability of hired murderers, acquiescent husbands, and lascivious lovers. Some negative aspersions on women are expressed even by the lover with whom Alice Arden commits the crime, a person far less constant than she, who distrusts his mistress by virtue of her strong love itself.[28] There is a great deal of imagery of savage *female* beasts (for example, at 3.109–13; 8.42–43).[29] Alice is associated not only with serpents and lionesses, but also with such traditionally female tactics as sorcery (8.93–97) and poison (1.360–69 and 609–32), and most importantly with the insubordination so dreaded in women, as when she pointedly asks, ". . . what hath he to do with thee, my love, / Or govern me that am to rule myself?" (10.84–85).

In the broadside ballads and pamphlets, as well as in these domestic tragedies, we have a poorer thing than the powerful drama which was still to develop in Elizabethan England. But these writings begin the process which is the major interest of this paper, the joining of life and art in portrayals of petty treason, the imbalance in the portrayals of the female, as opposed to the male villain, and the sustaining thereby of the hierarchical values which subordinated Renaissance Englishwomen.

Constructs of Petty Traitors in Selected
Conventional Dramas

Even the briefest review of portrayals of the petty traitor in English
Renaissance tragedy should note John Pikeryng's curious hybrid,
Horestes, possibly the earliest presentation of a Clytemnestra on the
English stage. Pikeryng's wobbly female villain is given such awkward
epitaphs as "mother most yll" and "mother most dyare" (Aii, lines
28 and 30). But even in this fledgling drama we find the core of
Renaissance doctrine which underlines the treatment of the petty
traitor: Clytemnestra is "[l]yke as a braunce once set a fyare, [which]
doth cause y tree to bourne" (Dii.v, line 967). A fiery, passionate,
diseased *appendage* of her husband, the necessarily single ruler of
the family, Clytemnestra has infected the main pillar of the home
through her disloyalty and must be eradicated. Hierarchical rule must
be maintained in the microcosm of the home, as in the macrocosm
of the state.[30]

We should also pause just to note that Shakespeare provides us in
his earlier plays with two instances of insubordinate adulteresses who
do not attempt to murder their husbands: Margaret in the *Henry VI*
trilogy and Tamora in *Titus Andronicus.* And, in the same context
of disorder and insubordination, he presents two instances of petty
traitors in his later works: Goneril in *King Lear* and Cymbeline's
queen in *Cymbeline.* These are full-blown Senecan revenge figures
based on chronicle accounts and enveloped by an atmosphere of
disorder and unnaturalness.

Surely the most brilliant of all the husband-murderers in the male-
authored tragedies is Vittoria, Webster's "Devill in crystal" (4.2.88).[31]
Nevertheless, even a recent analysis of duality in *The White Devil*
(Mc Leod) does not discuss the dual standard by which her participation, by innuendo at most, in her husband's murder (1.2.275–301
and 3.1.4–8) rates so much more virulent an attack throughout the
play than does Bracchiano's murder of his wife. If the play's thesis
is that "Next the devil, adult'ry, / Enters the devil, murder" (3.2.109–
10), then it is women who are held up as the greater demons: "No
woman keeper i'th' world, / Though she had practis'd seven year at
the pest-house, / Could have done't quaintlier" (5.3.181–83) is a comment that follows a murder committed by a man.

Underlying the play is an underpinning of misogynist judgment: "Fortune's a right whore," we are told in line four of scene one; women are "politic" (1.2.22), "like curst dogs" (1.2.243). Vittoria is a "debauch'd and diversivolent woman" (3.2.29). The root of all evil, women are defined as "Poison'd perfumes; . . . coz'ning alchemy; / Shipwrecks in calmest weather! . . . / . . . / the true material fire of hell" (3.2.82–86). They are the source of any male evil they may complain about, till even the benevolent image of the nurturing mother is inverted: "We sucked that [dissembling] . . . / From women's breasts, in our first infancy" (4.2.181–82).

Similarly, the love of man and woman, while celebrated by the intensity of the passion of Bracchiano and Vittoria, is fatal. In a dark moment, Bracchiano cries, "Woman to man / Is either a god or a wolf" (4.2.91–92). It is central to the play that Vittoria is, however daring, a woman subordinated in action because of her sex; it is to Bracchiano that she must look to " . . . seat [her] above law and above scandal" and "To keep [her] great" (1.2.307, 311). Vittoria's determination to "personate masculine virtue" (3.2.136) collapses in Bracchiano's absence, and she is thrown upon " . . . woman's poor revenge, / Which dwells but in the tongue!" (3.2.279–80). Bracchiano is left to range at will, while she is confined to a house of convertites. Finally, while Bracchiano's bravura continues till his end, Vittoria's heroism is diminished by her references to Bracchiano as "my good Lord" (5.3.87), by her confessions, after his death, that "I am lost for ever" (5.3.33) and that "this place is hell" (5.3.184), by her puling attempts to out-trick Flamineo, and by her final confession, "Oh, my greatest sin lay in my blood; / Now my blood pays for't" (5.6.241–42).

But the most important of the male-authored portrayals of the petty traitor for the purposes of this essay is Marlowe's early portrayal in his *Troublesome Reign and Lamentable Death of Edward the Second* of unhappy Isabel, the queen whom Edward mistreated to attend to his male favorites. Analysis of Marlowe's play is particularly valuable in juxtaposition to the protodrama by Elizabeth Cary on the same historical events. While Cary's "wedding," in Donald Stauffer's phrase, "of biography and the drama" (314) is discussed below, I will anticipate my argument just a bit by noting that she takes an even more unusual position on Isabel than Marlowe's.

Embroidering on and changing his source, Marlowe creates a fairly complex woman in Isabel. She is first introduced to us in a sympathetic light, as the loyal wife of a disdainful, harsh husband, a willing sufferer for the sake of England's peace (1.4.64–67), a woman wrongly impugned with aspersions of adultery by Edward (1.4.145–423).[32] Until late in the play, she is true to Edward and intent on preserving peace. And, at that time, when we see her indeed entangled with Mortimer, we tend, with perhaps a twentieth-century perspective, to feel that she was driven to that lord's protection (4.2.36–82) by her husband. Her fate and her son's would have been perilous without such allies as Mortimer, and we sympathize with her struggle against disorder when she asserts that "Misgoverned kings are cause of all this wrack" (4.4.9). This judgment, however, is not one which Isabel was allowed to make and act on in the Renaissance; it was her duty to remain submissive and loyal. Moreover, as a woman, she is herself inept at rule, as we see when Mortimer cuts her oratory short (4.4.22– 24), albeit in terms seemingly flattering to her.

We are initially charmed by Marlowe's portrayal of Isabel. She seems to embody powerlessness, submissiveness, and loyalty, and we find it hard to believe that "Mortimer / and Isabel do kiss, while they conspire; / And [that] yet she bears a face of love [to Edward]" (4.5.21– 23). But, indeed, by the end of the play Mortimer has become England's actual—though illegitimate—ruler and can gloat, "The Prince I rule; the Queen do I command; / . . . / I seal, I cancel, I do what I will" (5.4.48–51). Isabel is unmasked as "that unnatural queen, false Isabel" (5.1.17), that "Isabel, whose eyes, [being] turn'd to steel, / Will sooner sparkle fire than shed a tear" (5.1.104–05). After all, as a woman she is almost by definition a compound of treachery, disloyalty, and lust. Her degeneration is shown when she simultaneously sends presents to Edward as false pledges of her loyalty and tempts Mortimer to kill Edward "so 't were not by my means" (5.2.42–45).

In traditional (read male) Renaissance thought, Isabel is not justified by her husband's behavior; his disloyalty is not viewed, as hers is, as spotting the "nuptial bed with infamy" (5.1.31). Though Edward is shown as an inadequate husband and king, Isabel, who was first mistreated by him, is judged more harshly, as disloyal, scheming, insubordinate, and lustful. If at the end of the play we welcome her son's judgment that she is "suspected for his [Edward's] death"

(5.6.77), it is by minimizing her mistreatment and by an acceptance of the rhetorical, patriarchal question raised at Edward's death: "What eyes can refrain from shedding tears, / To see a king in this most piteous state?" (5.5.49–50). For under patriarchy, there is no justification for disloyalty to a legitimate ruler—in the kingdom or in the home. If we sympathize somewhat with Marlowe's Isabel, we are responding to a fairly complex, but still incompletely assimilated figure, and one, moreover, who is characterized in persistently pejorative ways.[33]

Constructs of Traitorous Wives by Elizabeth Cary

When we turn to Elizabeth Cary's protodramas on Edward II and her drama on Herod and Mariam, we find still ambivalent but even more sympathetic portrayals of the traitorous wife. Unfortunately, however, Cary never completely transformed her histories of Edward II into dramas, and so we lack a definitive contrast to Marlowe in the form of a woman author's construction of a voice for Queen Isabella. Although the Edward II protodramas were much later works, I shall therefore first comment on them and then discuss her *Mariam* at greater length; for *Mariam,* with an actual petty traitor and a wrongly suspected wife—both outspoken—offers much material to ponder.

In *Life, Reign, and Death,* her longer, and, as I have argued elsewhere, her more finished version of the history of Edward II,[34] Cary arguably takes her most sympathetic position toward the wife. Cary characterizes Isabella, for example, as "a Jewel, which not being rightly valued, wrought his [Edward's] ruine" (*Life* 19). The wrongs done Isabella by Edward are never lost sight of: "Had he not indeed been a Traytor to himself, they could not all have wronged him," she states (*Life* 160). Furthermore, she asks, ". . . what could be expected, when for his own private Vanities and Passion, he had been a continual lover and abettor of unjust actions" (*Life* 137). But Cary's negativism about women is also discernible in this play, as in her *Mariam.* She does not omit, for example, negative comments on the nature of women: "we may not properly expect Reason in Womens actions," she states at one point (*Life* 149). She is unbending in her condemnation of Isabella's treatment of her captive enemies, the Spencers, treatment which suggests a "Villanous Disposition, and a Dev-ilish Nature" (*Life* 129).

Her treatment of the more vexed issue of Isabella's adultery and complicity in Edward's murder is both more complex and more sym-pathetic than that of the relatively sympathetic Marlowe. Approached by Mortimer, "The Queen . . . is, or at least seems, highly discon-tented . . . and holds this act of too too foul Injustice. . . . She thinks it more than an act of Bloud, to kill a Husband, and a King, that sometimes loved her" (151). As in the case of Mariam, the individual woman's *feelings* concern the author as well as the more obviously sited questions of right and wrong. When Isabella acquiesces, cowed by Mortimer, it is to say, "Stay, *gentle* Mortimer . . . I am a Woman, fitter to hear and take advice than give it" (153).

Still I do not agree with Tina Krontiris' judgment that Cary con-dones Isabella's adultery (140). Extenuation and understanding are lavished on Isabella, but these do not amount to absolution. True, Cary states, "The Queen, who was guilty but in circumstance, and but an accessory to the Instruction, not the Fact, tasted with a bitter time of Repentance, what it was but to be quoted in the margent of such a story" (155). Quite sympathetic, yes. But Cary also writes that Edward, "this unfortunate King, . . . [is undone] . . . partly by his own Disorder and Improvidence, but principally by the *treacherous Infi-delity of his Wife, Servants, and Subjects*" (137; emphasis added). Cary, daughter of a harsh Renaissance judge, and reportedly well aware of judicial niceties, certainly knew that an accessory to a crime (like Anne Saunders) was liable to punishment (Simpson 4–5). On balance, Cary could and did evince considerable sympathy for the queen's misfortunes, but she did not reverse the Renaissance per-spective on a wife's disloyalty, and, of course, could not reverse the bitter historical ending of Isabella's life even when rewriting the neg-ative accounts of earlier male writers.

In her *Mariam*, the only known original play published in English by an Englishwoman during the Renaissance, Cary provides fasci-nating and explicit instances of both wifely rebellion and irresolute wifely smoldering, and again demonstrates the importance to her of the woman's perspective. It is striking that she concerned herself with the workings of the minds and with the outspokenness of subordi-nated women in a patriarchal society. In a more limited way than

Catherine Belsey has stated, I would agree that Cary "problematizes patriarchal absolutism and women's speech" (*Subject* 165).

As in the case of her *Edward II,* there are seemingly direct, male-authorized parallels to Cary's text in two versions of the Herod-Mariam love tragedy: Markham and Sampson's *The true Tragedy of Herod and Antipater: With the Death of faire Marriam* (1622) and Massinger's *Duke of Millaine* (1623). In fact, however, these two male-authored texts on the Mariam story do not center on the Mariam figure and are therefore not instructive.

The world of the play is Herodian Judaea, a kingdom ruled by a male despot. Several strong-willed women related to Herod are circumscribed by the explicit and tacit lines of male control in this world: Alexandra, Herod's mother-in-law, whose father and son have been murdered on Herod's orders, and who schemes ineffectually against her son-in-law by rousing her daughter Mariam's love for her kin; Mariam, Herod's wife, whom he adores but whom he suspects of infidelity, and whom he eventually executes on the basis of this false suspicion; Doris, his cast-off first wife, who plots ineffectually to regain the throne of Judaea for her son; and Salome, Herod's sister, who arouses and fans Herod's suspicion of Mariam, and who also successfully plots her second murder of a husband in the course of this play.

As I have noted at some length elsewhere ("Feme Covert"), *Mariam* is unique among Renaissance plays about the ill-fated love of Herod and Mariam (Valency) in centering on the marriage relationship and in analyzing the stirrings of personhood or independence in the wife as well as the jealousy of the husband. Mariam's ambivalent feelings toward Herod are certainly made understandable in human terms: she finds it hard to ignore her "loving" husband's murders of her grandfather and her brother. However, while Cary recognizes and voices the sorts of feelings that Mariam might well have experienced, she does not seem to accept Mariam's arguments as sufficient; while Mariam's physical fidelity to Herod is never brought into question for the audience, the chorus voices an apparently "official" expectation of a far more rigid wifely loyalty and subordination:

> When to their Husbands they themselves doe bind,
> . . . .

> . . . give they but their body not their mind,
> Reserving that though best for others pray?
> (3.3.1237–40)

In the course of the play, the chaste Mariam is sacrificed to Herod's jealous suspicions. Her crime is emotional disloyalty to a husband who, we might think today, had earned this distrust—she is executed, essentially, for thinking independently. Ferguson's comments on her outspokenness (esp. 107–10) are quite instructive. Still, although Ferguson does not deal with this question, Mariam's sister-in-law, Salome, who is guilty of the insubordination, lustfulness, and disloyalty which Mariam is accused of (in a word, of petty treason), is not disposed of in an equally appropriate fashion (by Renaissance standards).

Instead, the remarkably outspoken Salome is barely touched by remorse as she plots Mariam's death and the murders that will free her to marry the man she currently finds attractive. If we fail to empathize totally with Salome's lusty and violent aspirations, we are nevertheless privy to her uniquely stated aspirations for a single standard in marital freedom of choice and her unflagging, single-minded determination to achieve her ends: "My will shall be to me in stead of Law" (1.5.469)

Admittedly, Cary does apply negative imagery to Salome in the course of the play. She is a "painted sepulcher," and "a Serpent," comparable to "Tygers, Lyonesses, hungry Beares, / . . . / . . . the wreake of order, breach of lawes" (2.4.880, 889; 4.6.1581, 1601). Such descriptions, common in other dramas which have been cited above, evoke Jung's comments on the negative archetype. The internalization of negative imagery and thinking about women by a learned and pious woman writer is surely chilling evidence of the pervasiveness of the patriarchal attitudes that underlay woman's place in Renaissance society.

Admittedly, too, there is no question about Salome's guilt. At one point in the play, in a clear joining of familial and political treason, she states,

> Ile be the custom-breaker: and beginne
> To shewe my sexe the way to freedomes doore,
> And with an offring will I purge my sinne,

The lawe was made for none but who are poore.
(1.4.315–21)

Still, Salome *does not* suffer death, and Cary's failure to punish her and her depiction of her pluck in ways that win some reluctant admiration (or that displace audience wrath from the less insubordinate Mariam) suggest an ambivalence in the playwright's mind over woman's stark subordination in marriage in seventeenth-century England. While Mariam's execution by the jealous Herod seems to be upheld by the important commentators of the play, the message sent by Salome's lighter fate belies this thesis and perhaps attests to Cary's own doubts. We note that Cary simultaneously mouths pious platitudes on such woman's duties as submissiveness, loyalty, and chastity toward her husband and portrays plucky resistance toward those duties. In Ferguson's phrase, "Cary both interrogates and in some sense affirms the ideological link between unruly female bodies and unruly tongues" (105). Still, her modified disapproval is distinctly different from the less ambivalent attitudes which we have noted in the plays by Renaissance men on the petty traitor.

But even in these two works in which women's acts and speeches are constructed by a woman, Belsey's dictum stands:

In the family as in the state women had no single, unified, fixed position from which to speak. . . . [T]hey were only inconsistently identified as subjects in the discourses about them which circulated predominantly among men. . . . [D]uring the sixteenth century and much of the seventeenth the speech attributed to women themselves tended to be radically discontinuous, inaudible or scandalous. (*Subject* 160)

With the partial exception of Cary's plays, extant writings on the petty traitor express what we have seen to be disproportionate and almost unwavering condemnation. It is a sad fact to the student of woman's history that the "apparently transhistorical discourse of misogyny," once legitimized under the catchphrase "the dread of women," has been translated historically into codes which have repressed women more severely than they have men, with no bona fide justification for this repression. The patriarchal law of petty treason, or husband-murder, and its reflection in English Renaissance tragedy, is a case in point.

Notes

An earlier version of this essay was presented at the Patristic, Mediaeval, and Renaissance Studies Conference at Villanova University in 1984. I thank Carole Levin, Constance Jordan, and Ann Rosalind Jones for their helpful comments.

1. The female villain is defined here as a female literary character guilty of an act (technically a felony or trespass) which was considered criminal during the Renaissance, and which was triable by the secular courts. She is the literary correlative of the criminal, and is to be distinguished from the sinner, whose offense was considered a sin against God to be judged by the ecclesiastical courts. For discussions of Renaissance categories of crime, see Elton; Bingham, esp. 447–48; and Sharpe, esp. 188–89. And see Holdsworth, esp. 2: 357–65 and 449–64; 3: 287–317 and 372–73; and 4: 387–407.

2. Karen Horney introduced this term in her now-famous article. A much lengthier, but lucid and helpful discussion of the subject is that by Wolfgang Lederer, which argues that "denial [of this fear] . . . like the denial of any strong emotion, gave rise to varied psychopathology" (vii–viii).

3. For a provocative twist on the usual private-public axis, see Amussen, 2 et passim.

4. Anne, common report would have it, was told by Henry that she would have to tolerate his amours as her betters had done. She was condemned for adultery and incest despite the fact that her marriage to Henry had been annulled. For a careful discussion of her trial, see Schauer and Schauer. Katherine was not accorded even the mockery of a trial, but was condemned by an Act of Attainder. See Plowden, esp. 49–78 and 102.

5. Carol Z. Wiener observes that "the issue of sexual propriety was so much on women's minds and on the minds of men in dealing with them that it often intruded itself into quarrels about other matters; any argument involving a woman was likely to end up with shouts of 'whore' or 'bawd'" (47). And Stallybrass notes that "[a] man who was accused of slandering a woman by calling her 'whore' might defend himself by claiming that he meant 'whore of her tonge' not 'whore of her body'" (126).

6. In discussing the unusual degree to which Elizabethan women engaged in legal quarrels concerning their reputations for chastity, as opposed to their more passive behavior in general, Wiener underlines the significance of chastity to Renaissance women, remarking, "this was one of the few spheres of life in which [women] could possess any sort of reputation, good or bad" (46).

Indeed women were taught to live enclosed in silence. In the words of Juan Luis Vives, " . . . it neither becometh a woman . . . to live among men, or speke a brode and shake of her demurenes and honestie, eyther all together orels a great parte . . . let fewe se her, and none at al here her. . . . Let . . . women holde theyr tonges in congregations . . . nor they be nat allowed to speke but to be subjecte as the lawe biddeth . . . bicause a woman is a fraile thynge, and of weake discretion, and that maye lightlye be disceyved" (E2v).

7. Hull's thesis, that women were rigidly subordinated in Renaissance society and that they were evaluated as they conformed, or failed to conform, to these traditional

virtues, echoes Ruth Kelso's careful study. For further discussion of this requisite, see Travitsky, "Introduction."

8. The collection, according to the prefatory material, was originally compiled by one I. L., and later discovered by T. E., who then brought it to light (A3–A5).

For a twentieth-century evaluation of the "unity of person" that governed the relationship of husband and wife (*baron et feme*) in English Renaissance law, and in some cases until 1970, see Baker's standard text (258).

9. For sophisticated, recent discussions of the Renaissance ideal of order as it applied in both family and state, see the Jordan essays.

10. For a series of recent essays that focus on challenges to the social order, see Dollimore and Sinfield.

11. Two very popular such works were by Batty and Griffeth. In his definitive work on this subgenre, Chilton Powell notes the basic similarities among the different texts.

12. Among Grissill plays are those by Phillips; and Dekker, Chettle, and Haughton. Grissill-like figures appear in *Faire Maide, London Prodigall,* Wilkins's *Miseries of inforst Mariage,* and Snawsel's *Looking-glass for Married Folks* (1610). I thank Ann Jones for bringing Snawsel's Abigail and Eulalie to my attention. There are many parallel non-dramatic renderings of the sufferings of the perfectly meek wife. Judith Bronfman provides an overview on the Griselda story in the Renaissance.

13. Harris has provided a graphic account of the powerlessness of even a very well born noblewoman in the face of her husband's heavy-handed mistreatment.

14. The comparative lightness with which a husband's crimes are viewed, as compared to a wife's, is illustrated also in *A Yorkshire Tragedy,* a domestic tragedy based on the actual murders and attempted murders of Walter Calverly. Plays such as this and Cooke's *How a man may chuse* illustrate the pervasive extent to which the double standard obtained in the judgment of men and women and to which the mythos of terrible destructiveness was reserved for women. Powell commented long ago that "where the wife is the offender the plays result in tragedy, but where the husband performs equal and worse crimes they result in forgiveness and reconciliation . . . in strict keeping with the domestic ideals of the day" (200–201).

15. These are most easily studied in H. E. Rollins's *Analytical Index.*

16. Stanza 14 of "A warning for all desperate Women" reads,

> Good wives and bad, example take,
>   at this my cursed fall,
> And maidens that shall husbands have
>   I warning am to all:
> Your husbands are your Lords & heads,
>   you ought them to obey,
> Grant love betwixt each man and wife,
>   unto the Lord I pray.

In Jeaffreson (3: 107) there is an extant reference to the crime recorded in "The unnaturall Wife," a second ballad on petty treason.

A record of the crime recounted in "A warning for wives," can be found in Jeaffreson 3: 26. The refrain of this ballad reads, "Oh women, / Murderous women, / whereon are your minds?" Rollins comments here, "Marriage seems to have entailed many dangers to husbands of this period" (*Pepysian Garland* 299), thereby confirming the false impression of wifely violence that I have tried to demonstrate. (See below, notes 18 and 19.)

One example of a pamphlet account is *The Araignement & burning of Margaret Ferne-seede,* noted in Cockburn's *Calendar,* entries 168 and 170. Other pamphlets on petty treason include *STC* 7293, 14436, 15095, and 25980. Two other pamphlets are cited in note 22, below.

17. The Page murder was committed in Plymouth in 1591 by George Strangwidge and Ulalia Page, who were executed within two weeks of the crime. An extant pamphlet and three extant ballads were composed about this event, two ballads, "The Lamentation of Master Page's wife," and "The Sorrowful Complaint," in Ulalia's voice. The pamphlet is called *A true discourse of a cruel and inhumaine murder.* I have not yet found a legal record of the crime.

18. Wiener 45. She ascribes these proportions to "the relative dependence and passivity of Elizabethan women. . . . [M]ost Elizabethans thought it illegitimate for those on the subordinate side to use violence no matter what the provocation. . . . [W]omen were taught that tears, not force, were their proper remedy" (45). On the discourse of gender in the Renaissance, see Stallybrass and Ferguson.

19. On this disproportion between actual incidents and their notoriety, see Belsey, *Subject* 135–36.

20. Jung discusses the archetypal figure of the mother, and its "negative side," associated with "anything . . . that devours, seduces, and poisons, that is terrifying and inescapable," and that "may connote anything secret, hidden, dark, the abyss, the world of the dead." Archetypal images are located by Jung in man's "preformed psyche," where they are "derived from the unconscious predisposition" and "made visible in the products of fantasy" (78–82).

21. In "Appendix A" (193–203) Henry H. Adams lists many "Lost Domestic Tragedies," several of which probably dealt with petty treason. The few writers who have interested themselves in portrayals of the female criminal in Renaissance drama include Briggs, Barranger, Berggren, and, more recently, Belsey, Jardine, esp. 68–102, Lieblein, and Orlin.

22. "The complaint and lamentation of Mistresse *Arden"* relates to the Arden murder. Among legal records which refer to the crime are entries for the cost of executing Alice and Bradshaw in Canterbury, and excerpts from the Privy Council Book and from the Faversham Wardmote Book. A manuscript ballad relating to the events of *Warning,* "The wofull lamentacon of mrs. *Anne Saunders,"* has been reprinted by Rollins in *Old English Ballads.* The two pamphlets are by Golding and are almost identical. Aside from the Golding accounts and accounts by Stow and Munday, there is also a historical record in Dasent 8: 91, 92, 94, 105, and 121.

23. She is parallel in this respect to Heywood's Mistress Frankford, the *Woman Kilde with Kindnesse,* whose motives for her lapse are also incompletely and unconvincingly portrayed.

24. For a lucid account of the procedure of the courts during the period, see J. H. Baker, "Criminal Courts," who notes in passing, "It is doubtful whether the presumption of innocence had been formulated" (39).

25. The constant references to Mrs. Saunders's fecundity and the scenes with her children, as well as the association of her with such images as the moon, tend to mix our reactions to her and to blunt our negative feelings about her.

26. The chief source is Raphael Holinshed, 2nd ed.; M. L. Wine discusses the references in his introduction, xxxv–xliv.

27. The phrase is traditional among critics of the play; I take it from Sturgess 24.

28. He states, at one point,

> But what for that I may not trust you, Alice?
> You have supplanted Arden for my sake
> And will extirpen me to plant another.
> 'Tis fearful sleeping in a serpent's bed.
> And I will cleanly rid my hands of her.
>   (8.39–43)

29. Shakbag, for example, states,

> Such mercy as the starven lioness,
> When she is dry-sucked of her eager young,
> Shows to the prey that next encounters her,
> On Arden so much pity would I take.
>   (3.100–113; see also 8.42–43)

30. Other Clytemnestra figures from the early English drama include Guenevora, the adulterous queen of Arthur in Thomas Hughes's *Misfortunes of Arthur.* At first Guenevora appears to be a heroically disloyal Alice Arden, remorselessly plotting the murder of her long-absent husband, Arthur, with the help of her stepson lover, Modred. However, Guenevora's scheme dissolves suddenly in a decision to enter a nunnery, so that we see not a full-blown Clytemnestra, but an inconsistent portrayal. The reverse progression is true in *The Lamentable Tragedie of Locrine,* by W. S., where Guendoline, portrayed at first as a model of the wronged, submissive wife, suddenly becomes incensed at Locrine's love for Estrild and begins to wage a pitiless war to overthrow Locrine—her legitimate ruler as both husband and king.

Both plays are based mainly on Geoffrey's *History* and allude to mythological prototypes of female revengers (bk. 2: 1–6 [Gwendolen]; bk. 9: 9; bk. 10: 2, 13; bk. 11: 1 [Guenevere]). Both include elaborate and horrific speeches, not found in that source, which characterize these treasonous proto-Clytemnestras. Both, whether through ineptitude or design, present a petty traitor as a type of unpredictable, lustful, disloyal and insubordinate woman.

31. According to F. L. Lucas, Webster probably used an oral report as the basis of his plot, but deviated frequently from the source. He compressed the actual and recent

history of the two Italian lovers, omitting information that would have softened his portrayal of Vittoria (70–90).

32. His chief source is Holinshed's *Chronicles;* the less favorable portrait in the play has been attributed to "the unhistorical working up of the character at the beginning (of the play), and . . . the time-compression, that conduct seeming incomprehensible within a short period which in twenty-three years is only too credible" (Charlton and Waller 45–48).

33. Two important, additional portrayals of petty treason are those of Lucretia in Barnes's *Divils Charter* and of Beatrice-Joanna in *The Changeling.*

Barnes invented the portion of his play relating to Lucretia Borgia (Pogue 10–11), a "Thayis of the stewes" (1.3.291) to the mind of her jealous husband, Gismond. When she first appears on stage, she is bent on killing the husband who has restrained her, steeling herself with thoughts of "Impatient *Medeas* wrathfull furie, / And raging *Clitemnestraes* hideous fact," and invoking the ". . . griesly Daughters of grimme *Erebus* [to] / . . . Imarble more my strong indurate heart, / To consumate the plot of my revenge" (1.5.601–05). Lucretia's murder of her husband on stage, as well as her deadly dissembling to him, far outweigh, in impact on the audience, the extreme jealousy and power on his side which had enabled him to keep her a virtual prisoner, and which had moved her to murder him.

Beatrice-Joanna, the changeling, is betrothed to Alonzo De Piracquo when she conspires with De Flores to murder him. Entrapment is her motive, and she states,

> . . . would creation . . .
> Had form'd me man!
> . . . Oh, 't is the soul of freedom!
> I should not then be forc'd to marry one
> I hate beyond all depths! I should have power
> Then to oppose my loathings, nay, remove 'em
> For ever from my sight.
>
> (2.2.107–13)

But Renaissance discourse about female depravity dominates the play. Beatrice-Joanna discovers that she has become "the deed's creature" (3.4.138), and she comes to see herself as loathsome, styling herself, in her last moments, as "that of your blood was taken from you, / For your better health" (5.3.151–52).

Another minor representation of the same type occurs in Jonson's *Sejanus His Fall,* in the person of Livia, who is shown conspiring with Sejanus to poison her husband in one brief scene (2.1.1–138). Jonson's only change from history in his depiction of Livia was his omission of the fact that she was the sister of Germanicus, to avoid linking Sejanus's opponents to his allies.

34. *Paradise of Women* 211; "Feme Covert" 186. The shorter form of the play, *Most unfortunate Prince,* was included in the *Harleian Miscellany; Life, Reign, and Death* first appeared in 1680.

Works Cited

Adams, Henry Hitch. *English Domestic or Homiletic Tragedy, 1575–1642.* Columbia University Studies in English and Comparative Literature, no. 159. New York: Columbia UP, 1943.

Amussen, Susan Dwyer. *An Ordered Society: Gender and Class in Early Modern England.* London: Blackwell, 1988.

The Araignement & burning of Margaret Ferne-seede, for the Murther of her late Husband Anthony Ferne-seede, found deade in Peckham Field . . . . 1608. *STC* 724.

Baker, J. H. "Criminal Courts and Procedure at Common Law, 1550–1800." Cockburn, *Crime* 15–48.

———. *An Introduction to English Legal History.* London: Butterworths, 1971.

Barish, Jonas A., ed. *Sejanus His Fall.* The Yale Ben Jonson. New Haven: Yale UP, 1965.

Barnes, Barnabe. *Divils Charter: A Tragaedie Conteining the Life and Death of Pope Alexander the sixt* . . . . 1607.

Barranger, Milly S. "The Cankered Rose: A Consideration of the Jacobean Tragic Heroine." *CLA Journal* 14 (1970): 178–86.

Batty, Bartholomew. *Christian mans closet* . . . . London, 1581.

Bawcutt, N. W., ed. *The Changeling.* By Thomas Middleton and William Rowley. Cambridge: Harvard UP, 1958.

Beilin, Elaine. "Elizabeth Cary and *The Tragedie of Mariam.*" *Papers on Language and Literature* 16 (1980): 45–64.

Belsey, Catherine. "Alice Arden's Crime." *Renaissance Drama* ns 13 (1982): 82–102.

———. *The Subject of Tragedy: Identity and Difference in Renaissance Drama.* London: Methuen, 1985.

Berggren, Paula S. "'Womanish' Mankind: Four Jacobean Heroines." *International Journal of Women's Studies* 1 (1978): 349–62.

Bingham, Caroline. "Seventeenth-Century Attitudes toward Deviant Sex." *Journal of Interdisciplinary History* 1 (1970–71): 447–72.

Briggs, Katharine Mary. *Pale Hecate's Team: An Examination of the Beliefs on Witchcraft and Magic among Shakespeare's Contemporaries and His Immediate Successors.* London: Routledge, 1962.

Bronfman, Judith. "Griselda, Renaissance Woman." Travitsky, *Renaissance Englishwoman in Print* 211–23.

Cary, Elizabeth. *The History of the Life, Reign, and Death of Edward II, King of England, and Lord of Ireland. With the Rise and Fall of his great favourites, Gaveston and the Spencers. Written by E. F. in the year 1627. And Printed verbatim from the Original.* London: J. C. for Charles Harper, Samuel Crouch, and Thomas Fox, 1680.

———. *The History of the most unfortunate Prince, King Edward the Second; with choice political Observations on him and his unhappy Favourites, Gaveston and Spencer: Containing several rare Passages of those Times, not found in other Historians; found among the Papers of, and (supposed to be) writ by the Right*

Honourable Henry Viscount Faulkland, some time Lord Deputy of Ireland. Harleian Miscellany. 8 vols. London: John White, John Murray, John Harding, 1808. 1: 67–95.

———. *The Tragedie of Mariam, the Faire Queene of Jewry. Written by that learned, vertuous, and truly noble Ladie, E. C.* 1613. London: Charles Whittington and Co., at the Cheswick Press, 1914.

Charlton, H. B., and R. D. Waller, eds. *Edward II.* By Christopher Marlowe. New York: Gordian, 1966.

Cockburn, J. S. "The Nature and Incidence of Crime in England, 1559–1625: A Preliminary Survey." Cockburn, *Crime* 49–71.

Cockburn, J. S., ed. *Calendar of Assize Records, Surrey Indictments, James I.* London: HMSO, 1982.

———. *Crime in England, 1550–1800.* London: Methuen, 1979.

Coke, Sir Edward. *The Third Part of the Institutes of the Lawes of England: Concerning High Treason, and other Pleas of the Crown, and Criminal Causes.* 1644. 6th ed. London: Printed by W. Rawlins for Thomas Basset at the George near St. Dunstan Church, 1680.

"[The] complaint and lamentation of Mistresse *Arden* of [*Feve*]*rsham* in *Kent,* who, for the love of one *Mosbie,* hired certaine Ruffians and Villaines most cruelly to murder her Husband; and with the fatall end of her and her Associats." *STC* 732. [first extant version printed by Cuthbert Wright in 1633]. *Roxburghe* 8: 46–53.

Cooke, Joshua. *A Pleasant conceited Comedie, Wherein is shewed how a man may chuse a good Wife from a bad.* London, 1602. New York: AMS, 1912.

Dasent, John R., ed. *Acts of the Privy Council of England.* 32 vols. London: HMSO, 1890–1907.

Dekker, Thomas, Henry Chettle, and William Haughton. *The Pleasant Comoedie of Patient Grissill. . . .* 1600.

Dollimore, Jonathan, and Alan Sinfield, eds. *Political Shakespeare: New Essays in Cultural Materialism.* Ithaca: Cornell UP, 1985.

E., T. *The lawes resolutions of Womens Rights: Or, The Lawes Provision for Woemen.* London: John More, 1632.

Elton, G. R. "Introduction: Crime and the Historian." Cockburn, *Crime* 1–14.

"An exhortation, concernynge good order & obedience, to rulers and Majestrates." *Certayne Sermons appoynted by the Queenes Majestie, to be declared and read, by al Persones, Vycars, & Curates every Sundaye and holyday in their Churches: where they have curre.* London, 1562.

Faire Maide of Bristow. 1605.

Ferguson, Margaret W. "A Room Not Their Own: Renaissance Women as Readers and Writers." *The Comparative Perspective on Literature: Approaches to Theory and Practice.* Ed. Clayton Koelb and Susan Noakes. Ithaca: Cornell UP, 1988. 93–116.

Ferguson, Margaret W., Maureen Quilligan, and Nancy J. Vickers, eds. *Rewriting the Renaissance: The Discourses of Sexual Difference in Early Modern Europe.* Chicago: U of Chicago P, 1986.

Firth, C. H. "Ballads and Broadsides." *Shakespeare's England: An Account of the Life and Manners of His Age.* Ed. Sir Sidney Lee and C. T. Onions. 2 vols. Oxford: Clarendon, 1926. 2: 511–38.

Fischer, Sandra K. "Elizabeth Cary and Tyranny, Domestic and Religious." *Silent But for the Word: Tudor Women as Patrons, Translators, and Writers of Religious Works.* Ed. Margaret Patterson Hannay. Kent, Ohio: Kent State UP, 1985. 225–37.

Fullerton, Georgianna. *Life of Elizabeth, Lady Falkland, 1582–1639.* London: Burns & Oates, 1883.

Geoffrey of Monmouth. *History of the Kings of Britain.* c. 1138/39. Trans. Sebastian Evans. Rev. Charles W. Dunn. New York: Dutton, 1958.

Golding, Arthur. *A briefe discourse of the late murther of master George Saunders, a worshipfull Citizen of London: and of the apprehension, arreignement, and execution of the principall and accessaries of the same.* London, 1573. *STC* 11987.

———. *A briefe discourse of the late murther of master George Sanders, a worshipful Citizen of London: and of the apprehension, arreignement, and execution of the principall and accessaries of the same.* London, 1577. *STC* 11986.

Greene in Conceipt, New raised from his grave to write the Tragique Historie of faire Valeria of London. Wherein is truly discovered the rare and lamentable issue of a Husbands dotage, a wives leudnesse, & childrens disobedience. London: Richard Bradcocke for William Jones, 1598.

Griffith, Mathew. *Bethel: or a forme for families.* . . . London, 1633.

Harris, Barbara. "Marriage Sixteenth-Century Style: Elizabeth Stafford and the Third Duke of Norfolk." *Journal of Social History* 15 (1981–82): 371–82.

Henderson, Thomas F. "Elizabeth Cary, Lady Falkland [1585–1639]." *DNB* 3: 1149–51.

Heywood, Thomas. *A Woman Kilde with Kindnesse.* 1607.

Holdsworth, W. S. *History of English Law.* 7th ed. 12 vols. London: Methuen, 1903–38.

Holinshed, Raphael. *Chronicles of England, Scotland, and Ireland.* 1587.

Horney, Karen. "The Dread of Women; Observations on a Specific Difference in the Dread Felt by Men and by Women Respectively for the Opposite Sex." *International Journal of Psychoanalysis* 13 (1932): 348–60.

Hughes, Thomas. *Certaine Devises and shewes presented to her Majestie by the Gentlemen of Grayes-Inne at her Highnesse Court in Greenewich, the twenty eighth day of Februarie in the thirtieth yeare of her Majesties most happy Raigne.* 1587. *Early English Classical Tragedies.* Ed. John W. Cunliffe. Oxford: Clarendon, 1912. 217–96.

Hull, Suzanne. *Chaste, Silent, and Obedient: English Books for Women, 1475–1640.* San Marino, CA: Huntington Library, 1982.

Jardine, Lisa. *Still Harping on Daughters: Women and Drama in the Age of Shakespeare.* Totowa, NJ: Barnes, 1983.

Jeaffreson, John Cordy, ed. *Middlesex County Records.* 5 vols. Middlesex County Record Soc., 1888.

Jonson, Ben. *Sejanus His Fall.* 1607.

Jordan, Constance. "Feminism and the Humanists: The Case for Sir Thomas Elyot's *Defence of Good Women.*" Ferguson, Quilligan, and Vickers 242–58.

———. "Woman's Rule in Sixteenth-Century British Political Thought." *Renaissance Quarterly* 40 (1987): 421–51.

Jung, C. G. *The Archetypes and the Collective Unconscious.* Vol. 9, pt. 1. *The Collected Works of C. G. Jung.* Ed. Sir Herbert Read et al. Trans. R. F. C. Hull. Bollingen Series 20. Princeton: Princeton UP, 1959.

Kelso, Ruth. *Doctrine for the Lady of the Renaissance.* Urbana: U of Illinois P, 1956.

Krontiris, Tina. "Style and Gender in Elizabeth Cary's *Edward II.*" Travitsky, *Renaissance Englishwoman in Print* 137–53.

The Lamentable and True Tragedie of M. Arden of Faversham In Kent, Who was most wickedlye murdered, by the meanes of his disloyall and wanton wyfe, who for the love she bare to one Mosbie, hyred two desperat ruffins Blackwill and Shakbag, to kill him. Wherin is shewed the great mallice and discimulation of a wicked woman, the unsatiable desire of filthie lust and the shamefull end of all murderers. London, 1592.

The Lamentable Tragedie of Locrine, the eldest sonne to King Brutus, discoursing the warres of the Brittaines, and Hunnes, with their discomfiture. 1595.

"The Lamentation of Master Page's wife of Plimmouth, who being enforced by her parents to wed him against her will, did most wickedly consent to his murther, for the love of George Strangwidge; for which fact she suffered death at Barstaple in Devonshire. Written with her owne hand, a little before her Death." *STC* 6557.2. *Roxburghe* 1: 553–58.

Larner, Christina. "Crimen Exceptum? The Crime of Witchcraft in Europe." *Crime and the Law: The Social History of Crime in Western Europe since 1500.* Ed. V. A. C. Gatrell, Bruce Lenman, and Geoffrey Parker. London: Europa, 1980. 49–75.

Lederer, Wolfgang. *The Fear of Women.* New York: Grune, 1968.

Levin, Carole, and Jeanie Watson, eds. *Ambiguous Realities: Women in the Middle Ages and Renaissance.* Detroit: Wayne State UP, 1987.

Lieblein, Leanore. "The Context of Murder in English Domestic Plays, 1590–1610." *Studies in English Literature, 1500–1900* 23 (1983): 181–96.

The London Prodigall. 1605.

Lucas, F. L., ed. *Complete Works of John Webster.* 4 vols. London: Chatto, 1927.

Mc Leod, Susan H. "Duality in *The White Devil.*" *Studies in English Literature, 1500–1900* 20 (1980): 271–85.

Marlowe, Christopher. *The troublesome raigne and lamentable death of Edward the second, King of England: with the tragicall fall of proud Mortimer.* 1594. Spencer 101–42.

Middleton, Thomas, and William Rowley. *The Changeling.* 1653. Spencer 1015–50.

Murdock, Kenneth B. *The Sun at Noon: Three Biographical Sketches.* New York: Macmillan, 1939.

Orlin, Lena Cowen. "Man's House as His Castle in *Arden of Feversham.*" *Medieval and Renaissance Drama in England* 2 (1985): 57–89.

Phillip, John. *The commodye of pacient and meeke Grissill.* . . . c. 1570.

Pikeryng, John. *A Newe Enterlude of Vice Conteyninge, the historye of Horestes with the cruell revengment of his Fathers death, upon his one naturill Mother.* 1567.

Plowden, Alison. *Tudor Women: Queens and Commoners.* New York: Atheneum, 1979.

Pogue, Jim C., ed. *The Devil's Charter.* By Barnabe Barnes. New York: Garland, 1980.

Powell, Chilton Latham. *English Domestic Relations, 1487–1653.* Columbia University Studies in English and Comparative Literature. New York: Columbia UP, 1917.

Reynolds, John. *Triumphs of Gods Revenege against . . . Murther.* 1621.

Rollins, Hyder E. *An Analytical Index to the Ballad-Entries (1567–1709) in the Registers of the Company of Stationers of London.* Chapel Hill: U of North Carolina P, 1924.

Rollins, Hyder E., ed. *Old English Ballads, 1553–1625, Chiefly from Manuscripts.* Cambridge: Cambridge UP, 1920.

———. *A Pepysian Garland; Black-Letter Broadside Ballads of the Years 1595–1639, Chiefly from the Collection of Samuel Pepys.* Cambridge: Cambridge UP, 1922.

The Roxburghe Ballads. 27 parts in 9 vols. Ed. William Chappell [vols. 1–3] and J. B. Ebsworth [vols. 4–9]. Hertford: Ballad Soc., 1871–99. Rpt. [9 vols. in 8]. New York: AMS, 1966.

Schauer, Margery Stone, and Frederick Schauer. "Law as the Engine of State: The Trial of Anne Boleyn." *William and Mary Law Review* 22 (1965): 49–84.

Shakespeare, William. . . . *His True Chronicle History of the Life and death of King Lear and his Three Daughters.* . . . c. 1608.

———. *The Most Lamentable Romaine Tragedie of Titus Andronicus.* 1594.

———. *The Tragedie of Cymbeline.* c. 1608.

———. *The True Tragedie of Richard Duke of Yorke.* . . . 1595.

Sharpe, J. A. "The History of Crime in Late Medieval and Early Modern England: A Review of the Field." *Social History* 7 (1982): 187–203.

S[impson]., R[ichard]., ed. *The Lady Falkland, her Life from a ms. in the Imperial Archives at Lisle.* London: Catholic Publishing, 1861.

"The Sorrowful Complaint of Mistris Page, for causing her husband to be murdered, for the love of George Strangwidge, who were executed together." *STC²* 6557.4. *Roxburghe* 1: 561–63.

Spencer, Hazelton, ed. *Elizabethan Plays.* . . . Lexington, MA: Heath, 1933.

Stallybrass, Peter. "Patriarchal Territories: The Body Enclosed." Ferguson, Quilligan, and Vickers 123–42.

Statutes at Large, 15 Edward III–13 Henry IV, From Magna Charta to the End of the Eleventh Parliament of Great Britain, Anno 1761. Ed. Danby Pickering. 46 vols. in 48. Cambridge: by Joseph Bentham, 1762.

Stauffer, Donald A. "A Deep and Sad Passion." *Essays in Dramatic Literature: The Parrott Presentation Volume.* Ed. Hardin Craig. Princeton: Princeton UP, 1935. 289–314.

Sturgess, Keith, ed. *Three Elizabethan Domestic Tragedies.* Baltimore: Penguin, 1969.

Thomas, Keith. "The Double Standard." *Journal of the History of Ideas* 20 (1959): 195–216.

Travitsky, Betty S. "The *Feme Covert* in Elizabeth Cary's *Mariam.*" Levin and Watson 231–50.

———. "Introduction: Placing Women in the English Renaissance." Travitsky, *Renaissance Englishwoman* 3–41.

Travitsky, Betty S., and Anne M. Haselkorn, eds. *The Renaissance Englishwoman in Print: Counterbalancing the Canon.* Amherst: U of Massachusetts P, 1990.

———. *The Paradise of Women: Writings by Englishwomen of the Renaissance.* Westport, CT: Greenwood, 1981.

A true discourse of a cruel and inhumaine murder, committed upon M. Padge of Plymouth, the 11 day of February last, 1591, by the consent of his owne wife, and sundry other. 1591. *STC* 18287. *Shakespeare Society Papers.* 18 vols. London: Shakespeare Soc., 1844. 2: 79–85.

"The unnaturall Wife: Or, The lamentable Murther, of one goodman *Davis,* Locke-Smith in Tutle-streete, who was stabbed to death by his Wife, on the 29. of *June,* 1628. For which fact, She was Araigned, Condemned, and Adjudged, to be Burnt to Death in *Smithfield,* the 12. of July 1628." *STC* 6366. Rollins, *Pepysian Garland* 283–87.

Valency, Maurice J. *The Tragedies of Herod and Mariamne.* Columbia University Studies in English and Comparative Literature, no. 145. New York: Columbia UP, 1940.

Vives, Juan Luis. *The Instruction of a Christen Woman.* Trans. Richard Hyrde. London: Berthelet, 1529.

"A warning for all desperate Women. By the example of *Alice Davis* who for killing of her husband was burned in Smithfield the 12 of July 1628. to the terror of all the beholders." *STC* 6367. Rollins, *Pepysian Garland* 288–92.

A Warning for Faire Women. Containing The most tragicall and lamentable murther of Master George Sanders of London Marchant, nigh Shooters hill. Consented unto By his owne wife, acted by M. Browne, Mistris Drewry and Trusty Roger agents therin with their severall ends. As it hath beene lately diverse times acted by the right honorable, the Lord Chamberlaine his Servantes. 1599. Ed. Charles Dale Cannon. The Hague: Mouton, 1975.

"A warning for wives, By the example of one *Katherine Francis,* alias *Stoke,* who for killing her husband, *Robert Francis* with a paire of Sizers, on the 8. of Aprill at night, was burned on *Clarkenwell-greene,* on Tuesday, the 21 of the same moneth, 1629." *STC* 19280. Rollins, *Pepysian Garland* 299–304.

Webster, John. *The White Divel . . . With the Life and Death of Vittoria Corombona the famous Venetian Curtizan.* 1612. Spencer 925–80.

Wiener, Carol Z. "Sex Roles and Crime in Late Elizabethan Hertfordshire." *Journal of Social History* 8 (Summer 1975): 38–60.

Wilkins, George. *The Miseries of inforst Mariage.* 1607.

Wine, M. L., ed. *The Tragedy of Master Arden of Faversham.* London: Methuen, 1973.

"The wofull lamentacon of mrs. *Anne Saunders,* which she wrote with her own hand, being prisoner in *newgate,* Justly condemned to Death." Rollins, *Old English Ballads* 340–48.

A Yorkshire Tragedy, Not so New as Lamentable and True. 1608.

Giving up the Ghost in a World of Decay: Hamlet, Revenge, and Denial

ROBERT N. WATSON

THIS PROCESSION of black letters is intended as another reminder that we are all compelled to give up the ghost sooner or later. What dresses me in more than the customary suits of solemn black— maybe even in the black hat of the villain—is my polemical suggestion that we need to give up the ghost in a literal sense as well as the common figurative one, that we need to surrender the illusions of afterlife that *Hamlet* superficially encourages and deeply undermines. I share C. S. Lewis's sense that the entire play is haunted, not by "a physical fear of dying, but a fear of being dead" (147–52). *Hamlet* at once enables and fiercely interrogates the denial of death, a denial— channeled in this instance primarily through revenge—essential to the psychic survival of any human culture.[1] Despite the exclusionist claims of some political criticism, social hierarchy and private property are not the only aspects of cultural order that literature uneasily conspires to preserve. It seems ironic that the critics who (inspired by Michel Foucault, Clifford Geertz, and Stephen Greenblatt) have wonderfully expanded the areas in which we recognize the self-perpetuating strategies of the Elizabethan *episteme,* so often ultimately refer their discoveries back to a narrowly conceived political or economic hegemony. Thomas More's Utopia seems cozy enough in its communism; the threat it cannot tolerate is annihilationism, unbelief in any afterlife. A citizen who doubts that life has ulterior meaning is beyond control, and perhaps beyond sanity as well. A society lacking consensus on that meaning—lacking a univocal ghost—faces a perpetual crisis of morale and of *gestalt* as devastating as any rebellion. The vexed status of King Hamlet's ghost, both in the play and in its critical history—is it real or metaphorical, is it a psychological projection, a diabolical illusion, or a theatrical convention?—reflects a corrosive uncertainty in modern Western culture about the prospects for personal immortality.

Obviously the widely witnessed appearance of King Hamlet's ghost seems to affirm Catholicism and refute mortalism. But instead of spurring Hamlet to some pious resolution designed to alleviate or avoid his father's purgatorial agonies, the ghost makes Hamlet resolve to remember and avenge. The visitation renews the young man's hope, not of salvation, but of the lasting significance of mortal life, inspiring him to defend his father's memory against the ravages of time, and to attack the proximate cause of his father's death.

Ghosts are the standard-equipment starters of Senecan revenge-tragedies; my point is that this convention reflects a larger truth, namely, that the genre of blood-revenge is partly motivated by a need to sustain two beliefs. First, that our rights, our desires, and our consciousness continue to matter beyond our deaths. And, second, that revenge can symbolically restore us to life by defeating the agency of our death, conveniently localized in a villain.[2] Modern audiences need some version of these ghostly visitations for much the same reasons Renaissance playwrights needed them: to make our lives into meaningful plots that motivate our actions and allow us to perform something complete and significant. We each live in a "distracted globe," we demand that the culture haunt the theaters of our minds and our worlds with illusions of compelling meaning, and with diversions from the recognition of meaninglessness. So there are powerful and benevolent forces, sociological as well as critical and theological, arrayed to resist my exorcism. And perhaps I am like Gertrude, the sole observer to whom the ghost, holy or otherwise, chooses to be invisible. But it seems to me that a skeptical journey through *Hamlet* teaches us to see through this "illusion" (1.1.127).

In the first act, Horatio warns Hamlet not to follow the ghost; in the fifth act, he warns Hamlet instead not to focus "too curiously" on the inglorious indifference of corpses (Lyons 106). What if the lost father proves not to be a ghost, but instead a skull? Not the victim of extraordinary villainy, but of ordinary decay? When Hamlet encounters the remains of Yorick, the man who—kissing and carrying the boy "a thousand times"—seems to have been as loving a paternal figure as the biological father, the only tribute young Hamlet can pay him is a rising gorge (5.1.184–89). Revenge may be "a remedy for grief" (Welsh 488), but it is also a remedy for terror; it pretends to be a bloody horror, but it blocks another, paler kind of horror, one less susceptible to fictional adjustments into consolation. Pursuing the specter of a father (my essay will accept the male orientation of Shakespeare's symbolism on this point) allows one to flee the specters of decay and annihilation, of unaccommodated death.

My suggestion is not that we should dismiss the ghost as a mere hallucination (Greg), but rather that we exorcise it before it poisons or "blasts" us (1.1.127), that we follow the play in turning away from haunted battlements and accepting in their place a common grave-yard. If I cannot exorcise the vengeful ghost entirely (and my subtitle suggests an effort to go Eleanor Prosser one better), I want at least to isolate it as a fiction within a fiction within a fiction, an "illusion" within a drama within a cultural mythology of denial. No wonder this specter appears to be "a composite of what Catholics, Protestants, and skeptics thought about spirits" (Erlich 38–39), rather than an objectively consistent creation. Hamlet and Hamlet and *Hamlet*—the father, the son, and the ghostly play—creep in a petty pace from death to dusty death, for all their sound and fury. What I have to offer is less a strictly critical analysis than a series of meditations on that point.

The soldiers in the opening scene are standing on guard against some undefined threat to their world, an enemy that (for all its dis-guises) proves to be mortality itself, the foe against whom every soldier arms himself in vain, against which the wielded partisans of these sentries are naturally of no use: "For it is as the air, invulnerable, / And our vain blows malicious mockery" (1.1.145–46). The underlying story, as Horatio here explicates it, involves all the conventional strategies for overcoming mortality. This ghost is less "the devil of the knowledge of death" (as Knight, 39, maintains) than the tempter toward the denial of death. It encourages us to imagine life after death as a return to this living world, and it brings into focus the idea of a king's immortal presence in his nation. The vengeful quest of young Fortinbras makes us think, not only (as young Hamlet will wistfully observe) that life and death alike can be justified by honor, but also that the living can repair the losses of the dead, even that our children can triumphantly reconstitute us. If Fortinbras can undo one consequence of his father's defeat, the loss of territory, why not another, the loss of life?

Hopes of resurrection—whether by sons, symbols, or saviors—are timeless functions of human culture; they are also terrifying when they threaten to *mal*function. Both the timelessness and the terror are evident when Horatio turns to contemplating a previous eruption of politically ominous ghosts:

> A little ere the mightiest Julius fell,
> The graves stood tenantless and the sheeted dead
> Did squeak and gibber in the Roman streets.
> . . . .
> . . . and the moist star
> . . . .
> Was sick almost to doomsday with eclipse.
>   (1.1.114–20)

The doomsday comparison is more than casual, because Hamlet's diction generates a vision of the Last Judgment gone bad. The dead awaken to a nightmare. Though Rome was then a pagan world, the mightiest Julius fell just a little ere the meekest Jesus fell. This blurred vision suggests that, confronted by mortality, the state of Denmark is rotting from its spiritual core, just as Rome did. Presumably Shakespeare's own "distracted globe," where *Hamlet* followed *Julius Caesar,* was susceptible to the same disease.

Only a dozen short lines beyond this Caesarean mock-doomsday, Horatio attributes to the ghost a motive that, though conventional enough, here comes too close for comfort to the problems of bodily resurrection:

> if thou hast uphoarded in thy life
> Extorted treasure in the womb of earth,
> For which, they say, your spirits oft walk in death. . . .
> (1.1.136–38)

Perhaps the lost treasure for which the ghost mourns, which he wishes his audience would extort in a Caesarean rebirth from the tomb of earth, is nothing other than his own corpse. But at this moment the cock crows, and cuts off the speech. This "trumpet to the morn," as Horatio calls it, resumes the parodic echoes of the Day of Judgment. The Last Trumpet resounds here as a merely animal voice that sends the dead back to their graves instead of up into salvation.

Marcellus's rhapsodic response makes the Christian associations explicit, but again we seem to be stuck with a Savior who, instead of liberating the dead, remands them to their graves:

> It faded on the crowing of the cock.
> Some say that ever 'gainst that season comes
> Wherein our Saviour's birth is celebrated,
> This bird of dawning singeth all night long,
> And then they say no spirit dare stir abroad.
> (1.1.157–61)

So the cheer of the morning that now rises in its "russet mantle" is an equivocal cheer. For all Hamlet's eager hyperbole, his father is no Hyperion who resurrects with each morning (1.2.140, 3.4.56). The stage action reflects a psychological truth: that rising to the business of a new day means leaving behind the awareness of death and the memories of the dead. The mourning of the dead and the morning of the day are incompatible. That may partly explain why Hamlet complains of being "too much in the sun" and clings stubbornly to his midnight-black mantle of protracted sorrow.

This stubbornness is the problem Claudius confronts at the start of the second scene. He tries to bury the fact of death rhetorically in a subordinate clause—a syntactical analogue to the death-denying strategies of the culture as a whole—and tries to bury the same fact practically by evoking the role-based systems of marriage and royalty that subordinate the mortal body-natural to the successively immortal body-politic. It enrages Hamlet when Claudius identifies himself as

Hamlet's father and Denmark's king. Hamlet is determined to resist
this ordinary obliteration of the dead and of the facts of death, even
before he learns that this particular death demands a particular com-
memoration. So he attacks the neglect of mourning with his black
clothing, attacks the impersonal rhetoric of kingship with his ironic
wit, attacks the usurped roles on the throne and in the bed with his
outright diatribes.

Hamlet attempts to sustain his father's existence by identifying with
him, even if that means joining him in death (Leontes and Perdita
show a similar reaction to the image of the supposedly dead Hermione
in *The Winter's Tale*). He wishes not to be alive, even (in the famous
soliloquy at 3.1.55) "not to be" at all. In his gloom, passivity, and
silence, in the black of his mourning wear, in his closed or staring
eyes, and his wish to be out of the sun and into his grave, young
Hamlet tries to be a sort of medium at a seance, conjuring the dead
man into presence, with all his absentness intact. Gertrude is a worthy
monarch in the land of denial: she is no more willing to see the dead
than to see the mad Ophelia (4.5.1) or the "black and grained spots"
of her own mortal frailty (3.4.90). In deference to her own weaknesses
she strongly misreads her son's symptoms:

> Good Hamlet, cast thy nighted color off,
> And let thine eye look like a friend on Denmark.
> Do not for ever with thy vailed lids
> Seek for thy noble father in the dust.
> Thou know'st 'tis common, all that lives must die,
> Passing through nature to eternity.
>
> (1.2.68–73)

Hamlet's edged reply—"Ay, madam, it is common"—suggests that it
is precisely the commonness of death that horrifies him, the way it
erases distinctions.

Claudius then undertakes the same line of argument, but goes astray
in an interesting Freudian slip when he suggests that heaven, the
dead, nature, and reason all make up one voice that

> still hath cried,
> From the first corse till he that died to-day,
> "This must be so." We pray you throw to earth

> This unprevailing woe, and think of us
> As of a father, for let the world take note
> You are the most immediate to our throne.
>   (1.2.104–09)

The alternative to the utter unprevailingness of mourning is an acceptance of the figurations and distractions the culture offers: stepfathers in place of fathers, the deferred promise of glory and material reward. But who really was "the first corse"? Claudius seems to have forgotten, at least on the conscious level, that (according to his religion) it was Abel, murdered by his brother Cain. This unwitting but revealing allusion not only provides a first squeak of the guilt that will eventually be caught in "The Mousetrap"; it also compromises the larger cover story of natural decay by which Claudius's depredations—and perhaps those of all Creation—seek to disguise themselves as something orderly and acceptable, something controllable by a finite period of grievous memory ("for some term / To do obsequious sorrow," as Claudius puts it at 1.2.91–92).

From another perspective, the allusion points to the deeper things that this revenge story has in common with the Genesis story. Both narratives play to our profound need to perceive death as a contingency, and a correctable one at that. That is the fallacy at the pathetic heart of blood-revenge, the fallacy that inspired the "prophetic soul" of Hamlet himself to suspect his uncle of murdering as well as replacing his father (1.5.40). Just as the play vindicates the disgusted cynicism of adolescence by giving it objective correlatives, so too it vindicates—like many (other?) detective stories—the perversely satisfying suspicion that every ordinary death can be exposed as a murder. Every death is both banal and outrageous; nature becomes murder's alibi in Claudius's speech, in a way that reminds us how murder becomes nature's alibi in several popular genres of fiction.

Ordinary death is just what Hamlet wants to avoid:

> O that this too too sallied flesh would melt,
> Thaw, and resolve itself into a dew!
> Or that the Everlasting had not fix'd
> His canon 'gainst self-slaughter!
>   (1.2.129–32)

This is not merely (as he is commonly characterized) a man so disgusted and weary-spirited that he wishes to surrender to death. On the contrary, he is trying to find an alternative to death, or if he must die, to do so as a willed act, a conquest rather than a surrender. (Intriguingly, the other great voice of morbid intellect in this period, John Donne, appears to have been similarly obsessed by the possibilities of death as a pure melting, as in the "Valediction: Forbidding Mourning," or as a decisively violent suicide, as in *Biathanatos.*)

The alternatives to such lovely or sudden endings were much less attractive, as the vivid heritage of macabre medieval art would have reminded everyone involved. As so often in Renaissance literature, gardens become a subconscious euphemistic metaphor for graveyards:

> 'tis an unweeded garden
> That grows to seed, things rank and gross in nature
> Possess it merely. That it should come to this!
> But two months dead.
>
> (1.2.135–38)

At two months dead, the problem is not only faded memories above ground, but also decaying flesh below ground that nature grossly repossesses. Hamlet will talk explicitly about the "convocation of politic worms" that feast on Polonius's corpse (4.3.19–31), but the macabre *transi* image seems already to be on Hamlet's mind in his first soliloquy. When he recalls bitterly that Gertrude used to hang on King Hamlet "As if increase of appetite had grown / By what it fed on" (1.2.143–45), it sounds as if she were a coffin-worm, and their marriage had been the beginning of King Hamlet's vermiculation. Indeed, early in the bedroom confrontation, Hamlet construes Gertrude's marriages as a mindless feeding on her husbands (3.4.66–67). Again, it is convenient to have a villain to blame for mortality, and, since he has not yet learned about the murder as such, Hamlet edges toward the common misogynist suspicion that women (in the decadent sexuality they evoke, or in the fallible bodies they issue) are the source of men's mortality. "Frailty, thy name is woman" (1.2.146).

Some thirty-five lines after Hamlet's disgusted reference to the way Gertrude "fed on" King Hamlet, the suggestion of vermiculation becomes all the more disturbing in Hamlet's suggestion that

> the funeral bak'd-meats
> Did coldly furnish forth the marriage tables.
> Would I had met my dearest foe in heaven
> Or ever I had seen that day, Horatio!
> My father—methinks I see my father.
> (1.2.180–84)

Seeing him is one thing; eating him is another. Hamlet's father, already regurgitated by his tomb (1.4.50–51), becomes all too model a Host at this mixed sacrament, serving as a locus for the communion of his kin. A king may go a progress through the guts of a beggar, as Hamlet argues (4.3.30); he may also go a progress through the guts of his son. The wildest horrors of *Titus Andronicus* lie waiting to be recognized in every meal of our ordinary lives, as we repress the knowledge of the deaths our lives are built on.

Hamlet's reluctance to partake of this feast of renewal is understandable. He is much more willing to incorporate his father's returning spirit than his father's bodily remains; he prefers communication to communion. Yet the ghost's inspiriting message seems, in body language, to communicate nothing but death. Horatio shifts the conversation from the funeral meats to the apparition, which he describes as "very pale," its eyes "fix'd" (1.2.233).[3] It came "In the dead waste and middle of the night" and left the sentries "distill'd / Almost to jelly with the act of fear," so that they "Stand dumb and speak not to him" (1.2.198, 204–06). The blank staring, the collapse into silence, even the distillment into jelly (compare Donne again, describing corpses in the sermons), suggest that this ghost infects those he encounters with a version of his own unredeemed deadness. Marcellus turns for consolation to the idea of Christ as a bearer of Eternal Life (1.1.158–64), but the ghost is a parodic inversion of precisely that notion.[4]

Why, then, is Hamlet so jolly by the end of a ghostly visitation that hints at purgatorial torments, reveals earthly horrors, and assigns him a brutal and predictably fatal task? Perhaps Hamlet exults because the idea of death as ultimate closure and permanent stillness has been so strikingly refuted. What Hamlet emphasizes repeatedly in greeting the ghost is its bodily escape from the tomb, as if that physical resurrection were more valuable, or at least more plausible, than spiritual salvation:

                                                          tell
Why thy canoniz'd bones, hearsed in death,
Have burst their cerements; why the sepulchre,
Wherein we saw thee quietly interr'd,
Hath op'd his ponderous and marble jaws
To cast thee up again. What may this mean,
That thou, dead corse, again in complete steel
Revisits thus the glimpses of the moon . . . ?
                                        (1.4.46–53)

The ghost provides simultaneously an explanation and a disproof of
simple mortality. The gross decay of this old man's flesh resulted
from an evil aberration, and the rest of his spirit is not yet silent.
Better a murdered king on earth than a dead one at peace, if Hamlet's
response is any guide.

What Hamlet craves from this visitation is a sense of mission, provided now from the grave, the very place where he apparently lost
it. "Say why is this? wherefore? what should we do?" (1.4.57). If his
father still has a purpose in death, then Hamlet's life, rendered aimless
by his confrontation with mortality, can recover purpose also. "My
fate cries out," Hamlet insists over Horatio's warnings, "Still I am
call'd" (1.4.81, 84). "Fate" and "calling" are the words by which
countless Renaissance self-fashioners deemed valid the readings of
their lives that gave them narrative shape, and therefore value.

Shakespeare thus exposes the inner workings of the justifying narratives that rose rapidly to prominence during his lifetime: the call
of a conversion experience, the spiritual autobiography, the revenge
story. Without such provocative mythologies, we might not know
what, why, even how to desire, beyond the sleeping and feeding
Hamlet dismisses as merely bestial (4.4.33–35). Without such "reve-
lations" to dispel the banality of death, without them to shape for
us a meaningful task of defending "good" against "evil," we would
likely sink into the poisonous *accidie* that grips Hamlet in the opening
scenes. He has to find murder for the same reason most people have
to find God. Hamlet's responses to the visiting ghost, and even to
the visiting players, pressure us to evaluate our own appetites for
stories of murder and retribution, whether in the Book of Genesis,
the story of Pyrrhus, or the play of *Hamlet.* Revenge drama is, I
believe, overdetermined in its appeal to Renaissance audiences; but

instances of blood-revenge offer the supplemental incentive of hearing that death, rather than being the accepted order, is "most foul, strange, and unnatural" (1.5.28). And when the ghost reports further that it is the work of an evil "serpent" in the Garden (or at least the orchard, 1.5.35–39), against which the devout son must redeem him, Shakespeare both taps and anatomizes the appeal of Christian mythology. Our desire for Hamlet to kill Claudius, for the heir to defeat death on the father's behalf, is really another version of a standard dream of immortality regained.

Claudius assigns Rosencrantz and Guildenstern to elicit from Hamlet "What it should be, / More than his father's death, that thus hath put him / So much from th' understanding of himself" (2.2.7–9). But might not that clearest early warning of death most people encounter—the demise of the same-sex parent, a loss Shakespeare suffered about the time he was writing *Hamlet*—make it unbearable for us to recognize ourselves sanely, to understand ourselves as the heirs of graves no less than thrones? How should one sanely, self-knowingly, reconcile (as Hamlet attempts to do later in the same scene, 2.2.303–08) the magnificence of humanity with its destiny in dust? Gertrude diagnoses for Claudius the cause of Hamlet's madness as "His father's death and our o'erhasty marriage" (2.2.57). From Hamlet's perspective, those two events are two stages of the same crime, the commonplace and outrageous obliteration of King Hamlet by time and mortal frailty.

On one level, the revelation of Claudius as a murderer is merely the literal fulfillment of a fact that is already crucially true psychologically, symbolically. By replacing the perfect father with a mortal man, by showing that love and memory are ephemeral, and that roles such as husband and king are fungible, the transition from King Hamlet's reign to that of Claudius entails the invention of mortality in young Hamlet's psychic world. No wonder the comparison of Claudius to that first corpse-maker, Cain, keeps recurring. Again—to adapt Voltaire's aphorism about God—I am not denying that there was a murder, only adding that, if there had not been one, Hamlet would have been compelled to invent it. And in a work of fictional art, in the work of mythmaking, there can hardly be any absolute distinction between empirical reality and psychological invention. The need to make a hero and a villain out of father and stepfather respectively not only suggests a familiar psychological syndrome in Hamlet the man. It also reminds us that our pleasure in watching *Hamlet* the play, or other stories of blood-revenge, arises from a similar syndrome, a need to cast the world in polarities that give it meaning, to isolate a force of immortality that can finally be vindicated against the interim victories of mortality. Christianity, like most other religions that have thrived, seems well designed to capitalize on that need.

Claudius proves susceptible to the same convenient allegorization of his own mortality, pleading for England to eradicate Hamlet, "For like the hectic in my blood he rages, / And thou must cure me" (4.3.66–67). Hamlet is indirectly flesh of his flesh, more than kin and less than kind, the outward agency of Claudius's own susceptibility to death—which, indeed, he proves to be. He brings Claudius's own poison into Claudius's own bloodstream, gives him a taste of his own mortality. Claudius's plots to assassinate Hamlet derive from the same futile illusion, the same projective mythology, that shapes Hamlet's plots against Claudius: the idea of defeating death by a preemptive or retributive attack on the symbolic bearer of one's own vulnerability. The assurance God will not give him in the prayer scene, Claudius begs from the English executioners, through an assertion of his royal prerogative over life and death. The effort to "defy augury" (5.2.219), the futile struggle to elude a bitter destiny, becomes explicitly in *Hamlet* what it is implicitly in so many works of tragic art: a parable of mortality.

Laertes' determination to aid and comfort the dead Ophelia— indeed, his illusion that that is his motive—provides a vivid example of the culture's standard mechanisms of denial hard at work. Even at his most violently rebellious, Laertes is as much a safely conventional thinker as his father. He returns from France to Denmark unselfconsciously delighted to have been cast in such a juicy role as avenger, first on behalf of his father and then on behalf of his sister as well. He desperately needs to find a villain from whom to retake their lives, and Claudius is shrewd enough to cast Hamlet convincingly in that role. Claudius promises Laertes that Ophelia's "grave shall have a living monument" (5.1.297) in the killing of Hamlet, who supposedly caused her death. So the act of revenge is to serve the same purpose as funeral statuary, to give the deceased some representative immortality.

Claudius, furthermore, discusses Laertes' filial obligation in terms that underscore the notion that any reticence in revenge is itself a version of death: a submission to time, disease, and mutability (4.7.110–18). By raising for Laertes the same disturbing possibility that events have raised for Hamlet—that time erodes loving memory, the last hope of the dead father—Claudius compels Laertes to assert the contrary with bloodshed. Claudius demands, "What would you undertake / To show yourself indeed your father's son / More than in words?" (4.7.124–26). By accepting the conventional formula of consolatory vengeance, Laertes will indeed prove himself his complacent father's son. More specifically, when Laertes responds with predictable fervor, vowing "To cut [Hamlet's] throat i' th' church" (126), the immortality fantasies based in memory, progeny, and vengeance are set directly against the central immortalizing promise of Christianity. We are left uncertain whether revenge should be construed as the correction of murder, as revenge tragedies often suggested, or merely as further murder, as Elizabethan orthodoxies insisted. By these contradictions *Hamlet* deconstructs its own genre, forcing us to recognize the arbitrary designations by which we locate absolute immortal values within our incoherent mortal world.

What characterizes the latter part of this play is the sheer overdetermination of death—which allows one to overlook its binary nature and its basic and inevitable causes. As a mortal man, Hamlet must die within a few decades by course of nature; but we hardly notice that tragic fact in its own guise while we are watching him parry more vivid and specific threats: suicidal impulses, marauding pirates, mandated executions, poisoned swords and cups. Laertes says his poison is so powerful that

> Where it draws blood, no cataplasm so rare,
> Collected from all simples that have virtue
> Under the moon, can save the thing from death
> That is but scratch'd withal.
>
> (4.7.143–46)

But what balm can save anyone from death, even in the absence of a poison-tipped rapier? They should have died hereafter, unless the poison were the things it conceivably parodies here: the baptismal water and the blood of Christ that supposedly offer eternal life (comparably, Ophelia is apparently damned rather than saved by immersion). From this perspective, the duel is a kind of Black Mass that, under Claudius's satanic guidance, undoes all the promises of immortality. Like the guests at Claudius's hasty cannibalistic wedding-feast, these Danes are feeding on a deadly rather than a redemptive Host.

The black humor of the gravediggers performs the same kind of subversion as that Black Mass. Like the crowing of the cock and the recollection of Julius Caesar in the first act, the scene suggests a parody of the Last Judgment: skulls rise from their graves to endure Hamlet's sentences, and the gravedigger, Hamlet, and Laertes all climb from graves under their own power (Van Tassel 59). This is a place of skulls—"another Golgotha," to borrow a crucifixion reference from *Macbeth* (1.2.40)—but the only resurrection it can offer is exhumation. The clowns enter analyzing the causes and implications of Ophelia's death, and doing it so badly that they expose the underlying absurdity of allocating burial spots according to the state of mind that once inhabited the decaying corpse. Their indignation that the rich and powerful have more right than the poor to hang and drown themselves is itself revealingly absurd. The graveyard humor arises precisely from the way the decorous official metaphors collapse to a crudely physical level: "The crowner hath sate on her, and finds it Christian burial" (5.1.4). But that collapse is as scary as it is funny. Incoherent theology becomes a poor cover for implacable biology. Certainly, after seeing the attitude of the gravediggers toward the bodily remains—the way the props are treated by the stagehands after the funeral show is over—we cannot miss the empty pomposity of the priest's concern that a full Christian ceremony would "profane the service of the dead." They are already being served profanely enough, and served in fact to worms.

Laertes tries to answer the priest's chilly arguments with natural facts and feelings, but cannot help inventing his own death-defying miracles and his own supernatural cruelties in the process:

> Lay her i' th' earth,
> And from her fair and unpolluted flesh
> May violets spring! I tell thee, churlish priest,
> A minist'ring angel shall my sister be
> When thou liest howling.
>
> (5.1.238–42)

Laertes' passionate leap into the grave, Gertrude's speculations about marriage and strewing of flowers—how much of this can survive as convincing high sentiment after the gravediggers have sounded the low-comic keynotes? Hamlet accuses Laertes of "rant," then grandly demands to be buried with Ophelia too. Gertrude attributes Hamlet's reactions to "mere madness," but Ophelia's stark indifference to the debates and rivalries over her worldly love and her eternal soul exposes all these competitors and commentators as victims of a typically human madness, a delusive need to replace the indifference of death with the differentiations by which we define and preserve our sanity.

The incongruities of this burial scene suggest the shortcoming I perceive in most modern studies of Renaissance attitudes toward death. By engaging in elaborate explications of the *ars moriendi,* the rituals of funeral, and the traditions of tomb-making, such analyses tend to participate in the very mechanisms of distraction and denial they purport to be studying (Stein, Aries, Andrews). The moment of dying is not death; the responses of the living are not the experience of the dead. Furthermore, by studying the various ways death was represented, scholars tend to overlook the crucial premise that death is representable, the fact that visualizing death begs the question of whether death is finally mere blankness.

So while it is valid for a *Hamlet* scholar to inquire, say, whether aristocratic Renaissance widows were expected to mourn two months or twelve (Frye 82–102), it is also valid to ask why it should matter. Hamlet exclaims sarcastically to Ophelia, "O heavens, die two months ago, and not forgotten yet? Then there's hope a great man's memory may outlive his life half a year, but, by'r lady, 'a must build churches then . . ." (3.2.130–33). Patent as it may seem, this tirade still strikes a devastatingly direct blow to some familiar complacencies that expect to answer mortal annihilation with the memories of those who loved us, with the legacies of our good deeds and grand monuments, and with the prayers such things elicit for us from those we leave behind. Hamlet's anger reflects a special exasperation with the willingness of people—irrationally, but under the name of reasonableness—to measure responses to the infiniteness of death with finite numbers, to suppose that a month's mourning is the right amount for a permanent loss, even that a tanner's body will rot after nine years rather than eight. The popular aphorism about lies needs little revision to apply to denials of death: there are denials, damned denials, and statistics.

The persistence of the facts of deadness against all human constructions comes through clearly in the gravedigger's riddle that makes his profession the best builders, since "The houses he makes lasts till doomsday" (5.1.59). It comes through more subversively in his argument that Adam was the first gravedigger, which not only reawakens the Cain reference, but also suggests that all mankind has ever really done is tirelessly dig its own graves (the nuclear arms race may be the logical culmination of that process). The play focuses on this disturbing suggestion with increasing magnification. First we are told that this gravedigger began his job on "that day that our last king Hamlet overcame Fortinbras," suggesting that the earliest death mentioned in the play was in fact the start of the world's mortality. Moreover, the fact that young Fortinbras takes over young Hamlet's royal legacy at the end of the play demonstrates that time obliterates human achievements, that the essential things people fought and died for slip, by forfeit or random permutation, back to their opposites or starting-places. It finally makes no difference who survived and won that archetypal single combat between old Hamlet and old Fortinbras. The Old Testament keynote for *Hamlet* may thus be less the vengeful splendors of Genesis and Exodus than the clear-eyed weariness of Ecclesiastes.

The next step is the indirect revelation that this gravedigger's first day on the job was also "the very day that young Hamlet was born," as if this grave had been prepared for him (like the arriving-place in many stories of tragic irony) from the beginning of his existence as a physical individual, if not from the beginning of time itself. What was he "born to set . . . right"? Again the specific mission of revenge serves as a metaphor, or perhaps merely as a disguise, for the mysterious assignment implicit in being born a human being. Have we been summoned to perform justice, to defend honor, to protect our families and our nations? Or merely to chase illusions and to die?

Words, looks, and laws here lose their meaning; as the surface is scraped off the graveyard, the play exposes the shallowness of its culture's fabric of denial (however richly brocaded) beneath which it hides its dark obvious secrets. Culture is a shroud. Hamlet expresses surprise that this worker "sings in grave-making," and Horatio replies that "Custom hath made it in him a property of easiness" (5.1.66–68). This exchange builds on the preceding suggestions of universality, reminding us that, from one perspective, all our works and days constitute singing at grave-making, enabled by habit and by cultural customs that insulate us from the overwhelming facts of death that are always around and ahead of us.

Events forbid Hamlet to keep these observations at the comfortable distance of *contemptus mundi* and *memento mori* commonplaces, a process which serves to remind us that we too may not have truly confronted mortality merely by speaking about it sententiously in the abstract. He begins to identify achingly with the abused disinterred bones, then learns that one skull belonged to his old playmate, then discovers the funeral of his own beloved, and leaps into the grave with her. This leads to a sort of deathbed conversion. At the brink of death, with all his own *sententiae* about futility and anonymity still fresh in his ears, Hamlet begins seeking a final serenity within the Christian formula. This emerging attitude has often been interpreted as Hamlet's saving revelation, and as the central truth the play serves to inculcate. Such interpretations are appealing but finally unsatisfactory. Hamlet's attitude toward heaven consistently proves to be an index of how badly he needs belief at any moment; and the graveyard scene expands that pattern to the entire culture, positioning religion as one of the compulsive insanities provoked by the fact of death. And Hamlet's final "the rest is silence" (5.2.358) seems potentially disturbing for his religious followers in much the way Jesus' "Why hast thou forsaken me" might have been for his.[5]

Furthermore, it is hard to discern much divine care rewarding Hamlet's conversion, or much Christian benevolence in his own actions; the Denmark of act 5 is hardly a kinder, gentler nation. It is also hard at times to discern the Christianity behind the passivity. Stoicism is of course the last refuge of many a Renaissance hero, but Hamlet's acceptance of his role as a born avenger and a falling sparrow looks less like a positive declaration of faith than like an agnostic yielding to fate, as best one can read it. What Hamlet seems to posit is less a deity to save his soul than a co-author sufficient to legitimize the conversion of his life into a significantly shaped narrative, such that closure becomes a triumph rather than a surrender. God the Father in act 5 proves to be merely an extension (as Freud's theories of religion from the early *Totem and Taboo* to the late *Future of an Illusion* would predict) of the father's ghost in act 1. If my resistance to the Christian references places me in the critical pitfall Richard Levin calls "refuting the ending," my defense is a kind of *tu quoque:* to accept the conventional consolations as sufficient is to refute the ending of human life, to misrepresent as comic (however cleverly and appealingly) a plot of rise and fall.

Hamlet justifies his passivity with a parsing that—in its very absurdity and circularity—may be finally all the human mind can "reasonably" conclude about death:

> There is special providence in the fall of a sparrow. If it be now, 'tis not to come; if it be not to come, it will be now; if it be not now, yet it will come—the readiness is all.
>
> (5.2.219–22)

All one can do is blankly declare that each individual life is significant. All one can choose about death is to be ready—to mythologize the things that happen into a satisfactory story, to prepare a plausible reading of mortality as wholeness rather than emptiness. Hamlet hopes for a benevolent paternal deity behind this inscrutable omnipotence, but we see the duel arising instead from the feigned paternal benevolence of Claudius, the agent of death. Shakespeare even positions Horatio to encourage our exasperation with Hamlet for submitting to the scheme—thereby compelling us to challenge our own fatal attractions to schemes called honor and religion and revenge, things we choose to die for so that dying can have a "for."

What is there to fight for, what even to live for, in the world of Denmark? That is the question posed so memorably by Hamlet's early soliloquies, and we should not dismiss it as merely the conventional symptomology of the melancholic (though it may certainly be that) or forget its fundamental power when Hamlet conveniently receives an assignment that (in either sense) "distracts" him. Rosencrantz and Guildenstern expose friendship, if not as an outright fraud, as a weakling vulnerable to the brief passing of time and the least pressure of *Realpolitik.* Romantic love has been compromised, by Gertrude and Ophelia, in much the same way. Claudius poses as a Donne-like lover whose continued life depends on mutual attraction with Gertrude:

"She is so conjunctive to my life and soul, / That, as the star moves not but in his sphere, / I could not but by her." This, in turn, explains why he does not dispose of Hamlet promptly, since "The Queen his mother / Lives almost by his looks" (4.7.11–16). The entire Danish society—and it may not be extraordinary in this—becomes a kind of house of cards, people making the needy lives around them the justification for their own, in an endlessly circular argument of life-motivation.

Hamlet's survey of Fortinbras's "twenty thousand men / That for a fantasy and trick of fame / Go to their graves like beds" (4.4.60–62) defines honor as a thin, destructive invention to which one must nonetheless subscribe if one is to posit and preserve any transcendence of our status as physical animals. To avoid perceiving death as an ultimate defeat, one must declare something else more important, and validate that assertion by action. This is why the soldiers march, and it seems to Hamlet—while he acknowledges it is absurd and arbitrary—to be as good a reason as any.

Honor stands exposed, not only as this madness of Fortinbras's soldiery, but also as Ophelia's patchy prudery, and as the heartless heart of the duel with Laertes. The declared stakes of that duel—horses, decorations, reputations (5.2.147–64)—plausibly represent all the fripperies of worldly wealth and ostentation which generally serve, as they do in this specific instance, merely to distract us from the real situation until we are safely in the clutches of death. As on the level of plot, so too on the level of moral symbolism, these designated objects of rivalrous desire are mere delusive irrelevancies, mere excuses for holding the diverting contest. Acquisitive materialism, and the competition it breeds, keep us from recognizing our common grievance—and perhaps somehow making common cause—against mortality.

That recognition seems to be behind Hamlet's impulses to reconcile himself with Laertes, first in his mourning, then in his dying. Shortly before the fencing match, Hamlet declares that he feels

> very sorry, good Horatio,
> That to Laertes I forgot myself,
> For by the image of my cause I see
> The portraiture of his.
>
> (5.2.75–78)

The specific cause they share is the outrageous death of a father, but as Claudius pointed out in the play's second scene, the whole history of nature is "death of fathers," and it should not seem so particular with Hamlet and Laertes. We all share the simple doom that the revenge story buries and the gravediggers brutally unearth. To continue spilling each other's blood to cover up that fact—to perform vengeful human sacrifices in the service of an illusion—seems a terrible if commonplace mistake.

When Hamlet says that his imagination can "trace the noble dust of Alexander, till 'a find it stopping a bunghole," Horatio warns him that "'Twere to consider too curiously, to consider so" (5.1.203–06). It is not merely "the dread of something after death" that robs "enterprises of great pitch and moment" of "the name of action" (3.1.77–87); the dread of nothing after death can have a similar effect. Earlier in the play, when Rosencrantz tries to attribute Hamlet's distraction to his worldly ambitions, Hamlet replies, "I could be bounded in a nutshell, and count myself a king of infinite space—were it not that I have bad dreams" (2.2.254–56). The prospect of a universe infinite in space and time would disable human ambitions and destroy the human psyche, if it were not tamed by rituals, fictions, and selective perceptions. Better a king of a nutshell than a slave of the infinite. Hamlet's too curious dreams may have shown him that his worldly reign (like Alexander's) is nightmarishly lost in a vastness beyond measure.

If there is nothing to live for, at least there may be something to live *by,* and that something seems to be art as much as love, duty, honor, or (even) God. By the time Hamlet completes his revenge, he seems no longer to be working at the behest of the ghost, but on behalf of an unfathomable need to achieve shape and purpose in his own foreshortened lifetime. His metatheatrical consolation is that he dies as part of a meaningful and repeatable story. It is really the audience, on-stage and off, that is in danger of resting in silence, pallor, and oblivion:

> You that look pale, and tremble at this chance,
> That are but mutes or audience to this act,
> Had I but time—as this fell sergeant, Death,
> Is strict in his arrest—O, I could tell you—

But let it be. Horatio, I am dead,
Thou livest. Report me and my cause aright
To the unsatisfied.

                                    (5.2.334–40)

Anticipating his arrest to a new kind of prison, Hamlet here again resurrects his father's spirit in the process of avenging it: like the ghost, he turns his audience fearfully pale, withholds his secrets, but asks that he be remembered and thereby justified. This time Horatio will have to perform the moralizing and immortalizing work that Shakespeare himself performs, and in a similar way.

But all this telling will be lost to Hamlet, who concentrates on the completion of his earthly story, no longer on any prospect of a judgment beyond:

Fortinbras . . . has my dying voice.
So tell him, with th' occurrents more and less
Which have solicited—the rest is silence.
                    HORATIO
Now cracks a noble heart. Good night, sweet prince,
And flights of angels sing thee to thy rest!

                                    (5.2.356–60)

Under the immediate pressure of mourning, the stoic skeptic tries desperately to supply the transcendent music that seems to have forsaken his friend at the moment of death, tries at least to reinterpret that silence as a musical "rest" preparatory to an immortal song (Quinlan 306). But the music that immediately answers Horatio's plea is merely a drum, a sound—whether it proclaims victory or death—of determined destruction. Like the heartbeats of Henry King's "Exequy" that propel him inexorably closer to their silencing and his death, they speak of a forced march through time to timelessness.

When Fortinbras arrives, he sounds like a spokesman for a conventional view of heroic death that the play itself has rendered obsolete:

This quarry cries on havoc. O proud death,
What feast is toward in thine eternal cell,
That thou so many princes at a shot
So bloodily hast strook?

                                    (5.2.364–67)

The anthropomorphizing of death—even where it is disguised as a grim surrender, as it is here—is in fact a consoling fiction. Death (*pace* John Donne) is not proud; nor is it ashamed. The terror lies in its indifference, which steals away the differences by which and for which we live. At its Lasting Supper, "king and beggar are but variable service." The princes who fall bloodily at once would all soon enough have descended in age and sickness to their tombs, no more or less dead than paupers. As in the gravedigger's riddles, the high drama of a gallows must yield place to the sheer duration of a grave (5.1.41–59). A story of royal murder has become a story of human decay, death has become less a ghost than a skull, and the efforts to conceal it by hasty burial (of King Hamlet, Polonius, Ophelia) now yield to the stark deliberate staging of all available corpses (5.2.378, 396).

Shakespeare does not give his ghost the last word, as many revenge tragedians do. The final music of the play is not even that ominous drum, but the numbing, death-bearing sound of the soldiers' memorial shooting. The rest *is* silence, or might as well be. Fortinbras's closing suggestion that all this bloodshed would have been acceptable if it had occurred on the battlefield (5.2.402) reflects his psychological need to keep death safely contained within the ancient ritual known as war. It may also alert modern readers to a more urgent need that runs contrary to Fortinbras's conventional denial: the need, in a century of holocaust and potential holocaust, to eliminate the justifying, distancing category of war, to force ourselves to see in war all the individual deaths, which are each inherently tragic.

So why not give up the ghost? All that phantasm can give of life is a mission to lead it to its end, as Polonius and old Fortinbras and old Hamlet gave to their sons, as parents give to children in all times and places. The world is still full of Cold and Holy Warriors, armies propelled at each other in bloody vengeance by the ghosts of their fathers in armor. Perhaps Horatio is right that "there needs no ghost . . . come from the grave / To tell us" that a villain is a knave (1.5.125–26), but we certainly must be acting on supernatural information to conclude that people we have never met deserve for us to kill them. The ghost's words threaten Hamlet's ear with effects strikingly similar to those of Claudius's poison (compare 1.5.15–22 with 1.5.68–73); rumors "infect [Laertes'] ear / With pestilent speeches of his father's death" (4.5.90–91). Is there any worse poison that could

be poured in our ears than these legacies of blame and hatred? *Hamlet*
converts John's admonition in the New Testament—"Beloved, do not
believe every spirit, but test the spirits to see whether they are of
God"[6]—into a parable urgently applicable to a modern secular world.
Whether or not Prosser is correct in diagnosing a recognizable Elizabethan demon, this kind of ghost seems dangerously unholy, his
Annunciation a malediction. To identify the ghost as the incarnation
of Hamlet's feelings (Greg, Kirsch) may be to reverse the case: Hamlet
is martyred as an Incarnation of his father's desires, desires not for
mercy but for punishment. Again, revenge entails not just a violation,
but a parody, of Christian orthodoxy.

Recognizing the essential arbitrariness of the ghost's dictates and
Hamlet's obedience, recognizing in them desperate responses—by
father *and* son, by playwright *and* audience—to a situation to which
no response can be sensible, may liberate us in the opposite way
from Hamlet. We may be free to obey neither God the Father nor
the fathers' ghosts when they tell us to kill each other on behalf of
our immortality. If the world is, as Hamlet suggests, a prison, then
we should at least understand our sentence, and recognize our fellow-
prisoners. Denmark has gone from Eden to prison to killing-field to
graveyard. If we follow ghosts to a deadly brink, if we follow generals
to pointless battles, if we blindly trust some paternal deity to shape
our deadly ends, it will be easy enough to take our world along the
same path.

To interpret *Hamlet* this polemical way is to give up the ghost as
a real justification or consolation, isolating it instead within the fictive
form as a provisional projection of the various mythologies by which
we mortals sustain a sense of purpose. But exorcism is itself a risky
process, and not a simple one. Claudius convinces Laertes that abjuring revenge for our lost kin would mean abjuring love for them as
well. Hamlet fears the same equation, and fears more deeply that
giving up such ghosts might mean giving up entirely. My own lapsed-
preacher father, many years dead, comes in a transparency across the
mind's eye as I write. In many ways, the compelling ghost of a father
is a nightmare devoutly to be wished, but it will not tell the secrets
of its house, and at the crowing of the cock, it is gone again:

HAMLET
Do you see nothing there?

QUEEN
Nothing at all, yet all that is I see.
HAMLET
Nor did you nothing hear?
QUEEN
No, nothing but ourselves.
(3.4.131–33)

Notes

1. My inspiration in this line of thinking was Ernest Becker's devastatingly brilliant work of psychology, sociology, and philosophy. Since I began writing this piece, James L. Calderwood and Kirby Farrell have brought Becker's perspective to bear on Shakespearean drama. Also in this interim, Marjorie Garber has discussed the way absent presences help to construct and deconstruct the meaning of works such as *Hamlet*.

2. Alexander Welsh keenly recognizes that "revenge is a function of mourning" (482), but his sensible reminder that "two deaths do not make a life" (496–97) may not seem as true to the subconscious as it does to the conscious mind. As Welsh notes (486), the ancestors of *Hamlet* include Kyd's *The Spanish Tragedy,* in which the newly bereaved Hieronimo says, "To know the author were some ease of grief, / For in revenge my heart would find relief." Compare Ferenze's similar complaint in Marlowe's *The Jew of Malta,* 3.2.14, cited by Kirsch (17).

3. Hamlet mimics these symptoms when he visits Ophelia disguised as a sort of *memento amori,* "Pale as his shirt . . . / . . . / As if he had been loosed out of hell / To speak of horrors," letting out an expiration that seems to "end his being," and finds his way out "without his eyes" (2.1.78–95). Perhaps he is testing whether his dead self will be as pathetically rejected by his beloved as his father's dead self has been.

4. Avi Erlich (203) points out that this ghost makes "night hideous" instead of "wholesome," bringing news of a corruption through sexuality (the medium of Original Sin and hence mortality) that inverts the Glad Tidings enabled by Christ's virgin birth. Erlich puts this observation in service of a psychoanalytic diagnosis of Hamlet's "highly complex search, partially unconscious, for a strong father" (260); I prefer to associate this search with the more general symbolic need for some mission in life that death does not simply cancel.

5. Roland M. Frye (258) insists that Hamlet's remark is perfectly compatible with an expectation of Christian afterlife; but the contrast with the compelled speech of Hamlet's revenant father, and the correction ("flights of angels sing thee to thy rest") urgently offered by Horatio, suggest otherwise.

6. First Letter 4.1; see Joseph 493–94. See also Isaiah 8.19: "Should they consult the dead on behalf of the living?"

Works Cited

Andrews, Michael Cameron. *This Action of Our Death: The Performance of Death in English Renaissance Drama.* Newark: Associated Univ. Presses, 1989.

Ariès, Philippe. *Western Attitudes toward Death: From the Middle Ages to the Present.* Trans. Patricia M. Ranum. Baltimore: Johns Hopkins UP, 1974.

Becker, Ernest. *The Denial of Death.* New York: Free Press, 1973.

Calderwood, James L. *Shakespeare and the Denial of Death.* Amherst: U of Massachusetts P, 1987.

Erlich, Avi. *Hamlet's Absent Father.* Princeton: Princeton UP, 1977.

Farrell, Kirby. *Play, Death, and Heroism in Shakespeare.* Chapel Hill: U of North Carolina P, 1989.

Frye, Roland Mushat. *The Renaissance* Hamlet. Princeton: Princeton UP, 1984.

Garber, Majorie. *Shakespeare's Ghost Writers: Literature as Uncanny Causality.* London: Methuen, 1987.

Greg, W. W. "Hamlet's Hallucination." *Modern Language Review* 12 (1917): 393–421.

Joseph, (Sister) Miriam. "Discerning the Ghost in *Hamlet.*" *PMLA* 76 (1961): 493–502.

Kirsch, Arthur. "Hamlet's Grief." *ELH* 48 (1981): 17–36.

Knight, G. Wilson. *The Wheel of Fire.* 5th ed. Cleveland: World, 1964.

Levin, Richard. *New Readings vs. Old Plays.* Chicago: U of Chicago P, 1979.

Lewis, C. S. "Hamlet: The Prince or the Poem." *Proceedings of the British Academy* 28 (1942): 139–54.

Lyons, Bridget Gellert. *Voices of Melancholy: Studies in Literary Treatments of Melancholy in Renaissance England.* New York: Norton, 1971.

Prosser, Eleanor. *Hamlet and Revenge.* Stanford: Stanford UP, 1967.

Quinlan, Maurice J. "Shakespeare and the Catholic Burial Services." *Shakespeare Quarterly* 5 (1954): 303–06.

Shakespeare, William. *The Riverside Shakespeare.* Gnl. ed. G. Blakemore Evans. Boston: Houghton, 1974.

Stein, Arnold. *The House of Death: Messages from the English Renaissance.* Baltimore: Johns Hopkins UP, 1986.

Van Tassel, Daniel E. "Clarence, Claudio, and Hamlet." *Renaissance and Reformation* ns 7 (1983): 48–62.

Welsh, Alexander. "The Task of Hamlet." *Yale Review* 69 (1979–80): 481–502.

Reforming Prince Hal: The Sovereign Inheritor in 2 Henry IV

JONATHAN CREWE

THE "MATTER of Hal's redemption," as A. R. Humphreys, the Arden editor of *2 Henry IV,* calls it, may now seem too stale or tainted for further consideration.[1] It has certainly been discussed at length, and to go on talking about it now is to risk the charge of reviving the ideological discourse of the centered, sovereign, masculine subject. Resisting this possibility is in fact one imperative of a developing critique in Shakespeare studies, the stakes of which are declared to be high.[2] This risk aside, the notion of Hal's reform may still seem question-begging. The most influential current arguments deny that there is any substantive reform of Prince Hal's character. These are the arguments, associated mainly with Stephen Greenblatt, which insist on Hal's role-playing, and hence on the theatricality of his madcap character and of the metamorphosis he effects in *1 Henry IV.*[3]

Instead of confronting these arguments directly, I shall simply point out that, for better or worse, their privileged text is *1,* not *2, Henry IV.*[4] The definitiveness of this theatrical reading of Prince Hal, based on *1 Henry IV,* is implicitly challenged by *2 Henry IV,* and then again by *Henry V.* In each of these plays the matter of Prince Hal's reform is reinvestigated, while the reform itself is reattempted, either by Hal in his own person or—interpretively—by others on his behalf.[5] Yet the *repetition* of the reform-attempt begins to call for its own accounting. Its apparent compulsiveness (or sociopolitical compulsoriness) implies that a good deal is invested in it, not just by Hal, but by those in the plays who expect it of him—and then also by Shakespeare, by subsequent interpreters, and perhaps by a political imperative of "reform" that Shakespeare receives and transmits. At the same time, the sheer fact of repetition makes it increasingly difficult to imagine in what successful reform would consist.

In fact, *2 Henry IV* confronts us with just those issues. As already noted by the Arden editor, the play proceeds as if the reformation effected (or enacted) by Prince Hal in *1 Henry IV* had never happened. In his own eyes, in his father's eyes, and evidently in the eyes of the world, Prince Hal is still the unreformed scapegrace prince.[6] This seemingly burdened prince keeps anticipating—or is it desperately resisting?—his own reform right up to the moment of his father's death:

> O, let me in my present wildness die,
> And never live to show th'incredulous world
> The noble change that I have purposed!
> (4.5.152–54)

What is implied by such deferral, resistance or incapacity? What is at stake *in* reform? What is to be understood by the noble change Hal claims to purpose—and with which he is credited by his father at the moment in which the crown changes hands?[7]

These questions will lead on to further questions if, as I believe, *2 Henry IV* reveals a deepening Shakespearean preoccupation with mechanisms of "legitimate" change and succession, not just in the historical narrative of the Henry plays, but at every level including that of his own textual composition.[8] What I suggest, in effect, is that the fluid, somewhat facile, theatrical and/or metamorphic dynamics of reform invoked in *1 Henry IV,* enabling Hal as "Renaissance prince" to effect his own spectacular transformation at Shrewsbury, come into question in *2 Henry IV.* On one hand, mysterious resistances to reform surface in the latter play, while on the other hand the ever-questionable attainment of reform is staged in such a way as to pose more fundamentally than in *1 Henry IV* the question of Hal's legitimizing transformation: in what does it consist, or how, *faute de mieux,* is it managed? While no simple counter-model to that of spectacular metamorphosis necessarily emerges, *2 Henry IV* reopens the question of change-as-reformation; in doing so, it calls upon us to discover new interpretive resources or at least adapt existing ones to deal with the important as well as time-honored question of this reform.

To begin with a sidelong glance at some interpretive leads that I shall not pursue, it could be argued that the inconclusive repetition of Hal's reform in *2 Henry IV* skeptically exposes the emptiness or *un*thinkability of the historical reform-scripts Shakespeare inherits, or even of the Prince Hal character he inherits from earlier texts. Enough Pyrrhonism is in the air Shakespeare breathes—and in the Rumor prologue to *2 Henry IV*—for this to be entirely possible. Shakespeare's apparent derealization of reform in *2 Henry IV* could also be an effect of its displacement. The failure of "reform" to materialize where one is looking for it, for example in the life of Prince Hal, does not mean that it simply fails to materialize. Indeed, Greenblatt implies that a displacement of reform *is* effected in the Henry plays. Prince Hal's onstage reform may be empty in the sense of being merely played, yet "reforming" Prince Hal also becomes the one who, occupying the inside/outside position of the master-anthropologist in relation to the realm, will learn all its languages before substantively re-forming it as Henry V.[9] The reform, in other words, will not be the interior one that Prince Hal undergoes as a character, but the one he effectively imposes as a centralizing, homogenizing, and nationalizing ruler, appropriating and transmuting all the wild, polyglot diversity of an unreformed Britain. Yet this critical displacement of reform, which is also a strong, conservative reclamation of it, again relies primarily on *1 Henry IV,* and confirms the tendency in Shakespeare criticism to read *2 Henry IV* as a straightforward narrative and logical extension (if not a diminished repetition) of *1 Henry IV.* The surprising annulment, however, of the previous play's reform action in *2 Henry IV* constitutes a virtual starting over. Implicit in this curious new beginning is the suggestion that the reform-mechanisms of *1 Henry IV,* which Prince Hal has exploited with a certain opportunistic brilliance, are no longer effectual—or were so only in appearance. These seemingly discounted mechanisms of "reform" will include theatrical metamorphosis, in which Hal has certainly been adept, but also various equivalent forms of facile change or exchange troped in *1 Henry IV* and consciously manipulated by Hal. It is he, after all, who appropriates and reverses his father's thesis that he is a misbegotten changeling while Hotspur is the real princely son. It is he who thinks that characters can be "reformed" by positional changes since they are not real in the first place. It is he, finally, who thinks that the commodity-form of character enables one to be exchanged for another (Harry Percy for Harry Monmouth), or enables a good composite character to be acquired through the appropriation of others' desirable properties, including, as Hotspur complains, their "stolen" youth. Yet if none of this has really worked, we may have to conclude that reform doesn't mean change or exchange, nor does it mean the staged appearance of change. What then, to repeat the question, does or could it mean in *2 Henry IV?* How are we to construe it?

Let us briefly recall some of the data concerning the young Henry V that Shakespeare incorporates and revises. Various chronicle accounts of the young Henry V, including near-contemporary ones, mention not just that the unconstrained prince was a reveller, but that he gathered a formidable popular following which included gentry and commoners. Most Tudor accounts of Henry V, including those in Elyot's *Boke of the Gouernor* (1531), Redmayne's *Vita Henrici Quinti* (1540), Holinshed's *Chronicles* (1587), and Stow's *Annales* (1592) mention Henry's having given the Chief Justice a box on the ear, but also mention punishments that include the young Henry's imprisonment and dismissal from the Privy Council (Humphreys xxix–xlii). The assault on the Chief Justice was, in other words, taken seriously as the political gesture of a popular usurper-manqué threatening to repeat his father's history. In *The Famous Victories* the young Henry behaves, as Humphreys puts it, like a hooligan, though this so-called hooliganism can also be read as a legitimate popular politics of festive (and theatrical) revolt. Recognizing here a difficulty of critical description, but perhaps also of dramatic characterization, we might say that Shakespeare produces a disconcertingly censored and/or agreeably refined version of the young Henry V of folklore, chronicle, and *The Famous Victories of Henry V.* At all events the Arden editor describes Hal's alleged madcap revelling in *1 Henry IV* as harmless, and as essentially nonexistent in *2 Henry IV* (Humphreys xli). This is a marked departure from the sources on Shakespeare's part—or, to put it differently, it is a conspicuous rewriting of the young Henry. Insofar as Shakespeare renders the wild prince surprisingly tame or inactive—and apparently less political—he may appear self-defeatingly to void the dramatic action of reform by removing in advance any real need or occasion for it.

Despite this apparent voiding, a persistent "need" for reform as well as an action supposedly effecting it continues to be inscribed in *2 Henry IV.* As external or objective conditions giving rise to this need vanish, however, the need itself may increasingly seem to belong to an order of shared psychic compulsion rather than political or moral obligation. Indeed, the tame, passive, and increasingly ironized Prince Hal who finds himself subject to the widespread demand that he reform begins to resemble his chronological near-twin in the Shakespearean canon, namely Prince Hamlet, an "inward" protagonist oppressed and divided by a troublesome demand.

Such an interior shift, in which psychic (in)action is "substituted" for physical and/or overtly political action, is by no means unusual in Shakespeare. Yet it is not necessarily a shift *from* the political to the psychological. Rather, it is a move in which, characteristically, the psychic interior is politicized while the political exterior is correspondingly psychologized—that is, subjected to psychic "laws."[10] This crossing isn't one in which the differentiated and *prima facie* opposed realms of the political and the psychological are simply deconstructed, but rather one in which a certain reciprocal reconstruction is effected between these orders without the difference between them ever being effaced. A proposal simply to shift *from* political to psychoanalytic reading of *2 Henry IV* would accordingly be misplaced; what is required, I believe, is a reading that takes account of this putative crossover. Whether we want to speak in the final analysis of a psychologized politics or a politicized psychology, it is in such hybrid terms that the reform action of *2 Henry IV* takes on whatever degree of intelligibility can be claimed for it. That, at least, is the proposition according to which I shall now proceed.[11]

* * *

Whatever initial effect of unintelligibility may be produced by the reform-action(s) of the Henry plays does not arise from any shortage of models and contexts, historical and otherwise, for Prince Hal's reform. Well-recognized models, which are neither fully discrete nor fully successive, include those of a New Testament theology of the "new man," of medieval psychomachia, of disciplinary humanist pedagogy, and even of ego-psychology. Coercive vectors of reform include those of Renaissance subject-formation, of censorship and "courtly" refinement in the public theater, and—broadly speaking—of what Norbert Elias has called the civilizing process.[12] The dominant model that has been applied to Hal's reform is also, however, one that renders it less rather than more intelligible: this is the model of the prodigal son.[13] The prodigal-model is a tellingly *failed* one partly because it is not a narrative of primogeniture—of the scapegrace *eldest* son who is nevertheless to be the sovereign inheritor—but if anything a narrative somewhat subversive of that rigorously "unjust" principle. It is above all a model that acknowledges no parricidal impulse or dynamic in the process of reform and hence of "legitimate" or "authentic" succession. If anything, once again, that dynamic is forestalled, or displaced into sibling rivalry and reconciliation, in the prodigal son story. This refusal in any sense to license parricide is the condition on which patriarchal law and order properly so called can be maintained.

The action (or inaction) of reform in the Henry plays conspicuously does take account of the parricidal moment in the process of sovereign succession. So, implicitly, do the chronicles in presenting the young Henry as a usurper-manqué who raises his hand against the paternal lawgiver in the person of the Chief Justice. So does *The Famous Victories,* in which Hal's impatience for his father's death is an explicit motif, assimilated to his general wildness.[14] This parricidal recognition is accompanied in *2 Henry IV* by an increased emphasis, rising to the pitch of apocalyptic hysteria in a late speech by Henry IV, on Hal's "wildness" as covert murderous savagery rather than mere youthful excess. In the eyes of Henry, the ailing, threatened father, the son's wildness constitutes an unreformed interior that must always be socially dissimulated. Correspondingly, any innocuous revelling or even show of reform on the part of Prince Hal will be taken as dissimulation, the hidden content of which can be expected to emerge once he has succeeded to the throne. Thus Henry IV prophesies a wild apocalypse brought on by the unreformed, and perhaps unreformable, prince:

> Harry the fifth is crown'd! Up, vanity!
> Down, royal state! All you sage counsellors, hence!
> And to the English court assemble now
> From every region, apes of idleness!
> Now, neighbour confines, purge you of your scum!
> Have you a ruffian that will swear, drink, dance,
> Revel the night, rob, murder, and commit
> The oldest sins the newest kind of ways?
> . . . .
> . . . the fifth Harry from curb'd licence plucks
> The muzzle of restraint, and the wild dog
> Shall flesh his tooth of every innocent.
>
> . . . .
> O, thou wilt be a wilderness again,
> Peopled with wolves, thy old inhabitants!
> (4.5.119–37)

Despite its prophetic hysteria, Henry's vision isn't wholly inconsistent with the expanded *potentiality* given in *2 Henry IV* to resistant wildness and the "need" to reform. Nor is it inconsistent with the threatened tragic declension of wildness from relatively harmless masquing and revelling in *1 Henry IV* to savagery in *2 Henry IV*. In other words, it is not just the issue of parricidal succession, but of a corresponding predatory "wildness" resistant to any transformation—a wildness anterior and *interior* to civility, to the process of lawful inheritance, and to legitimized political rule—that *2 Henry IV* appears to take more seriously than does its predecessor. As this issue surfaces, the historical contingencies of Bolingbroke's "parricidal" usurpation and Hal's wildness may seem increasingly to belong to an order of necessity—in which case Henry IV's prophecy may also begin to sound like hysterical denial.

Insofar as succession is conceived to be wild in *2 Henry IV*, and to be so of necessity, its dynamic may seem to originate or inhere in the male character or specifically male *agency*, not as a natural fact but as the consequence of what I have already referred to as a politicized psychology or psychologized politics of sovereign succession. It is this agency that is "missing" in *1 Henry IV*, and from the reform that would, in effect, make Hal the inheritor in a theater-state. Under the "post-theatrical" regime of *2 Henry IV*, the sovereign inheritor will be required to reform in order to legitimize himself, but will also (contradictorily) be required not to reform in order to succeed. Moreover, the paternal demand for reform will seem like an effort to forestall rather than facilitate succession by taming—emasculating—the sovereign inheritor. Under these circumstances, Hal's constant anticipation and *deferral* of reform become intelligible, as do his curious paralysis and avoidance of his father. Yet it is not through Prince Hal and his father alone that the difficulties or even contradictions of reform are precipitated out in the play. Falstaff is exultantly unreformed and unreformable; he and his cronies, fond recallers of their wild youth, help at least as much as do Prince Hal and his father to unpack reform in the play.

At one level, the Falstaff-Shallow-Silence episodes function as a wickedly satirical exposure of "original" male deficiency rather than wild excess. There is no need to belabor the point that the wild youth of Shallow and Silence is a nostalgically recalled condition, denied by their contemporary, Falstaff. Their wild youth as unreformed students belongs to a commonplace nostalgic script, beloved of the law-abiding elderly. No need either to belabor the point that, insofar as Falstaff has claims to be the real wild man of the play, he is a wild *old* man. If anything, wildness is more plausibly the social condition of the old man than the young one, and it is more plausibly a function of social denial, marginalization, and conscious impotence than of any supposedly untamed or untamable excess in the "true" male character. In this satirically reductive setting, the name of Fall-staff speaks him no less than do those of Shallow and Silence.

The genuinely funny satirical comedy, as distinct from festive heartiness, of the Falstaff-Shallow-Silence episodes may thus seem to contest the "wild" male character and its ontological violence of agency as well as the process of succession in which it is justifyingly subsumed. Yet the zero-point of final reduction is one at which we never quite arrive. Or, more accurately, the satirical vanishing-point of "wild" maleness turns out to be indistinguishable from its mythic origin, glimpsed in and through Falstaff's alleged recall of the young Shallow:

I do remember him at Clement's Inn, like a man made after supper of a cheese-paring. When a was naked, he was for all the world like a forked radish, with a head fantastically carved upon it with a knife. A was so forlorn, that his dimensions to any thick sight were invisible; a was the very genius of famine, yet lecherous as a monkey, and the whores called him mandrake.
(3.2.302–09)

What this strange "recall" produces is a subhuman or inhuman grotesque of indeterminable sex, or of no sex at all, like the bare, forked animal Lear thinks he sees on the heath. (The apparition here is fully in keeping with Elizabethan folklore regarding the mandrake root: it can look male, female, or androgynous; human or non-human.) Apparently open to any construction—or to no determinate one— the root-like apparition of the young Shallow may all too literally mock any aspiration to get to the root of the matter of reform in terms of gendered character. What we find at the end of the line is literally a root.

At the critical moment, however, the interposition of a "thick-sighted" observer relativizes and equivocates any ontological determination. Furthermore, while the stark-naked Shallow is seen from the start as a remainder—a cheese-paring—rather than a bodily totality, and while he is always and already subsumed in an order of figurative likeness—he is cheese-like, radish-like—this characterization through deficiency is tantamount to masculine *re*characterization in terms of insatiable appetite rather than substance or "matter." Appropriately, it is Falstaff who effects this particular recharacterization. He assimilates any male sexual deficiency to a psychic and bodily economy of "prior" starvation, while, as characteristically, he recalls Shallow in the guise of an edible vegetable—a garden radish— and thus as an object as well as subject of insatiable appetite. It is left to the whores to translate this garden radish (ironically?) into the exotic and erotically mythologized mandrake root. Exotic sexual desire is thus superinduced upon domestic appetite in a novel etiology of the ontologically violent male character. It is evidently in terms of this prior "deprivation" and consequent appetite that greedy Falstaff not only resists reform, but considers himself entitled (and driven) by "law of nature" (3.2.326) to make a regal mouthful of such dace as Shallow—or Prince Hal as inheritor of the kingdom. If it were to be suggested that Falstaff fails in his more extravagant ambitions because he is captive to a dysfunctional conception of ontological necessity and empowerment, it should be recalled that an intuition of the same drive may inform Henry IV's prophecy that Hal's reign will be one of unbridled appetite: "fleshing the tooth on every innocent."

The point to be made here is that the "need" to reform as well as the sources of resistance to it remain curiously undetermined *and* overdetermined in *2 Henry IV* without ceasing to be invoked as crucial to the play's action(s) and outcome(s). I have already suggested that this situation gains a certain intelligibility if it is critically linked to what I have called a psychologized politics or politicized psychology of masculine sovereignty; this linking does not constitute an explanation so much as an attempt to (re)situate the problem where it belongs. At a minimum, the "return" of an ontological violence seemingly displaced from *1 Henry IV* is at issue in *2 Henry IV,* as it is in *Julius Caesar* and *Hamlet.* That this attempt to resituate isn't wholly misplaced is suggested by the terms in which Hal's "reform" and the royal succession are finally staged—or perhaps, *faute de mieux,* stage-managed. This event transpires in the complicated bedroom scene between Hal and his father.

Briefly to reprise, Prince Hal's reform in *1 Henry IV,* climactically staged on the battlefield of Shrewsbury, may seem, in the extended perspective offered by *2 Henry IV,* like a dress rehearsal. There, Prince Hal stages his own spectacular apotheosis for such wondering "choral" onlookers as Vernon, but also kills his rival-twin Hotspur in an act of virtual *Brudermord, unbestraft* in this case. (Falstaff finishes off the job but also decodes it, as the saying goes, by wounding Hotspur in the groin.) Hal then gives full credit for the deed to Falstaff in a way that conveniently masks the doer from most of those onstage if not from the audience. It is as if Henry IV sees through just *this* dissimulation of savagery; his deathlike sleep in *2 Henry IV* accordingly seems like a device of entrapment designed to make Prince Hal show his murderous hand—as Henry believes Hal has done when he seizes the crown and tries it on.

Furthermore, as Henry IV approaches his end, he increasingly sees Prince Hal not just as the feral harbinger of universal wildness/wilderness (wild-boy as wolf-boy) but, in a totalizing projection of sovereign male appetite and desire, as the original totemic despot reborn: a savage "Amurath" rather than a gentle Harry. (Though this is not what Warwick understands to be happening, his observation that the Shakespearean Prince Hal is studying his companions to "gain the language" [4.4.69]—to engross *all* language?—is consistent with this dread.)[15] As if confirming this anticipation, toward the end of the play as well as Henry's life, Hal is suddenly everywhere onstage in the guise of sibling-delegates including the notoriously "cold" Prince John; in Henry's view, however, he also threatens to consume those sibling-agents along with everyone else in the kingdom. This feared outcome is what Henry attempts to forestall by belatedly imploring his son Clarence to become Prince Hal's civilizing mediator while sentimentally fabricating a more humane (if still disturbingly "mixed") character for Prince Hal:

> For he is gracious, if he be observ'd,
> He hath a tear for pity, and a hand
> Open as day for melting charity:
> Yet notwithstanding, being incens'd, he's flint,
> As humorous as winter, and as sudden
> As flaws congealed in the spring of day.
>
> (4.4.30–35)

These scarcely tractable anxieties, which threaten to bedevil any smooth or consensual transfer of power between a threatened father and a supposedly unreformable son, are, however, mitigated by a certain identification on Henry's part with Prince Hal: identification in the sense both of sympathetic recognition and recognition of likeness. Indeed, Henry's dread is also the projection of an unsatisfied appetite upon Prince Hal: specifically, an appetite for the power that he has desired but conspicuously failed to concentrate in himself during his troubled reign. The differences between himself and Prince Hal on which he keeps harping are thus undercut, even in his own mind, by the perception of likeness:

> Most subject is the fattest soil to weeds,
> And he, the noble image of my youth,
> Is overspread with them.
>
> (4.4.54–56)

> This part of his conjoins with my disease,
> And helps to end me.
>
> (4.5.63–64)

It is partly Henry's recognition of likeness that allows a political settlement of the parricidal succession to transpire between him and Hal. It allows Henry to be reconciled to his own deep mortification, and to displacement by one who can be a surrogate-success as well as a rival. It allows Hal's reform to be effected in a mode of vertical rather than horizontal exchange, Harry for Harry again. It allows Henry's own putative hunger and wished-for engorgement to be glimpsed, even as it does Hal's putatively corresponding insatiable appetite:

> How quickly nature falls into revolt
> When gold becomes her object!
>
> .   .   .   .
>
> For this [fathers] have engrossed and pil'd up
> The canker'd heaps of strange-achieved gold.
>
> (4.5.65–71)

Finally, since the "wildness" to be reformed does not constitute a category of absolute difference, or definitively characterize anyone in particular, its putative form and location can be shifted around in the process of settlement.

Briefly, what this situation allows is that wildness in its various aspects as criminality, natural excess, inordinate appetite, and even fulminating disease can *consensually* be transferred from the scapegrace son to the father as original usurper, on one hand allowing it to be buried with the corpse and on the other permitting the instantly reformed son to become the legitimate heir. Hal can then ostentatiously place himself under the paternal law, embodied in the Chief Justice, and begin laying down the law himself. As soon as Henry "confesses," the reforming and legitimating bargain is sealed:

> For all the soil of the achievement goes
> With me into the earth. It seem'd in me
> But as an honour snatch'd with boist'rous hand.
>   (4.5.189–91)

The sole acknowledgment of this parricidal "boisterousness" will not only be in the past tense, but will occur in the moment in which the violent hand is being transferred for burial from son to father.

This relatively diplomatic transaction does, however, have a price. It is paid by neither party to the transaction, and the payment exacted is such as to suggest that the dynamics of the play do indeed belong to a psychologized politics or politicized psychology of specifically masculine sovereignty. In the complicated transfer we witness, the Oedipal scenario is conspicuously reconstructed as one of exclusively male agency, empowerment and succession. It is Prince Hal as inheritor who, in a state of sublime innocence or Machiavellian callousness, reads the Oedipal situation as one in which the woman is always and already displaced by the crown as substitute-object, which is to say as object substituted for her, but also as object constituted in her likeness:

> Why doth the crown lie there upon his pillow,
> Being so troublesome a bedfellow?
> O polish'd perturbation! golden care!
>   (4.5.20–22)

Syntactically, as Hal presumably doesn't register, it remains undetermined which bedfellow is troublesome to which, yet the woman has been displaced by the crown as the pursued and piously denied object of appetite, while the void figure of the feminine (*res nulla*) has been appropriated and transmuted into the substantial figure of masculine sovereignty.[16] If this displacement and transmutation of the woman can't be effected without a remainder of "feminine" meretriciousness or troublesomeness, that remainder can in turn be identified as the cause of any violent disturbance, not just in men but between them. Indeed, it enables the *crown* to be incriminated as the real parricidal agent, threatening and coming between generations of men, but also, once identified as the source of the trouble, facilitating their diplomatic reconciliation:

> Accusing it, I put it on my head,
> To try with it, as with an enemy
> That had before my face murder'd my father,
> The quarrel of a true inheritor.
>
> (4.5.165–68)

"The quarrel of a true inheritor"—the bad yet still seemingly "necessary" parricidal one—is realigned to become the good quarrel of the inheritor with the intermediate parricidal agent/object, while this object can in turn be reclaimed as the sullied/solid currency of a benign transaction between father and son. What is *sacrificed* to the settlement of parricidal succession is evidently the woman; what is appropriated for it is women's agency. Political Shakespeare with a vengeance.[17]

This version of reform as parricidal transfer and place-changing, in which the parricide is also backdated to Henry's usurpation of Richard II, is of course no more absolute or final than the theatrical metamorphosis enacted in *1 Henry IV.* It is undone again in *Henry V,* while the brutal exclusionary reduction of the woman is "liberalized" inasmuch as Henry V's legitimation turns out to depend on the lawfulness of female inclusion in the royal line. Henry V must also eventually confront a French Catherine as potentially troublesome and usurping bedfellow, whose language he is far from having engrossed, and in relation to whom his provincial tongue seems disabled. Moreover, in the process of translation during the courtship, language is punningly "engrossed" again in the sense of being resexualized; this dirty talk isn't Henry V's *forté.*[18]

Inconclusiveness notwithstanding, what I should like to suggest in conclusion is that our critical tendency to elide or "forget" *2 Henry IV* in this tetralogy, at the same time critically and affectively privileging *1 Henry IV,* is related to an apparent displacement of ontological violence and corresponding, agreeable theatrical facilitation in *1 Henry IV.* This tendency to overlook *2 Henry IV* is heightened by a certain critical tradition in which its disillusioning traits, including the waning, sickening, or fading in it of the bright stars of *1 Henry IV,* are emphasized, as is the devaluation of the royal currency. Yet in addition to getting down to some *Realpolitik* glossed over in *1 Henry IV, 2 Henry IV* marks the "return" of an ontological violence neither fully locatable nor fully erasable in the contexts of Shakespeare's production. It is the critique of such violence, which cannot be regarded as fully performed even if it is desired in our own political and professional contexts, that recalling *2 Henry IV* facilitates.

Notes

1. By "matter" Humphreys means primarily the extensive chronicle materials on which Shakespeare draws in the Henry plays (as in the traditional phrase "the matter of Britain"), but the term resonates beyond that denotation (xix). His term "redemption" appropriately invokes the religious and morality-drama context(s) of Hal's putative betterment. My choice of the term "reform" emphasizes secular contexts, including that of a disciplinary, character-forming humanism. Mention of Hal's "reformation" will, however, recall the Protestant epoch in which the play was written. See also Dickinson 33–46.

2. This critique is widely implied in radical new historicism and/or feminism, partly in response to the reading of Prince Hal in Stephen Greenblatt's "Invisible Bullets: Renaissance Authority and Its Subversion." Traditional readings subject to this critique would include all ego-psychological ones as well as C. L. Barber's festive-political reading, in which Prince Hal progressively manifests his "sovereign nature" (192–221).

3. "Invisible Bullets" is the *locus classicus* for this argument. It does envisage some changes in Prince Hal in *2 Henry IV*, but not of the positive kind associated with self-improvement.

4. The theatrical reading depends partly on Hal's self-unmasking in the "I know you all" soliloquy in *1 Henry IV* (1.1.192–214). The revisions effected in *2 Henry IV* suggest that this speech embodies the young prince's fantasy of masterful knowledge as theatrical knowledge, soon to be dispelled.

5. Interpretively by various interested characters in the Henry plays, including the politic archbishop of Canterbury in *Henry V,* who finds that, at the moment of Henry IV's death, Hal's "wildness, mortified in him / Seem'd to die too . . . consideration like an angel came / And whipp'd th' offending Adam out of him / Leaving his body as a paradise" (1.1.27–31). Quite soon, however, the clerics get down to postlapsarian business, which consists in making a preemptively large contribution to Henry's military budget.

6. This peculiarity is extensively discussed by Humphreys, who properly relates it to the problem of the relationship between *1* and *2 Henry IV.* While questionably accepting that "redemptions" do occur in both plays, he concludes that "naturalistically speaking these twin-redemptions are an incoherence, [yet] dramatically and by folktale or morality canons they are acceptable" (xxviii). Humphreys concludes, moreover, that the two versions of Hal's "redemption" are radically incompatible: while the playful version in *1 Henry IV* comes from Daniel and *The Famous Victories,* the serious, father's-deathbed version comes from Holinshed.

7. "Noble change" is a peculiarly resonant phrase. While the change effected in *1 Henry IV* hardly merits the description "noble," the phrase invokes such change in

the field of the play's representation but also in contexts such as those of Elizabethan upward mobility, of disciplinary humanism, of ruling-class appropriation of popular culture and theater, and even of self-sacrificial assumption of the burden of kingship. It is understandable, then, that the process of noble change may seem at once bafflingly complex, compulsory, and subject to endless resistance. I shall deal with the question largely in terms of the play's representation rather than of its implied contexts.

8. Jonathan Goldberg's *Writing Matter* enables us to conceive of this particular displacement of the reform-action. It could be said that the action is displaced to the level of Shakespeare's "reforming" authorship and textual revision, to which considerations similar to those of Hal's reform may apply. Under this assumption, questions regarding Shakespeare's authorial "character" and the notoriously troublesome *text* of *2 Henry IV* take on paramount importance. The process of "theatrical legitimation" that Timothy Murray sees being pursued by Jonson as author and editor is also, *mutatis mutandis,* pursued by Shakespeare.

9. The republication of Greenblatt's "Invisible Bullets" in *Shakespearean Negotiations: The Circulation of Social Energy in Renaissance England* brings it under the purview of new categories of displacement, circulation, etc.

10. The apparent phenomenon of the interior shift generally results in a critical shift toward psychological (psychoanalytic) reading of Shakespeare. What can easily be overlooked is the simultaneous shift in the other direction in Shakespeare, such that the represented political world seems increasingly governed by psychological "laws."

11. I take it that implicit recognition of psychologized politics and/or politicized psychology has been widespread during the past decade, notably in politically conscious Freudian (often feminist) criticism. This is the critical recognition which, without necessarily crystallizing into a fully coherent model, informs my discussion. An essay that importantly embodies this recognition with reference to Shakespeare is Jacqueline Rose, "Sexuality in the Reading of Shakespeare: *Hamlet* and *Measure for Measure."*

12. The pertinence of courtesy literature and conduct books need hardly be insisted upon. Part of Hal's "reforming" consists in his "fashioning" (self-fashioning?) as a courtier and a gentleman. However, see Elias for the most sweeping contextualization of this process.

13. We have been taught to recognize the sophisticated refinement, allegorization, and economic transcription of the prodigal reform-model during the English sixteenth century by critics, notably including Helgerson and Hutson. Nonetheless, my point stands.

14. I don't assume that "wildness" is mere code for parricide in the play; rather, parricide appears to inhere in a more diffuse wildness. It is around parricide, nevertheless, that diffuse wildness seems to become centripetally organized toward the end of the reform-action in *2 Henry IV.* Harold Jenkins notes that the young Henry V is not just a historic figure but a folkloristic wild-boy, hence some of the "trickiness" of his reform in the Henry plays (Humphreys xxvi–xxvii). A pervasively invoked "wildness" in the Henry plays can sometimes be construed as that of the wild sign in an otherwise stable signifying system, or of the wild card—the joker—in a pack otherwise stably denominated. If Hal is the character most often associated with these forms of

wildness, perhaps especially as the changeling-figure in *1 Henry IV,* he is by no means exclusively so. Part of the difficulty in staging any reform-action is the elusive, boundary-crossing character of this "wildness"; however, the "solution" in *2 Henry IV* depends on this mobility.

15. Here it is pertinent to recall that "engrossing" means writing in the sixteenth century—Shakespeare's all-engrossing mastery of the language clearly makes him a threatening figure for the paranoid or even just anxious interpreter.

16. Some of my locutions here are indebted to Eve Kosofsky Sedgwick, *Between Men: English Literature and Male Homosocial Desire.* It would appear that the transactions she identifies "between men" can occur vertically between father and son as well as horizontally between sibling-like rivals. See also Berger and Holland.

17. The atrocities ascribed to the Welshwomen at the beginning of *1 Henry IV* include mutilation of men's corpses on the battlefield. Sure enough, this "unmanly" power will be appropriated and re-gendered by Falstaff-Hal in the killing of Hotspur. The falling-silent and disappearance of women in the course of the so-called Henriad (the English epic-manqué constructed by modern critics) is conspicuous.

18. Some of the oddity of Prince Hal's character comes from his overt sexual apathy, idle Falstaffian talk of his sexual adventures notwithstanding. The repression of an indeterminate sexuality, which will include at least a homosexual component, is inevitably to be suspected. The word "wild" could be applied to homosexuality, though not exclusively to it as a sexual practice, in the sixteenth century (Bray 25–27).

Works Cited

Barber, C. L. "Rule and Misrule in *Henry IV.*" In his *Shakespeare's Festive Comedy: A Study of Dramatic Form and Its Relation to Social Custom.* Princeton: Princeton UP, 1959. 192–221.

Berger, Harry, Jr. "Psychoanalyzing the Shakespearean Text: The First Three Scenes of the *Henriad.*" Parker and Hartman 210–29.

Bray, Alan. *Homosexuality in Renaissance England.* London: Gay Men's Press, 1982.

Cohen, Walter. "Political Criticism of Shakespeare." Howard and O'Connor 18–46.

Dickinson, Hugh. "The Reformation of Prince Hal." *Shakespeare Quarterly* 12 (1961): 33–46.

Dollimore, Jonathan, and Alan Sinfield, eds. *Political Shakespeare: New Essays in Cultural Materialism.* Ithaca: Cornell UP, 1985.

Drakakis, John, ed. *Alternative Shakespeares.* London: Methuen, 1985.

Elias, Norbert. *The Civilizing Process: The Development of Manners.* Trans. Edmund Jephcott. New York: Urizen, 1978.

Faber, M. D., ed. *The Design Within: Psychoanalytic Approaches to Shakespeare.* New York: Science House, 1970.

Goldberg, Jonathan. *Writing Matter: From the Hands of the English Renaissance.* Stanford: Stanford UP, 1990.

Greenblatt, Stephen. "Invisible Bullets: Renaissance Authority and Its Subversion, *Henry IV* and *Henry V.*" Dollimore and Sinfield 18–47.

———. *Shakespearean Negotiations: The Circulation of Social Energy in Renaissance England*. Berkeley: U of California P, 1988.

Helgerson, Richard. *The Elizabethan Prodigals*. Berkeley: U of California P, 1976.

Holland, Norman. "Introduction to *Henry IV, Part 2*." Faber 411–28.

Howard, Jean E., and Marion F. O'Connor, eds. *Shakespeare Reproduced: The Text in History and Ideology*. New York: Methuen, 1987.

Humphreys, A. R. "Introduction." *2 Henry IV*. Shakespeare xi–xci.

Hutson, Lorna. *Thomas Nashe in Context*. Oxford: Clarendon, 1989.

Murray, Timothy. *Theatrical Legitimation: Allegories of Genius in Seventeenth-Century England and France*. New York: Oxford UP, 1987.

Parker, Patricia, and Geoffrey Hartman, eds. *Shakespeare and the Question of Theory*. New York, Methuen, 1985.

Rose, Jacqueline. "Sexuality in the Reading of Shakespeare: *Hamlet* and *Measure for Measure*." Drakakis 95–118.

Sedgwick, Eve Kosofsky. *Between Men: English Literature and Male Homosocial Desire*. New York: Columbia UP, 1985.

Shakespeare, William. *The Second Part of King Henry IV*. Ed. A. R. Humphreys. The Arden Shakespeare. New York: Vintage, 1967.

King Lear *and the Royal Progress: Social Display in Shakespearean Tragedy*

BRUCE THOMAS BOEHRER

I WANT TO START by describing life as King Lear would like it. To do so should help cast some light on Lear's tragic loss, which is after all an immediate consequence of his plan for an ideal retirement; and, as I hope to demonstrate, the project of envisioning Lear's ideal future is not entirely as whimsical as it might seem.

Imagine, then, that Lear has divided his realm and his cares equally among his three adoring daughters, and that nothing more remains for him but, in his own words, to "crawl toward death" (1.1.41) unburdened. By his own arrangement, the route to that destination passes through all three of his daughters' estates, which he visits in sequence; and we may thus visualize him approaching, say, Goneril's castle with his retinue. Goneril's servants, informed of his approach, meet him and his select company of one hundred knights (with their horses, grooms, servants, baggage, etc.) some miles before the castle proper; there they entertain him with food and drink in a large tent erected specifically for the purpose. The entire company then proceeds onward to its final destination, where pasteboard figures of gigantic proportions are placed upon the battlements, with "huge and monstrous Trumpettes counterfetted, wherein they seem . . . to sound: and behind them [are] placed certaine Trumpetters who sound . . . in deede" (Gascoigne 2: 92). Lear is then treated to a grandiloquent speech of welcome delivered by a figure attired as Hercules, and then another, spoken by the Lady of the Lake from a floating island in the castle moat; and when Lear finally proceeds, at the end of his day's journey, to his rooms in the castle's inner court, his arrival is greeted with "sweet Musicke" and a decorative arrangement of "wine, corne, fruites, fishes, fowles, instrements of musicke, and weapons for martial defence" (Gascoigne 2: 95)—all illustrating the inexhaustible bounty to be placed at his disposal.

These gestures mark the beginning of an extended entertainment schedule, in which Lear is treated to round after round of hunting, tilting, picnicking, musical serenades, bear-baiting, quintains, tumbling, dancing, masquing, and banqueting, all punctuated by sententious speeches of welcome and praise (Dunlop 146–48). Evening meals characteristically include as many as three hundred separate dishes (Erickson 281)—all provided out of Goneril's apparently boundless generosity and even more boundless *richesse*. Lear stays for about a month; and when he chooses to depart, the figure of Sylvanus appears, running by his stirrup, begging him not to leave, and promising to double the number of deer for the hunt and to bring perpetual spring if only Lear will condescend to remain Goneril's guest forever (Gascoigne 2: 124). And so on to the next castle, where the entertainment begins anew.

The details of this description are of course drawn from historical event: specifically from Leicester's celebrated entertainment of Queen Elizabeth at Kenilworth—nineteen days of festivities that climaxed the royal progress of 1575. But it is also clear that Lear's own plans for retirement generally agree with the scene just presented. Thus, for instance, his abdication predicates itself upon the very sort of sycophantic verbal performance Elizabeth witnesses constantly while at Kenilworth. "Which of you shall we say doth love us most?" (1.1.51) is a question that could prompt Sylvanus's parting pleas to the queen as easily as it does Goneril's opening speech. Moreover, Lear is careful to furnish his old age with courtiers and attendants— the "reservation of an hundred knights" (1.1.133) that will prove so offensive to Goneril and Regan. He specifically insists on retaining

"The name and all th' addition to a king" (1.1.136), thus monopolizing the supreme ceremonial status within pageants and festivities like those of Kenilworth. And by requiring his daughters to entertain him constantly (while specifically stipulating that they pay for his and his followers' amusements—"By you to be sustain'd" [1.1.134]), Lear in effect commits himself to a schedule of endless mobile merrymaking. He plans to go on progress forever.

Although never specifically mentioned in *Lear,* the idea of the royal progress thus permeates the structure of the play, which develops as a tragedy when its hero elects to separate the progress as social practice from the material circumstances that permit it to exist—most particularly the king's multiform capacity to *make* others freely entertain him. Moreover, by 1604, the earliest possible date of composition for Shakespeare's play, the royal progress itself would begin to change its function as a social institution, conforming to the expectations of a new ruler, assuming a new protocol, and embodying a new set of presuppositions about the monarch's relation to his/her subjects. We may therefore suggest that *King Lear* functions at one level as an exercise of the political unconscious: as a play about problematical changes in current social practice, and specifically in the display of royal power.

This proposition assumes, in Fredric Jameson's words, that literature works to "project decorative or mythic resolutions of issues that [one is] unable to articulate conceptually"—that is, that one of the literary work's principal (albeit undeclared) functions is to construct "symbolic resolutions of real political and social contradictions" (Jameson 79, 80). And thus, taking Shakespearean drama as the articulation of "a political *pensée sauvage*" (Jameson 80), the present study of *King Lear* relates the play's "decorative or mythic" modality to problems in the conduct of Renaissance monarchy itself. In this respect the critical tradition on *Lear* is rich and useful; Alvin Kernan, for instance, describes the play as enacting a conflict between "two world views, the medieval and the modern" (13); Jonathan Dollimore relates these diverging "world views" to oppositions between "the realities of property-marriage" and "the language of love and generosity" (199); and Rosalie Colie, in a profound and compelling essay, similarly remarks that "*King Lear* is tied to the problems of an aristocracy caught between an old ethos of unreckoned generosity, magnificence, and carelessness, and new values stressing greater providence, frugality, and even calculation" (212). While substantially agreeing with all of these formulations, the present essay seeks to avoid characterizing thrift as a modern, bourgeois virtue opposed to the essentially medieval or feudal qualities of display and generosity. Instead we will contend that a major aim of royal self-representation in Renaissance England is to deny the mutual exclusivity of these concepts—to reformulate display and thrift and generosity in such a way as to render them inseparable and coextensive within the person of the monarch.

From this standpoint it is oversimple to read *Lear* as a conflict between aristocratic and bourgeois values; we may more accurately read the play as dramatizing the moment at which such conflict comes into being as a conceptual possibility. Hence the problems of what we may call royalty on vacation (how to fund one's pleasures, how to relate those pleasures and that funding to the notion of productive work, etc.) are the most apparent in the play's opening scenes—precisely the scenes in which Lear's England is still more or less a traditional royal state; thereafter, developments lead the tragedy away from any narrow focus upon courtly politics and toward larger questions of justice, duty, and personal sacrifice. Yet these larger questions are only asked (and arguably *can* only be asked) in the absence of orthodox political assumptions and processes; and thus the tensions within Lear's royal behavior serve as an important triggering mechanism for the play's subsequent events.

II

Lear's retirement plan, as it emerges in the opening scene of his play, affords a primary instance of royal self-contradiction. Initially framing itself as a request ("Tell me how much you love me"), it transforms itself into a command through the agency of a single dependent clause:

> Tell me, my daughters,
> (Since now we will divest us both of rule,
> Interest of territory, cares of state)
> Which of you shall we say doth love us most?
> That we our largest bounty may extend
> Where nature doth with merit challenge.
>
> (1.1.48–53)

Lear's words seek to mediate between the expression of unforced loyalty and the imposition of rewards and punishments. On the one hand, his daughters' love must be freely offered because—as Goneril claims—it is "Beyond what can be valued" (1.1.57); yet on the other hand that very love is subject to an elaborate set of pressures and constraints—as suggested by Lear's warning to Cordelia, "Mend your speech a little, / Lest you may mar your fortunes" (1.1.94–95). Moreover, the very terms of Lear's abdication render the process equivocal; he insists upon retaining "The name and all th' addition to a king," while in the very next breath he assigns "the sway, / Revenue, execution of the rest" to his "Beloved sons" (1.1.136–38) and seals the bequest with a coronet, thus distributing the symbols of power equally among himself, Albany, and Cornwall. Nor does Lear attempt to explain how he may retain "all th' addition to a king" while conferring upon Cornwall and Albany "*all* the large effects / That troop with majesty" (1.1.131–32; emphasis added); for apparently, in vintage Jacobean fashion, Lear's "darker purpose" (1.1.36) is to be both a king and no king—at the same time.

A king and no king: this popular phrase effectively characterizes the difficulties of any Renaissance monarch on progress; for the spectacle of royalty at play, accepting the gracious hospitality of dutiful subjects, bluntly engages the very contradictions implicit in Lear's retirement plan. The Renaissance monarch on progress is beset with a series of nagging problems: how to force one's subjects into entertaining one freely and generously; how to solicit the hospitality—and financial support—of others, while maintaining that such largesse is finally neither necessary nor important; how to construct one's pleasures so that they have the same general appearance and effect as one's work. These are, by and large, Lear's problems too. In this sense Marie Axton is demonstrably right to call the play "a tragedy of kingship" (138); and while the politics of *King Lear* are by no means limited to those of the Stuart court, the play's larger themes of justice and equity thus arise, at least in part, from incoherencies in the function and structure of kingship itself. Critics have regularly accounted for this incoherence in terms of intellectual and/or social conflict; John Danby, for one instance, distinguishes between the "two Natures and two Reasons" represented in the play by Edmund and Edgar, arguing that these characters' separate discourses "imply two societies" (46)—one modern, scientific, and bourgeois, and the other medieval, theocentric, and aristocratic. And Paul Delany similarly equates the Edgar/Edmund dichotomy with the transition from "a feudal-aristocratic ethic that promotes display, generosity and conspicuous consumption [to] a bourgeois ethic that values thrift" (434). The present study regards Lear's own character as a prime locus of such conflict; in short, it argues that Lear's world fails to make sense because Lear himself—and the mode of government he represents—fails to make sense.

The issue of money provides a clear case in point; for having resigned the sway and revenue of royalty, deploring them as "cares and business" (1.1.39), Lear nonetheless continues to behave as a limitless source of revenue and preferment for others; as Goneril remarks, he seeks precisely to "manage those authorities / That he hath given away" (1.3.18–19). Thus when Kent has earned Lear's favor by tripping Oswald, Lear bestows gold on him as "earnest of [his] service" (1.4.98–99); and when overcome by a fevered vision of universal "Luxury," Lear exclaims, "Give me an ounce of civet, good apothecary, / To sweeten my imagination. / There's money for thee" (4.6.119, 132–34).[1] Cash appears miraculously as soon as the old man desires it; moreover, if it is physically unavailable, his imagination supplies it anyway, equally miraculously. And this miraculous appearance, we may suppose, is a precondition for the king's finely honed contempt of his own "revenue." For Lear's retirement plan unfolds in a setting of Edenic plenitude coextensive with and sustained by the king's own presence: a world in which one can give away all one's revenue and still have plentiful gold for one's servants. The fool twits Lear with the idea of turning an egg into two crowns (1.4.162–71); and he can do so precisely because for Lear life is a Brueghel landscape, with eggs trotting around already soft-boiled and cracked for serving.

Thus, as Joseph Wittreich has observed, Lear "perpetuate[s] the process of division by which paradise ha[s] been lost" (24); and he does so by locating paradise, with relentless literalism, in himself, by identifying himself as its inexhaustible essence. It is a gesture typical of James I, who undertakes the task of "restoring paradise" (Wittreich 24) through a program of extravagant court expenditure; and Lear's ungrateful daughters adopt much the same position with their inheritance. Goneril resents her father's retinue very largely because it interferes with the rhetoric of limitless indulgence—with what Rosalie Colie has called "the projected image of [her] own greatness" (201); Lear's knights cost money to maintain, and they detract from the comfort and status of Goneril's own people. Thus she complains that Lear's "disorder'd rabble / Make servants of their betters" (1.4.264–65); and thus too she denounces them for behaving like paying customers at an entertainment house:

> [T]his our court, infected with their manners,
> Shows like a riotous inn: epicurism and lust
> Makes it more like a tavern or a brothel
> Than a grac'd palace.
> (1.4.251–54)

Such talk leads naturally to the bargain-basement markdown of Lear's status in 2.4, where the king naively insists to Goneril that "thou art twice [Regan's] love" (262), because she has cut the number of his followers to fifty rather than to twenty-five. Goneril, activating the limitless rhetoric of sovereignty, reduces the number still further, while reconstructing the severest privation as a geometrically expansive luxury:

> What need you five-and-twenty, ten, or five,
> To follow in a house where twice so many
> Have a command to tend you?
> (2.4.263–65)

As Leonard Tennenhouse has noted, Lear's followers "take on the features of carnival and inversion" and hence "pose a potential threat to legitimate authority" (136). And they do so largely because they take the language of royalty at face value; behaving as if they were in paradise, they prove that they are not.

III

Thus, oddly, Lear and Goneril find themselves propelled toward the same general kinds of behavior; both at various times maintain that more (land, revenue, retinue) is less, that everything is nothing;

and both assert their authority as *fons et origo* of the social order
by cutting themselves off from the sources of their power (in Lear's
case, lands and revenue; in Goneril's case, her father). Political equilibrium reemerges in the play only when, by a kind of *deus ex
machina,* a new ruler appears whose authority does miraculously
seem self-contained, who is indeed at once nothing ("Edgar I nothing
am" [2.3.21]; "my name is lost" [5.3.121]) and everything. But Lear's
retirement plan itself denies such self-containment, for it functions
within the realm of economic exchange, while seeking to preempt
exchange itself; and thus its immediate result is what Terry Eagleton
calls "a bout of severe linguistic inflation" (76). Framing itself as a
mercantile transaction (whose governing principle is that "nothing
will come of nothing" [1.1.90]), Lear's design seeks paradoxically to
escape the realm of economic necessity, to "shake all . . . business
from [his] age" (1.1.39)—to *buy* a life in which cash really is as
unimportant as his rhetoric requires it to be.

Comfort without money—or rather, without the appearance of
money: it is the Club Med principle of royal retirement, and it is
already potentially present within the conceptual framework of the
Elizabethan progress. Thus in 1579, when presented by the mayor of
Norwich with "a faire standing cup of silver and guilt" and one
hundred pounds in gold, Elizabeth could accept the gift with a speech
embodying most of Lear's contradictions:

Princes have no need of money: God hath indued us abundantly, we come
not therefore, but for that which in right is our own, the hearts and true
allegiance of our subjects, which are the greatest riches of a Kingdom.
(Dutton 71)

Like Goneril's professed love for her father, the "hearts and true
allegiance" of Elizabeth's subjects transcend value, catapulting the
monarch out of the realm of financial considerations. Thus "princes
have no need of money"; and yet, affirming the existence of a quality
beyond value, Elizabeth's remarks subject that very quality to valu-
ation, defining it metaphorically as "the greatest riches of a Kingdom"
while the queen slyly accepts a hundred pounds in gold with her
left hand. Elizabeth successfully inhabits two distinct social and political orders at once; money is for her both valuable and valueless; and

her subjects' affection is at once both an incalculable quantity and a direct function of the splendor with which they entertain—and *sustain*—her.

Nor are such baffling ambiguities at all remarkable; indeed, they comprise a central mystery of the queen's behavior. Thus, on one hand, George Puttenham records the apparent distaste with which Elizabeth greeted her subjects' extravagant expenditures on her behalf:

King *Henry* the seuenth her Maiesties grandfather, if his chaunce had bene to lye at any of his subjects houses, or to passe moe meales then one, he that would take vpon him to defray the charge of his dyet, or of his officers and houshold, he would be marvelously offended with it, saying what priuate subiect dare vndertake a Princes charge, or looke into the secret of his expēce? Her Maiestie hath bene knowne oftentimes to mislike the superfluous expence of her subjects bestowed vpon her in times of her progresses. (sig. Kk2r)

In Puttenham's account, what offends Henry is clearly the *lèse-majesté* of looking into a king's "secrets"—the implication that a subject can presume to become a monarch's patron, even if only for a night. Elizabeth similarly objects to the effrontery of such a gesture; yet she nonetheless discreetly allows new precedents to be set for the entertainment and subsidizing of royalty. Thus early in her reign, when she visits Oxford in 1566, the mayor, aldermen, and burgesses of the town present her with "a cup of silver, double-gilt, worth £10. and in it about £40. in old gold" (Nichols, *Elizabeth* 1: 208). And John Nichols, the early chronicler of Elizabeth's progresses, remarks that "this gift was the first in money that ever, as I can yet learn, was presented to a Prince" (*Elizabeth* 1: 208); evidently the queen's scruples were quite selective.

Certainly Elizabeth betrays a measure of nervousness over such gifts, as the infinite variety of her acceptance speeches shows. Thus in 1572, during her visit of that year to Warwick, she once more takes money (this time "a purse very faire wrought, and in the purse twenty pounds, all in sovereignes") while seeming to decline it:

I thank . . . you all, with all my heart, for your good willes; and I am very lothe to tak any thing at your handes nowe, because you at the last time of my being here presented us to our great liking and contentacion; . . . and I

am the more unwilling to tak any thing of you, because I knowe that a myte
of their haunds is as much as a thowsand pounds of some others. (Nichols,
Elizabeth 1: 315)

Again, Elizabeth bluffs through her embarrassment by both refusing
and accepting the gift at one and the same time; and in the process
she once more subjects her people's cash to re-valuation. All gold
sovereigns are valuable, she says, but some are more valuable than
others, for they are dignified by the "haunds" through which they
pass. The nature of the dignity conferred remains equivocal, but the
queen's remarks succeed at unfixing the value and importance of the
gift relative to her; and she then concludes with a brilliant reversal,
accepting the money not for its face value, but for its worth as a
token of "good wille": "Nevertheless, because you shall not think
that I mislike of your good willes, I accept [the gift] with most hearty
thanks" (Nichols, *Elizabeth* 1: 315). Elizabeth, whose regular progresses very clearly served to relieve pressure on a cash-poor government (Dutton 70), and who rewarded her hosts on such a rigidly
codified basis that one could regularly expect a knighthood for entertaining her three days or more (Dutton 72), clings resolutely to the
myth that her acts—and her subjects' love—are somehow both valuable and free.

IV

King Lear tests the literal validity of this myth on the stage at the
same time that King James is beginning to test it elsewhere. Thus
Shakespeare's tragedy enacts a fundamental "separation of forms of
power" (Tennenhouse 139) in the wake of Lear's retirement; pursuing
filial affection and freedom from expenses, Lear sacrifices paternal
dignity and the authority of patronage. Similarly, King James begins
his reign by openly separating the powers of social title from those
of cash, and by seeking to exchange the one for the other; his proliferation of honors soon frames them as an item of purely mercantile
value (by 1606, knighthoods are not merely bought and sold; they
are the stuff of financial speculation [Stone 77]). And Kent's own jibes
at Oswald—"a base, . . . hundred-pound, filthy worsted-stocking
knave" (2.2.13–15)—suggest disgust at the practice of keying social

status to buying-power alone. Yet if, on one hand, the honorific significance of noble or gentle status seems imperiled by the open sale of knighthoods, James's attitude toward the nature of his progresses seems equally to threaten all honest and fair economic exchange. For James quickly redefines the progress as an exclusive domain of the royal pleasures, which are apparently as free as knighthoods are constrained. (Recall that on 17 July 1603 the king *commands* all subjects worth £40 or more to receive the order of knighthood [Harrison 47].) Thus the king's country-excursions hold little room for tedious public appearances; indeed, they take the king ever more often to his own estates, rather than to those of his subjects; and in early 1605, for instance, while hunting at Thetford, he flees the field when beset by a "press of company, which came to see him" (Lodge 3: 138). James's pleasures are private and exclusive, holding no space for his subjects; and his subjects' honors are public and mercantile, allowing less and less room for any special relation with the sovereign who confers them.

Thus the delicate tissue of contradictions sustaining the Elizabethan progress is torn to tatters by both Lear and James. "Nothing will come of nothing": Lear's cautionary insistence that there is no free lunch resonates sourly throughout the play, impeaching the king's own behavior with cruelty and precision:

> FOOL
> . . . Can you make no use of nothing, Nuncle?
> LEAR
> Why, no, boy; nothing can be made out of nothing.
> FOOL
> [*To Kent.*] Prithee, tell him, so much the rent of his land comes to.
> (1.4.136–41)

And when challenged by Goneril and Regan to justify the size of his progress-train, Lear ironically winds up maintaining that the best things in life, including servants and retainers and "ceremonious affection" (1.4.62), are free—or at least that they *should* be:

> O! reason not the need; our basest beggars
> Are in the poorest thing superfluous:

> Allow not nature more than nature needs,
> Man's life is cheap as beast's.
>
> (2.4.266–69)

Like Nero in his golden house, Lear is driven by his own rhetoric to insist that he can only live like a human being if he is treated like a king.

As a result, Lear's language oscillates ever more wildly between separate and competing notions of economy. Applying the nothing-will-come-of-nothing principle to his own behavior, Lear convicts himself of tyranny and folly in his punishment of Cordelia:

> If you have poison for me, I will drink it.
> I know you do not love me; for your sisters
> Have, as I do remember, done me wrong:
> You have some cause, they have not.
>
> (4.7.72–75)

From this standpoint, Cordelia's kindness makes no sense, for Lear has done nothing to earn it; and similarly, Lear invokes a kind of metaphysical ledger-sheet to extenuate his own behavior, claiming that his credits overbalance his debits, that he is "a man / More sinn'd against than sinning" (3.2.59–60). And yet against such remarks, he opposes a vision of free, unforced, and almost prelapsarian content-ment—located in, of all places, prison:

> Come, let's away to prison;
> We two alone will sing like birds i' th' cage:
> . . . .
> . . . and we'll wear out,
> In a wall'd prison, packs and sects of great ones
> That ebb and flow by th' moon.
>
> (5.3.8–19)

For this second side of Lear's discourse, plenitude and comfort consist by definition in the *absence* of buying-power; one purchases them precisely and only by having nothing; and in this sense, Lear sets out literally to demonstrate, with Hamlet, how a king may go a progress through the guts of a beggar.

But if *King Lear* deconceals the contradictions implicit in social displays like the royal progress, that is arguably because the progress itself, as an institution, is rapidly collapsing under the weight of its own incoherencies. On one hand, the progresses of James I (among which we may reasonably include his initial journey south from Edinburgh in 1603) resolutely maintain the illusion of unforced and infinite largesse—of a golden age restored, in which both the king and his subjects may entertain themselves readily and limitlessly. Reaching York on 16 April 1603, James found a triumphal reception awaiting him—including, at York Minster, "a conduit that all day long ran white and claret wine, every man to drinke as much as he listed" (Nichols, *James* 1: 78); and in Cambridgeshire Sir Oliver Cromwell of Hinchinbrook, equally committed to re-figuring England as the Land of Cockaigne, received James with

such entertainment, as the like had not been seen in any place before, since his first setting forward out of Scotland. There was such plentie and varietie of meates, such diversitie of wines, . . . and the cellers open at any man's pleasure. (Nichols, *James* 1: 100)

For their part, James's subjects invoked the old Elizabethan rhetoric repeatedly in public displays, as when Sir Henry Montague and the aldermen of London presented James with a gift of three golden cups as a token of unforced affection:

Twentie and more are the Soveraignes wee have served since our Conquest; but, conqueror of hearts, it is you and your posteritie, that we have vowed to love. . . . In pledge whereof, my Lord Mayor, the Aldermen, and Commons of this Citie, wishing a golden reigne unto you, present your greatnes with a little cup of gold. (Nichols, *James* 1: 360)

And for James, as for Lear, this is to live like a human being.[2]

Yet counter to—and concurrent with—these Jacobean visions of plenitude, one detects a competing sense of niggardliness and penury. Giovanni Scaramelli, Venetian Secretary in England during 1603, thus complains in a letter that the English "Government are re-introducing the ancient splendours of the English Court, and almost adoring his Majesty" (*C.S.P. Foreign Archives* 10: 46); yet Scaramelli is perceptive enough not to ascribe this development to the king's improvidence alone. Conspicuous consumption is a corporate vice, he remarks, noting that "the King, . . . of his own accord, would probably hardly

have changed his modest habit of life which he pursued in Scotland"
(*C.S.P. Foreign Archives* 10: 46). In September of the same year Sir
Thomas Edmonds records difficulties in "raising of money for sup-
plying of the King's necessities" (Lodge 3: 30); and in 1604 both the
Commons and the Privy Council make formal motions to restrain
what Jonathan Goldberg has called the "royal pleasures" (83).[3] Thus
a committee of Parliament petitions James on 27 April to restrict the
activities and excesses of the royal purveyors (Harrison 135)—a
request certainly not alien to Elizabeth, but gaining stridency under
James; and by 17 December the Privy Council has approached James
concerning the cost of court entertainments, noting that "it will be
very disadvantageous" for the expense of such events to "be laid on
noblemen and gentlemen, for few are able to undergo such charges"
(Harrison 171). Finally, in 1608, only two years after *Lear* is performed
at court, one subject bluntly describes a prospective royal visit to
Northamptonshire as being "as unwelcome as raine in harvest" (Stone
454). As for James himself, John Chamberlain describes him as proceeding in January of 1605 to Royston (i.e., to Theobalds) for the
hunting there, claiming it to be "the only meanes to maintain his
health" (Chamberlain 2: 201), and charging his council—in language
reminiscent of *Lear*—to "undertake the charge and burden of affaires,
and foresee that he be not interrupted nor troubled with too much
business" (Chamberlain 2: 201). The rhetoric of limitless indulgence
no longer coexists with that of economic exchange, even in pretense;
and thus the delicate subject of the king's entertainment emerges as
a point of conflict between two distinct and opposed social config-
urations. In short, James—like Lear—has defined the progress as a
space of *retirement.*

V

King Lear thus develops by stressing the incompatibility of feudal
loyalty and royal patronage; it constructs a world in which unforced
obedience and coercive power are mutually preemptive; and it
redeems that world only on condition that the king himself be spurned
and abandoned. In its larger thematic concerns, *King Lear* certainly
transcends the limited politics of a Jacobean (or an Elizabethan) progress; yet it begins with the very problems that confronted King James

on vacation at Theobalds, or Queen Elizabeth on display in Norwich. And finding those problems insurmountable within the courtly context, the tragedy thus resolves itself—contrary to Holinshed's example, Johnson's objections, and Tate's adaptation—only at the expense of the king's own individual and dynastic life.[4]

This paper has aimed to correlate social practice (specifically the forms and conventions of the royal progress) and literary practice (the tragedy of *King Lear*) by viewing both as what Jameson has called "'utterances' in an essentially collective or class discourse" (80). Both seek, from this standpoint, to work around the same political antinomies in different ways. Adopting Jameson's terminology further, we may suggest that the formal discourse of the Elizabethan progress functions in the world of romance, presupposing "a transitional moment in which two distinct modes of production, or moments of socioeconomic development, coexist" (148); and it is precisely that world that the tragedy *Lear* works to interrogate and arguably to deny. It strikes me as, at the very least, a noteworthy coincidence that *Lear* should enact such denial just when the rhetoric and practice of the royal progress are themselves registering new figural difficulties.

This being said, we must return to our initial picture of Lear on his ideal progress, enjoying the same homage and "ceremonious affection" reserved for Elizabeth at Kenilworth; and we must note that this picture is quietly but fundamentally inaccurate. For while its external details conform well to the conventions Lear invokes, the Elizabethan progress performs a clear symbolic function that Lear's endless holiday cannot. Elizabeth's appearances service the myth of royal absolutism by manifesting the queen's transcendent and controlling duality, presenting her as both host and guest, both patron and protégée, and thus integrating her into the very social arrangements from which it declares her to be aloof; whereas Lear's retirement plan, like James's progresses, is "almost entirely designed for his own and not his people's pleasure" (Dutton 75). Thus it operates not to display power but to enclose it, alienating the monarch in one apocalyptic gesture from the mechanisms of economic exchange and thereby disowning its own practical function. Instead of traveling *to the country,* like Elizabeth, James and Lear travel *from the court,* away from the cares and business of rule; instead of employing the royal progress to perpetuate the royal myth, James and Lear employ the royal myth to perpetuate the royal progress. As Stephen Greenblatt argues with reference to exorcism, *"King Lear* is haunted by a sense of rituals and beliefs that are no longer efficacious, that have been *emptied out"* (119); and this draining of the symbols of power conforms to the privatization of courtly pleasures under James.

Thus we may end not with a historical parallel to life as Lear would like it, but rather with a historical emblem of life as Lear *makes* it: the royal mansions of Theobalds and Holdenby. King James first visits Theobalds, the renowned family seat of the Cecils, in 1603, during his initial progress south from Edinburgh. It is at Theobalds, in effect, that Sir Robert Cecil hands James the practical apparatus of government, for it is there that the new monarch first meets the assembled household and principal ministers of Queen Elizabeth. The meeting is clearly cast as an old-style royal entertainment, set in a mansion that was enlarged specifically to accommodate Queen Elizabeth during her progresses (Dunlop 168). (Holdenby, the near-duplicate of Theobalds built by Sir Christopher Hatton, is said to have been "consecrated" to the queen's memory [Erickson 294].) And Cecil clearly spared no expense for the occasion of James's arrival; as one contemporary description of the event notes:

His Majestie stayed at Theobalds four dayes; where, to speake of Sir Robert's cost to entertaine him, were but to imitate Geographers, that set a little *round* O for a mighty Province; words being hardly able to expresse what was done there indeed. (Nichols, *James* 1: 111)

"Now thou art an O without a figure" (1.4.200), the fool tells Lear, and his remark applies equally well to the fate of Theobalds and the Stuart monarchy. For Cecil's expense in maintaining the mansion (an expense that, although aggravated by the king's visit, remained steady and spectacular even without the royal presence)[5] would prove more than the monarchy itself could shoulder. James, unwilling to tolerate the ambiguities of the progress-visit—which would enable him periodically to enjoy such an estate without having to pay for its maintenance—quickly arranged that Theobalds should become crown property. And this acquisition would contribute to an unprecedented surge in royal household expenses and thus lead to the eventual destruction of the estate itself during the Commonwealth (Dunlop 123–24).[6] Similarly in 1610 the estate of Holdenby, purchased three years earlier by James, would stand empty and derelict, "by reason whereof the rooms grow musty, the walls decay and the chimneys fall down" (Dunlop 122).[7] James's empty house stands as the perfect complement to Shakespeare's houseless king, an O without a figure: empty ceremonial presences, drained of their social utility. That loss—of function, purpose, and hence of identity—pervades the social context of Shakespeare's play, as well as the play itself.

Notes

An earlier version of this essay was presented at the 1989 conference of the Renaissance Society of America. I am indebted to my co-panelists and session organizers—especially Arthur Kinney—for their assistance and encouragement. I am likewise grateful to Walter Cohen and Mary Beth Rose for their help with the process of revision.

1. Colie, for one, directs this remark at the blind Gloucester and argues that Lear in fact hands him a purse (207). And although Colie does not deal much with the references to cash in *Lear,* she does note valuably that "despite all its moments of exact social observation and commentary, [the play] is surrounded by questions neither directly met nor directly answered" (191)—questions that involve the practical management of the kingdom, how it is to be divided, where Lear holds court, how letters move, etc. The equivocations about cash are of a piece with these others, forcing the play's language "into areas of meaninglessness and incalculability" (Colie 213).

2. Glynne Wickham has already argued for the presence of a Jacobean pageant-mentality in *King Lear.* Correlating Shakespeare's revisions of the Lear story with events in the early years of James's English reign, Wickham maintains that *King Lear* is a reflection of the political optimism with which James's succession was generally greeted (38–43). Yet Wickham's argument ignores the unmistakable disapproval in, for instance, Kent's reference to hundred-pound knighthoods (2.2.13–15), while equally overlooking the clear political and economic tensions that were already developing in 1604 between James and his new subjects. Thus if the play's pageantic features seek to compliment James, we must conclude, they do so in an uneasy and highly equivocal fashion.

3. Goldberg's important remarks about the royal pleasures emphasize the disparity between James's rhetoric and his behavior; thus, as Goldberg notes, "it was only in verbal strategies that James joined pleasure and business" (83). And despite James's repeated and "sanctimonious statements defending his pleasures" (Goldberg 83), Goldberg cites telling instances of the king's failure to convince others that he was in fact a working monarch.

4. Holinshed is of course not the only version of the Lear story in which Cordelia survives to maintain Lear's threatened dynasty; and thus Samuel Johnson is at least partly justified in remarking that Cordelia's death is "contrary to the natural ideas of

justice, to the hope of the reader, and, what is yet more strange, to the faith of chronicles" (155). Tennenhouse responds that Cordelia's death is necessary because the play calls into question "the patriarchal principle itself" (141) and thus needs to reaffirm a specifically male image of sovereign authority. For present purposes, we may simply suggest that in dispersing the symbols of his power, Lear has abandoned a royal relation that cannot be preserved by any intrinsic means—certainly not by heredity. The natural place to position sovereignty, after Lear's bequest to his daughters, is as far away from Lear and his issue as possible.

5. As an instance of such upkeep expenses, it is worth noting that the regular operation of Hatfield House cost Robert Cecil roughly £8,500 per year. Cecil's annual income during the last years of his life was approximately £25,000 (Worden 55).

6. Thus, discussing the gradual erosion of royal credit under the Stuarts, Robert Ashton notes that "in the years following 1606 [i.e., immediately after James's acquisition of the property at Theobalds] there had been a notable expansion of the royal demand for loans. This was the period during which the carefree extravagance which had marked the opening years of the reign was beginning to bear fruit in the form of an alarmingly enhanced debt" (157–58).

7. Ironically enough, Hatfield House, the principal crown property given to Cecil in exchange for Theobalds, still stands as an outstanding example of the Renaissance progress palace, illustrating "the place of conspicuous expenditure in Jacobean politics" (Worden 55). Yet, although Robert Cecil enlarged Hatfield at an initial cost of £40,000, King James himself did not choose to visit it.

Works Cited

Ashton, Robert. *The Crown and the Money Market, 1603–1640.* Oxford: Clarendon, 1960.

Axton, Marie. *The Queen's Two Bodies: Drama and the Elizabethan Succession.* London: Royal Historical Soc., 1977.

Calendar of State Papers and Manuscripts, Foreign Archives. 37 vols. London, 1900. Liechtenstein: Kraus-Thomson, 1970.

Chamberlain, John. *The Letters of John Chamberlain.* Ed. Norman Egbert McClure. 2 vols. Philadelphia: American Philosophical Soc., 1939.

Colie, Rosalie L. "Reason and Need: *King Lear* and the 'Crisis' of the Aristocracy." *Some Facets of* King Lear: *Essays in Prismatic Criticism.* Ed. Rosalie L. Colie and F. T. Flahiff. Toronto: U of Toronto P, 1974. 185–219.

Danby, John F. *Shakespeare's Doctrine of Nature: A Study of* King Lear. London: Faber, 1961.

Delany, Paul. "*King Lear* and the Decline of Feudalism." *PMLA* 92 (1977): 429–40.

Dollimore, Jonathan. *Radical Tragedy: Religion, Ideology, and Power in the Drama of Shakespeare and His Contemporaries.* Chicago: U of Chicago P, 1984.

Dunlop, Ian. *Palaces and Progresses of Elizabeth I.* London: Cape, 1962.

Dutton, Ralph. *English Court Life, from Henry VII to George II.* London: Batsford, 1963.

Eagleton, Terry. *William Shakespeare*. Oxford: Blackwell, 1986.

Erickson, Carrolly. *The First Elizabeth*. New York: Summit, 1983.

Gascoigne, George. *The Princely Pleasures at Kenelworth Castle*. *The Complete Works of George Gascoigne*. Ed. John W. Cunliffe. 2 vols. Cambridge: Cambridge UP, 1910. 2: 91–131.

Goldberg, Jonathan. *James I and the Politics of Literature: Jonson, Shakespeare, Donne, and Their Contemporaries*. Baltimore: Johns Hopkins UP, 1983.

Greenblatt, Stephen. *Shakespearean Negotiations: The Circulation of Social Energy in Renaissance England*. Berkeley: U of California P, 1988.

Harrison, G. B. *A Jacobean Journal: Being a Record of Those Things Most Talked of During the Years 1603–1606*. London: Routledge, 1941.

Jameson, Fredric. *The Political Unconscious: Narrative as a Socially Symbolic Act*. Ithaca: Cornell UP, 1981.

Johnson, Samuel. *Johnson on Shakespeare*. Ed. R. W. Desai. New Delhi: Orient Longman, 1979.

Kernan, Alvin B. "*King Lear* and the Shakespearean Pageant of History." *On* King Lear. Ed. Lawrence Danson. Princeton: Princeton UP, 1981. 7–24.

Lodge, Edmund. *Illustrations of British History, Biography, and Manners*. 3 vols. London: Chidley, 1838.

Nichols, John, ed. *The Progresses, Processions, and Magnificent Festivities of King James the First*. . . . 4 vols. London: Soc. of Antiquaries, 1828.

———. *Progresses, Public Processions, etc. of Queen Elizabeth*. 3 vols. London: Soc. of Antiquaries, 1828.

[Puttenham, George.] *The Arte of English Poesie*. Amsterdam: Da Capo, 1971.

Shakespeare, William. *King Lear*. Ed. Kenneth Muir. 8th ed. Cambridge: Harvard UP, 1952.

Stone, Lawrence. *The Crisis of the Aristocracy, 1558–1641*. Oxford: Clarendon, 1965.

Tennenhouse, Leonard. *Power on Display: The Politics of Shakespeare's Genres*. New York: Methuen, 1986.

Wickham, Glynne. "From Tragedy to Tragi-Comedy: *King Lear* as Prologue." *Shakespeare Survey* 26 (1973): 33–48.

Wittreich, Joseph Anthony. *"Image of That Horror"*: History, Prophecy, and Apocalypse in King Lear. San Marino, CA: Huntington Library, 1984.

Worden, Blair, ed. *Stuart England*. Oxford: Phaidon, 1986.

Notes on Contributors

MICHAEL D. BRISTOL is professor of English at McGill University in Montréal. He is the author of *Carnival and Theater: Plebeian Culture and the Structure of Authority in Renaissance England* (1985) and of *Shakespeare's America / America's Shakespeare* (1990).

M. LINDSAY KAPLAN is assistant professor of English at Lewis and Clark College. She is currently revising a book on slander in the work of Spenser, Jonson, and Shakespeare entitled *"Slander to th' state": The Poetics and Politics of Defamation*.

JANET M. SPENCER is assistant professor of English at Wingate College, Wingate, North Carolina. She is completing a book which examines the interactions among public spectacles, royal appropriations of popular forms, and the emergence of an individuated conception of the human body in English Renaissance drama and culture.

CHRISTOPHER HIGHLEY is a Ph.D. student at Stanford University and is finishing his dissertation on the imaginative mapping of the Celtic fringe in Spenser, Shakespeare, and Elizabethan culture. He was recently appointed assistant professor of English at Ohio State University.

DAVID H. THURN teaches English and humanistic studies at Princeton University. His essay on Marlowe's *Tamburlaine* appears in a recent issue of *English Literary Renaissance*. He is currently engaged in a study of demonological literature of the English Renaissance.

GEORGE MARISCAL is assistant professor in the Department of Literature at the University of California, San Diego. He has published articles on Calderón and Shakespeare, early modern Spanish literature, and the Chicano novel. His *Contradictory Subjects: Quevedo, Cervantes, and Seventeenth-Century Spanish Culture* will be published by Cornell University Press in 1991.

BETTY S. TRAVITSKY, consultant archivist at the Billy Rose Theatre Collection (NYPL), is editor of *Paradise of Women: Writings by Englishwomen of the Renaissance* (1981; rpt. 1989), coeditor of *Renaissance Englishwomen in Print* (1990) and of *Women in the Renaissance,* a special issue of *Women's Studies* (Summer 1991), and author of a number of essays in a variety of anthologies and journals. She is currently at work on a critical edition of Elizabeth Egerton's manuscript journals.

ROBERT N. WATSON, professor of English at the University of California, Los Angeles, is the author of *Shakespeare and the Hazards of Ambition* and *Ben Jonson's Parodic Strategy.* He is currently writing a book on the fear of death in Renaissance England.

JONATHAN CREWE, a graduate of the University of California at Berkeley, has taught at The Johns Hopkins University, University of Tulsa, and Dartmouth College, where he currently teaches Renaissance literature and critical theory. In addition to many articles, he has published *Unredeemed Rhetoric: Thomas Nashe and the Scandal of Authorship, Hidden Designs: The Critical Profession and Renaissance Literature,* and *Trials of Authorship: Anterior Forms and Poetic Reconstruction from Wyatt to Shakespeare.*

BRUCE THOMAS BOEHRER is assistant professor of English Renaissance literature at Florida State University. His work has appeared most recently in *PMLA* and *Journal of the History of Sexuality.*